From Self to Selfie

Angus Kennedy • James Panton
Editors

From Self to Selfie

A Critique of Contemporary Forms of Alienation

Editors
Angus Kennedy
West Sussex, UK

James Panton
Magdalen College School
Oxford, UK

ISBN 978-3-030-19193-1   ISBN 978-3-030-19194-8 (eBook)
https://doi.org/10.1007/978-3-030-19194-8

© The Editor(s) (if applicable) and The Author(s) 2019
This work is subject to copyright. All rights are solely and exclusively licensed by the Publisher, whether the whole or part of the material is concerned, specifically the rights of translation, reprinting, reuse of illustrations, recitation, broadcasting, reproduction on microfilms or in any other physical way, and transmission or information storage and retrieval, electronic adaptation, computer software, or by similar or dissimilar methodology now known or hereafter developed.
The use of general descriptive names, registered names, trademarks, service marks, etc. in this publication does not imply, even in the absence of a specific statement, that such names are exempt from the relevant protective laws and regulations and therefore free for general use.
The publisher, the authors and the editors are safe to assume that the advice and information in this book are believed to be true and accurate at the date of publication. Neither the publisher nor the authors or the editors give a warranty, express or implied, with respect to the material contained herein or for any errors or omissions that may have been made. The publisher remains neutral with regard to jurisdictional claims in published maps and institutional affiliations.

Cover illustration: © yipengge / iStock / Getty Images Plus

This Palgrave Macmillan imprint is published by the registered company Springer Nature Switzerland AG
The registered company address is: Gewerbestrasse 11, 6330 Cham, Switzerland

For
Maddy and Claudia
&
Mira and Alexandra

Personality implies that as this person: I am completely determined on every side and so finite, yet nonetheless I am simply and solely self-relation, and therefore in finitude I know myself as something infinite,—universal, and free.
—Hegel, Philosophy of Right

Acknowledgements

This book is a collection of essays based on lectures delivered at the Academy of Ideas *Academy* in 2017. All the chapters in this book were originally delivered as a lecture or talk in some form. We have edited them into prose, but inevitably many of them retain a more informal and colloquial tone than might be expected in a publication intended exclusively for an academic audience. We hope that will make the book—in its broad brush, if not cursory, treatment of a hugely complex and difficult subject—open to a wider readership, but we do seek to excuse neither the limitations that result nor the errors our editing will have introduced.

We would like to thank all the contributors to this collection—many of whom are long-term supporters of the Academy—for agreeing to include their lectures and for their commitment of time and effort in making them ready for publication. Frank Furedi and Claire Fox deserve special mention for their ongoing inspiration and support. In addition, we owe a debt to all those regulars at the Academy over the last eight years without whose support, commitment, and intellectual input, these ideas would not have developed in the way and at the pace they have.

We are very grateful to Sharla Plant at Palgrave Macmillan for entertaining the original idea and taking the project on board. And to Poppy Hull and all the team there for making it a reality.

Gae Kennedy helped with transcribing two of the original lectures. We would both like to thank Gae and Sara Beck for all their support in too many ways than we have space to list here.

West Sussex, 2019   A.E.K.
Oxford, 2019   J.K.P.

Contents

Part I 1

1 **Introduction: Classical and Contemporary Forms of Alienation** 3
   James Panton

2 **The Emergence of the Self in History** 13
   Frank Furedi

3 **In Praise of Selfish Individualism** 27
   Jamie Whyte

4 **Self-Enlightenment** 45
   Angus Kennedy

5 **'Of Individuality, as One of the Elements of Wellbeing.' J.S. Mill and the Nineteenth-Century Liberal Individual** 69
   James Panton

| 6 | The Rise and Fall of the Rule of Law
Jon Holbrook | 85 |

Part II   103

7	Autonomy and the Birth of Authenticity *Tim Black*	105
8	Self, Society, Alienation: From Marx to Identity Politics *Josie Appleton*	129
9	Anti-humanism and the Deconstruction of the Liberal Subject *James Heartfield*	147
10	Narcissism and Identity *Claire Fox*	167
11	New Forms of Alienation *Frank Furedi*	193
12	Conclusion: The Self and Its Prospects *Angus Kennedy*	207

Index   225

Notes on Contributors

Josie Appleton is the director of the Manifesto Club (www.manifestoclub.com), which campaigns for freedom in everyday life, and is the author of dozens of reports about contemporary civil liberties. She studied sociology and politics at the University of Oxford (undergraduate) and the University of London (graduate). She worked as a journalist and editor for five years and has good contacts with political/current affairs desks on all major newspapers where her research is reported every three months or so. She is the author of *Officious: Rise of the Busybody State* (2016) and she writes about the history and philosophy of freedom at notesonfreedom.com

Tim Black is the editor of the essay-and-review magazine, the spiked review, and a columnist at *Spiked*. He has also written for the *EU Observer*, the *Australian*, the *Independent*, *La Republica*, and others. He did a PhD at the University of Sussex on 'The Ideology of Modernism'.

Claire Fox is the director of the Academy of Ideas (AoI), which she established to create a public space where ideas can be contested without constraint. She convenes the yearly Battle of Ideas festival and initiated the Debating Matters Competition for sixth formers. She also co-founded the AoI's residential summer school, the Academy, with the aim to demonstrate 'university as it should be'. Fox is a panellist on BBC Radio 4's *The Moral Maze* and is frequently invited to comment on developments in culture, education, media and free-speech issues on TV and radio programmes in the UK such as *Newsnight* and *Any Questions?* and regularly appears on Sky News' evening paper review. Fox is a columnist for *TES* (*Times Educational Supplement*) and *MJ* (*Municipal Journal*). She is the author of a book on free speech, recently republished as *I STILL Find That Offensive!* (2018), and *No Strings Attached! Why Arts Funding Should Say No to Instrumentalism* (2007). Fox is involved at a board level in the international debate network, Time to Talk. In 2018, she did a three-month residency as a presenter of the weekly three-hour radio magazine show *Fox News Friday* on Love Sport Radio.

Frank Furedi is a sociologist and social commentator. Since the late 1990s, he has been widely cited about his views on why Western societies find it so difficult to engage with risk and uncertainty. He has published extensively on controversies relating to issues such as health, parenting children, food and new technology. His book *Invitation to Terror: Expanding the Empire of the Unknown* (2007) explores the way in which the threat of terrorism has become amplified through the ascendancy of precautionary thinking. It develops the arguments contained in two previous books, *Culture of Fear* (2002) and *Paranoid Parenting* (2001). Both of these works investigate the interaction between risk consciousness and perceptions of fear, trust relations and social capital in contemporary society. His new book, *How Fear Works: Culture of Fear in the 21st Century*, returns to his original theme—as most of what he predicted has come true. It seeks to explain two interrelated themes: why has fear acquired such a morally commanding status in society today, and how has the way we fear today changed from the way that it was experienced in the past? Furedi has also written extensively about issues to do with education and cultural life. His book *Wasted: Why Education Is Not Educating* (2009) deals with the influence of the erosion of adult authority on schooling. *On Tolerance* (2011) offers a restatement of the importance of this concept for an open society. *Authority: A Sociological History* (2013) examines how the modern world has become far more comfortable with questioning authority than with affirming it. Furedi is committed to promoting the ideals of a humanist education, and his writings on higher education are devoted to affirming the value of the liberal arts. His book *Power of*

Reading: From Socrates to Twitter (2015) outlines the case for a liberal humanist conception of a culture of reading. One of his most recent publications *What's Happened to the University?* is devoted to a study of the infantilisation of the academy and its relation to wider cultural influences. Furedi's books and articles offer an authoritative yet lively account of key developments in contemporary cultural life. Using his insights as a professional sociologist, he has produced a series of agenda-setting books that have been widely discussed in the media. His recent book *Populism and the European Culture Wars: The Conflict of Values Between Hungary and the EU* argues that the EU Establishment has succeeded in distorting the true meaning both of populism and of the principle of national sovereignty. Furedi's books have been translated into 13 languages. Furedi regularly comments on radio and television. He has appeared on *Newsnight*, Sky News and BBC News, Radio Four's *Today* programme and a variety of other radio television shows. Internationally, he has been interviewed by the media in Australia, Canada, the United States, Poland, Holland, Belgium, Brazil and Germany. Follow Furedi on Twitter @Furedibyte.

James Heartfield is a British writer and lecturer. He has published widely on international politics and Empire. He wrote *The Aborigines' Protection Society, 1837–1909* (2011), *Who's Afraid of the Easter Rising?* (2015), and *An Unpatriotic History of the Second World War* (2012). His PhD thesis (awarded by the University of Westminster) was published as *The European Union and the End of Politics*, by Zero Books in 2013. His most recent publication is *The Equal Opportunities Revolution* (2017), though his 2006 *The Death of the Subject Explained* is maybe the most immediately relevant to this project. Heartfield has also written for *Art Review*, Spiked Online, and *The Times Education Supplement*. Heartfield has had articles published in the *Guardian*, the *Telegraph*, *The Times*, *Blueprint*, the *Architects' Journal*, the *Review of Radical Political Economy*, *Rising East*, *Cultural Trends*, and the *Platypus Review*.

Jon Holbrook has been a practising barrister for over 25 years. He started his legal career in 1991 in what became a leading human rights chambers (Garden Court Chambers) by doing mostly legal aid work for individual service users, but in 2004 he moved to a different sort of chambers where he built a practice acting mostly for local authorities and service providers. He changed his practice in order to swim against the tide that was moving in an ever-stronger rights-based direction. The author is recognised as a leading barrister for public law by the legal directories. In 2017 Chambers & Partners described Holbrook as 'terribly good—you get a QC service when you go to him'. When not in his wig and gown Holbrook has been politically active, and after a brief spell in the Labour Party he joined, in 1985, an organisation that developed into *Spiked* and the Academy of Ideas, two organisations for which he regularly writes and speaks. In 2014 Holbrook was shortlisted by the legal publisher, Halsbury, for its Legal Journalism award for his *Spiked* articles on the politics of law. He tweets for 'more politics and less law' at @JonHolb. Holbrook has also written for the *New Law Journal* and Judicial Power Project. Earlier this year Policy Exchange published his critique of Global Governance (co-authored with Professor James Allan).

Angus Kennedy is the convenor of the Academy of Ideas' educational initiative the Academy, which he established in 2011 as a modest attempt to demonstrate—over a weekend of reading and discussion—what university should be like and so rarely is. He is interested in and writes on the philosophy of freedom and is the author of *Being Cultured: In Defence of Discrimination* (2014). He has MAs in Classics from Christ Church, Oxford and Linguistics from Birkbeck College London as well as an MPhil in Artificial Intelligence from Dundee University. He works in information technology and is working on a book titled *Borders: The Foundation of Freedom and Security*.

James Panton is the head of upper sixth and head of politics at Magdalen College School, Oxford, and associate lecturer in philosophy at the Open University. He previously taught political theory and intellectual history at St John's College, Hertford College, and Balliol College, Oxford, and he was responsible for setting up the tutorial teaching training programme for graduate students in the department of politics and international relations, University of Oxford. Panton continues to teach politics, philosophy, and intellectual history regularly for the department of continuing education at the University of Oxford. He is the author of academic and mainstream media articles and commentaries. Panton has also campaigned around politics and civil liberties. He was a founder member of the pressure group *The Manifesto Club*, which campaigns against the hyper-regulation of everyday life, and a founding member of *Pro*Test in defence of animal research at Oxford University.

Jamie Whyte is a journalist. From 2017 to 2018 he was Director of Research at the Institute of Economic Affairs (IEA). In 2014 he was leader of the ACT Party of New Zealand, a position he resigned upon failing to be elected to parliament in the September general election. Whyte has previously worked as a management consultant for Oliver Wyman and the Boston Consultant Group. He lectured in philosophy at Cambridge University, from where he also holds his PhD. Whyte is the author of *Quack Policy* (2013), *Free Thoughts* (2012), *A Load of Blair* (2005), and *Crimes Against Logic* (2004). He won the Bastiat Prize for Journalism in 2006 and was runner-up in 2010 and 2016.

Part I

1

Introduction: Classical and Contemporary Forms of Alienation

James Panton

This book is a collection of essays based on lectures delivered at the Academy of Ideas *Academy* in July 2017. The Academy that year was devoted to an exploration of the rise and the fall of the self. As organisers of the event, Angus Kennedy, Josie Appleton, Tim Black, and I were particularly interested in exploring the peculiar ways in which selfhood is problematised in contemporary society—for example, on the one hand, there is our increasing obsession with the fixed corporeality of selfhood (biology, sex, colour, and so on) which, on the other hand, sits beside a rather hollowed out, and increasingly abstract, form of universal selfhood (the cosmopolitan self who is a citizen of the world but with nowhere to call home). We began by considering a more or less classical, Enlightenment-liberal, notion of the self which emerges historically through the location of human subjectivity in some variant of individual freedom or autonomy: freedom or autonomy is taken to be the condition for individuals to undertake projects, often in collaboration with other individuals, in the pursuit of common interests. By contrast, formulations of the self

J. Panton (✉)
Magdalen College School, Oxford, UK

that we can begin to uncover in much contemporary social and political discussion seem to begin from a disavowal of the self as a subject or agent in the world in favour of a self that is conceptualised in terms of more rigid categories of identity: what I am, it seems, has become more important than what I might make of myself.

The trajectory we have sought to uncover is a movement *from self to selfie*: from a model of an autonomous agent, the author of their own being, to a model of a more heteronomous individual whose existence is realised through continuous external validation; the self really only exists as a selfie, and its existence becomes more determinate the more *likes* it receives. To the extent that this trajectory from self to selfie is real, we are concerned that the ground of the existence of the individual is moving from a pursuit of agency to a condition of objectivity; from the pursuit of truth and knowledge to a one-sided acceptance of the facts of being. Where once the alienation of the self from its possibilities was a condition to be overcome, now those erstwhile alienated conditions of selfhood are embraced and celebrated.

A problem for any attempt to study the self is the difficulty one encounters in attempting to capture the subject itself: the answer to the question 'what is the self?' is always elusive. The self, as Frank Furedi suggests in Chap. 2, 'is always in the process of changing, mutating, and developing new dimensions of itself.' It 'does not, and cannot, stay still.' This fact of the self, that it is in a state of constant flux, explains why some of the most significant attempts to conceptualise what it is that forms the essence of being human often have an intangible character. Marx's famous definition of the essence of man in the *Theses on Feuerbach*, for example, that 'the essence of man is no abstraction inherent in each single individual' but rather the 'ensemble of social relations' (1845 [2002], §6) suggests that the essence of what it is to be a human being must be sought somewhere outside the boundaries of the individual: somewhere in the relationships through which society is produced and reproduced. However, this essential character of man must also find its expression in the individual men and women who are, essentially, humanity. The construction of the self as an individual in society and the possibility for that self to realise itself are differently conditioned by the organisation of society in different historical moments. 'The abstract individual,' notes Marx, 'belongs in reality to a particular social form' (1845 [2002], §7). This historically situated character of the individual self is the foundation of our attempt to make sense of the peculiarities of the self, and in particular, the unique form taken by the problematisation of selfhood in the contemporary period.

The problem of pinning down the nature of the self is not, however, merely historical. The restless nature of the self, whereby its definition must be sought and yet its boundaries are (never quite) discovered somewhere outside of itself, is true in any one period just as much as it is true across different historical moments. Neither biological nor spiritual nor temporal definitions of the self ever quite get at its essence. This is the truth in Sartre's paradoxical assertion: 'We have to deal with human reality as a being which is what it is not and which is not what it is' (1943 [1996]: 58). To other selves, the individual exists as a particular being: observable, embodied, biologically bounded, sexed, and gendered, with a particular skin colour and determinable way of being in the world. This is, of course, who one is to others, and it may also form an important aspect of who one is to oneself. Yet Sartre's point is that we are these more or less fixed and determined, factical aspects of ourselves, *only in the sense of not being them*. For we are also *so* much more. We are subjects of our own lives and experiences. As the philosopher Thomas Nagel notes, 'to yourself, more intimately, you appear as "I", the mental subject of your experiences, thoughts, feelings, memories and emotions' (2009: 33). The opacity of my inner subjectivity to others is one aspect of Sartre's paradoxical assertion. A further and important aspect is the extent to which I am constantly and necessarily going beyond the limits of my facticity: I am constantly and unstoppably in a process of *becoming*. *I am what I am not* (my objective, given, factical, self) because it is what I outwardly am, and yet I am so much more than this; and *I am not* (yet) *what I am* (my subjectively determined and determining, experiencing, conscious, becoming, self) because this aspect of my selfhood remains always and forever in the realm of possibility.

The intention of this book is to explore the problematisation of the self in contemporary society using the necessarily changing dynamic of selfhood as the foundation for our investigation. The way we approach this often intangible object is through a comparison between the models of selfhood which seem to underpin discussions of the self today with the models of selfhood which emerged in an earlier age, and which seemed to be relatively more optimistic about the human condition. The lectures from which the chapters in this book are drawn are diverse in their exploration of different accounts of selfhood from different historical moments and perspectives. The contributors do not necessarily agree in their diagnosis of the problem, but they share a sense that there is a new problematic of the self in contemporary society which is worthy of exploration.

We have organised the book into two parts from which certain core themes and questions emerge. The chapters in Part I trace the emergence of ideals of selfhood in different historical periods, including classically liberal accounts of the self and its possibilities as seen in philosophy, economics, law, and politics. These reach a high point in late-Enlightenment accounts of the self: ideas of the primacy of individual reason, self-determination, natural rights, freedom, and autonomy.[1] The chapters in Part II then examine more contemporary examples of what can be understood as the decline or eclipse of the self in a reaction that expresses new forms of determinism, whether they lay claim to a need to be true to a supposedly authentic self or through the determinations, even self-imposed, of class, race, gender, and identity.

* * *

In Chap. 2, Frank Furedi traces the emergence of self-consciousness to the Renaissance, and to Luther's distinction between the inner and external life of the individual. The space that was opened up, as external authority was weakened, created the possibility for the self to become self-authorising. However, this self-authorising self necessarily existed on shaky foundations, precisely given the weakening of external authority. This meant that the emergence of selfhood in this period established the self, from the moment of its possibility, as a problem. For Furedi, the

---

[1] This 'Enlightenment' model should not be read too crudely: the model of Enlightenment universalism in opposition to Romantic particularism has always missed the point that Hegel, perhaps more than any other thinker, understood: that the universal 'is neither seen nor heard,' it is realised only in the form of the particular (1830 [2010]).

transformative dynamic of selfhood is positively driven by the capacity for imaginative self-determination 'which engages the individual in a project of testing the boundaries of necessity' in order to 'create a space in which we can determine for ourselves certain dimensions of our lives' (Chap. 2). Jamie Whyte, in Chap. 3, gives a superficially less problematic account of the self as the individual, which underpins classically liberal models of free-market capitalism: the self as selfish individual. Here, the pursuit of self-interest is fundamental to the human condition, and for Whyte, it is free-market individualism which best harnesses that selfish drive in positive terms: 'That is why,' he claims, 'people who live in capitalist countries are freer and richer than people living in countries that reject selfish individualism.' This model of the self as a rationally self-interested agent is something I pick up in Chap. 5 in discussing John Stuart Mill's individual as conceived in *On Liberty* as the apotheosis of the Enlightenment-liberal model of the self. I argue that this self is far more socially engaged than the more classically liberal free-market account suggests, and in its social engagement, this self is also far more robust than contemporary models of the self are wont to allow. For Angus Kennedy, in Chap. 4, the tension between the social and the individual is but one of the antithetical tensions in which the Enlightenment self is located: including nature and society, authenticity and autonomy, individual freedom and self-government in society. The challenge of the Enlightenment subject to create the world in its own image, and of the liberal individual to seek truth as the foundation of its being in the world, establishes a project of the self which is at the same time an impossible attempt to authorise itself as a self in the absence of external structures of authority and determination.

Resolution to this crisis of authority of the individual self has at different times been attempted by various forms of external authority, but such attempted resolutions may be more transient than they often appear. In Chap. 6, Jon Holbrook considers the transforming model of selfhood underpinning the ideal of the liberal 'rule of law': the legal subject. However, the notion that rule of law is fundamental is, as he suggests, to mistake what was in reality the role of law for a particular period in the middle of the twentieth century, for the entire structure of law throughout the history of liberal democracy. Holbrook believes that where once law could assume a more or less stable consensus between individuals within which it enabled personal autonomy to flourish, there has been ever since an expanding juridification of relations between individuals whose autonomy can no longer be assumed; the rule *of* law has been replaced with the rule *by* law; individual latitude hemmed in by contract.

* * *

The capacity for the self to exist beyond the boundaries and determinations of itself is, on the one hand, the foundation for the dynamic and creative potential that we as individual human beings represent. On the other hand, it explains the fact of our alienation: our dislocation from ourselves as potential selves; our disconnection from the world we inhabit as our world; our tendency to experience our freedom as unsettling, and our facticity as all determining. One core theme that emerges from Part II of this book is that the peculiarity of the present is the extent to which contemporary culture encourages us to embrace and to celebrate our alienation rather than to experience that alienation as a challenge, as something to be overcome. As the self, the rational conscious subject, has become more and more important from the Reformation onwards, so too have external forms of authority been weakened or rejected, leaving the self victorious (as it were) but alone and decentred: the battle won, but the war lost. The self becomes acutely aware of its own fragility and centrality and shrinks from the limelight, looking to find validation and guidance outside its self. In the past the self struggled to leave itself behind, to transcend its limitations, but now the selfie turns instead to demanding recognition and protection for what it is, for its identity, not for what it has become or made of itself. It appears, ironically, that reaching the very heights of subjectivity—seeing no limits to what the self can achieve—has left us without limits to transcend and, as a result, we are left with ourselves. As individual selves we are wont to then explain away this situation, listing various excusatory external factors that make it so: the fashionable determinations of neuroscience, genetics, culture, or gender, for example.

In the opening chapter of Part II, Tim Black begins with the notion of authenticity as the defining ideal of selfhood in the contemporary world and then traces that ideal back through two and a half centuries of the problematisation of the self. Black argues that over that period, amongst other things, there has been a change in the nature of *authenticity*: where once it was seen as expressing the ability of the authentic self to stand independent and unconcerned, free from the judgement of others, it has now turned into a demand for the judgement of others to fall in one particular way, in recognition of the identity in question. In Chap. 8, Josie Appleton argues that we have seen an erosion of the mediation between the individual and society, resulting in increasingly estranged elements of the individual and the social. For her, this process is most clearly expressed in contemporary identity, and she suggests the conceptualisation of the individual is now largely hostile to the social (and by contrast, the social is conceived in ways that are hostile to the individual). Appleton's chapter seeks to make sense of the ways in which the contemporary estrangement of people from their social existence is expressed at the level of social policies which develop and elaborate the disconnection between individual people. The growth and expansion of external forms of mediation between individuals—bureaucracy and therapy, and we might now add social media—were key to Christopher Lasch's groundbreaking exploration of the changing dynamics of selfhood in the twentieth century (1979 [1991]). In Chap. 10, Claire Fox notes that according to the *New York Times*, narcissism is now 'the go-to diagnosis' for commentators. Fox critically explores different explanations for narcissism as a defining cultural characteristic of the present, from affluence, through 1960s permissiveness, to overindulgent parenting; from a loss of confidence in the future to a demonization of the past. In Chap. 9, James Heartfield traces the intellectual upsurge in different strands of philosophy—from the linguistics of the structuralists, Levi-Strauss's anthropology, Louis Althusser's reconsiderations of the basis of Marxism, Derrida's deconstruction of ontology, Lacan's deconstructions of Freud and the unconscious, and Michel Foucault's historical genealogy—whereby the centrality of Man and the model of a human-centred moral and intellectual universe was radically reconsidered. These 'post-modern' theories were of course once derided by those of an Anglo-American analytic bent as the harbingers of relativism and the destruction of truth. Yet it should be clear that what is explicit in the work of these so-called Continental thinkers is already implicit in the intellectual tradition traced throughout Part II of this book: the decentring of a self who, diminished in stature and lacking recourse to reason and agency, becomes unable to make claims to truth or understanding beyond the dimension of immediate experience. This is why for Heartfield what has often been seen as the triumph of subjectivity over objective reality in these theories of deconstruction is really a critique of the *subject* itself.

* * *

Throughout the chapters in this book, contributors explore different aspects of the changing dynamics of selfhood. Today we see a retreat into forms of denial of the possibilities of the self, in the sense that the scope and importance of autonomy and self-conscious reason are played down in neurological or biological reductionist accounts of the self, and through the re-emergence of the concept of fate in the form of pre-given, off-the-shelf, identities. What people are has become more important than what they want to become: rather than the agency of the self, venturing out and discovering itself in the making of a world fit for selves, we now have a self which finds itself already constituted, thrown into a world in which we are fixed and pre-determined. This modern condition of selfhood is paradoxical. The identity of the self has become both entirely free floating, on the one hand, to be changed almost at whim, and entirely determinate, on the other hand, in the sense that the given identity of the individual becomes the overriding and unassailable condition of their existence.[2] These competing characteristics of selfhood are two sides of the same coin. However, complete determination and complete indeterminacy both miss the fundamental character of our personhood: that we are both determinate products of a world we do not choose, and agents capable of choosing ourselves in that world.

As an attempted resolution to the contemporary modes of alienation of the self from itself and from its possibilities, the selfie self is tilting at

---

[2] Recent research by Mastercard has found that the use of 'I' and 'me' in pop songs has eclipsed that of 'you,' rising by 43 per cent in the 20 years to 2018. Songs about sex are out (it takes a you to tango after all) with a fall of 69 per cent, but the words 'body' and 'pretty' have increased by 428 and 2300 per cent, respectively (MasterCard Social Newsroom 2019).

windmills. It declares itself unique and individual on the basis of nothing more than the bare fact of being there and the incantation of the spell: 'I identify as...' It bolsters its claim by inflating the extent of external threats it imagines it finds in social 'phobias' ranged against its identity of choice. It then demands that society—the state—police and regulate these supposedly hostile identities in order to create a safe space for its own, vulnerable, selfie. The selfie proclaims itself homeless and says that is what the condition of being is these days (think of Generation Rent). It then demands that the state provide housing: seemingly unaware that one might be 'housed' but will never be 'at home'—for the latter is a matter of creating oneself and fashioning the space in the world into which one can fit, rather than being squeezed into a ready-made box.

Hence the individual self, the selfie, in its action, reaffirms and embraces its alienation not only from the world but from its own active engagement in that world. One consequence of the arguments put forward in this book is that the decline of the self into particularism and identity politics has shattered the shared universal foundation of the individual which rested in the mutual recognition of autonomy. When the self demands recognition for what it is—for its difference—it closes the door on what we have in common: the self stays locked in; unable to transcend those limits the existence of which it has already denied; unable to develop its own identity because it lacks any social identity.

We conclude with arguments as to why we need to find a new balance between the desire to leave ourselves behind and the need to recognise the reality and value of the constraints and limits that serve to make us what we are. In its simplest form this means accepting that for every 'I' there is a 'You' and that if I am to receive recognition it can only be on the basis that You do too: in the shared recognition of our mutual independence.

References

Hegel, G. W. F. (1830 [2010]). *Encyclopaedia of the philosophical sciences in basic outline: Part 1: Science of logic*. Cambridge: Cambridge (Cambridge Hegel Translations).

Lasch, C. (1979 [1991]). *The culture of narcissism: American life in an age of diminishing expectations*. New York: W.W. Norton.
Marx, K. (1845 [2002]). *Theses on Feuerbach*. Marx/Engels Internet Archive. Retrieved from https://www.marxists.org/archive/marx/works/1845/theses/theses.htm.
MasterCard Social Newsroom. (2019). *Selfie generation's music is all about me, me, me....* [Online]. Retrieved January 6, 2019, from https://newsroom.mastercard.com/eu/press-releases/selfie-generations-music-is-all-about-me-me-me/.
Nagel, T. (2009, November 5). The I in Me. *London Review of Books, 31*(21), 33–34.
Sartre, J.-P. (1943 [1996]). *Being and nothingness: An essay on phenomenological ontology* (H. E. Barnes, Trans.). London: Routledge.

2

The Emergence of the Self in History

Frank Furedi

I want to start to explore the way the self has been conceptualised—throughout history—by focusing on a number of recurring themes: using them as a way of isolating the key questions we need to reflect upon to make sense of the emergence and transformation of the self.

The question I posed to myself when I started to write this chapter was to ask what had been the nature of my own thinking in relation to the question of the self in the course of my intellectual development. I remembered that as an undergraduate, a very long time ago, my final thesis in my last year at university was on the self: particularly on the alienated self. I still have notes on the self that go back almost four decades, and I thought I would look back through them in preparation for writing this chapter and see the ways in which my own concerns and ideas have evolved: an approach which I think was actually quite useful because just as one goes back and forth in history in one's reading, so it is often profitable as well to go back and forth in terms of one's own intellectual development, and see how these things interweave.

F. Furedi (✉)
University of Kent, Canterbury, UK

One of the things that really struck me when I looked at my notes and looked again at the literature dealing with the question of the self—reacquainting myself with the different philosophers, theologians, and psychologists dealing with the issue—is that actually the title I had chosen for this chapter, that is to say the topic I had committed myself to exploring, namely the nature of the emergence of the self in history, was not quite accurate; the real focus of the chapter should be on the *emerging* self. The wonderful thing about the self is that it is always in the process of changing, mutating, and developing new dimensions of itself. In many respects how we view the self, the things that we attribute to it, and above all the way we experience ourselves, is always changing because, whether we like it or not, we are always in the business of remaking ourselves, refashioning, and reimagining ourselves. It is one of the central dimensions of the human experience that in response to it the self does not, and cannot, stay still. In an important sense any project that sets out to 'discover' the self must invariably end in failure for the simple reason that the self can never be discovered, found, or cast into any fixed and immutable form as long as we continue to imagine: it is only when one ceases to imagine and to reflect on the world that the self can, finally, stay still.

The attitudes we have about the self are invariably related to the way we view the relationship between the self and society. Throughout history, the discussion on the self has always been about what forces—spiritual or physical or material—impinge upon the self. What are these external forces that constrain and compel the self to conform to certain patterns of behaviour? How do they operate?

Now my own concern in this chapter, and also in my work more broadly (see especially Furedi 2011, 2013), is to establish the case for an idea of the self that combines a voluntarist dimension of self-formation with the recognition that self-determination has its limits and must always be prepared to settle accounts with the constant and unpredictable demands of external necessity. We have to be able to formulate a view that can understand that, on the one hand, the self has this voluntaristic idealised form of existence where it is continually striving to free itself of every encumbrance, but at the same time, even in the best of all possible worlds, there is an ever-present material, physical, and social reality that one has to relate to and upon which one is in some sense dependent.

2 The Emergence of the Self in History

What is genuinely interesting is to what degree one can hope to construct and defend an ideal of the possibility of self-creation through the self-conscious cultivation of the self without falling into idealistic and sometimes mystical solutions which attempt to transcend the self. As we can see, for example, in mystical religions, and also in some forms of Christianity, when hermits go off to the desert and spend years and years looking into their own souls: leading their lives on quests for something that they can never hope to really discover given that the self is not something hidden inside us. No matter how hard you look, you cannot hope to find it. It is something that emerges through our action in the world and interaction with others.

* * *

We have inherited some wonderful ideas about the self from different philosophical traditions, such as the Stoics for example, or the important modern version of the self that emerges with the writings of John Locke. Locke claimed that the 'self is a conscious thinking thing' (Martin and Barresi 2006: 92). For myself, however, the most important contribution towards understanding the workings of the self is to be found in Marx. The third thesis on Feuerbach is absolutely critical for understanding how the self works. If you recall, what Marx did was to provide us with a very useful concept of self-emancipation, an idea that he developed over a period of time.

Importantly, Marx argued that human activity means self-change. To quote the third thesis in full:

> The materialist doctrine concerning the changing of circumstances and upbringing forgets that circumstances are changed by men and that it is essential to educate the educator himself. This doctrine must, therefore, divide society into two parts, one of which is superior to society.
>
> The coincidence of the changing of circumstances and of human activity or self-changing can be conceived and rationally understood only as *revolutionary practice*. (Marx 1985: 121)

The idea of self-change is something that is essential to Marx's theory: as far as Marx was concerned *being human* and *the transformation of the self* were synonymous. The two ideas overlap each other in such a fundamental way that Marx is able to draw the conclusion that any activity which is not self-changing is, therefore, not human. For Marx the term 'self-change' implies the mutual transformation of an active subject, on the one hand, which does the interpreting and changing, and an object, on the other, which is interpreted and changed. And I think that kind of relationship is eloquently set out in some of his earlier writing.

* * *

For now, however, let us just take a step back and ask the question, what is the self? What is this notion or idea of a self that we are trying to examine? As I suggested, it is a fluid concept, one that changes with time and through history, but whenever we think about the self what we commonly mean is the particular being of a person, any person: whatever it is about each of us that distinguishes you or me from others, draws the parts of our existence together, persists through changes, or opens the way to becoming who we might be or should be; it includes the future-oriented dimension of the self as well.

By far the most interesting historical study of the self to come from political theory in recent years is Jerrold Seigel's *The Idea of the Self* (2007). Seigel claims that there are three important dimensions through which the self has been approached in Western culture since the modernist conception of the self emerged from thinkers such as Descartes and Locke. The first dimension is the bodily or material dimension of the self which 'involves the physical, corporeal existence of individuals, the things about our nature that make us palpable creatures driven by needs, urges, and inclinations' (Seigel 2007: 5) which influence our temperament. This material dimension is a presupposition of the self. The second dimension Seigel considers is the relational dimension of the self, which 'arises from social and cultural interaction, the common connections and involvements that give us collective identities and shared orientations and values, making us people able to use a specific language or idiom.' In this dimension, 'our selves are what our relations with society and with others shape or allow us to be' (Seigel 2007: 5). And thirdly, and for me very importantly, there is a third dimension which is the reflective dimension of the self: 'the human capacity to make both the world and our own existence objects of our active regard... putting ourselves at a distance from our own being so as to examine, judge, and sometimes regulate or revise it' (Seigel 2007: 6). This third dimension of the self is particularly important for those of us who are concerned to understand the self's relation to freedom and autonomy or to cultivate a sense of autonomy.

Depending on where people stand on this question of autonomy will determine how they assess the importance of self-reflection. They will either seek to exalt the power of reflection or, alternatively, to diminish it and think of it as only of marginal importance. Of course, self-reflection is not the only power that can be mobilised against the limits of individual and social existence—there are other ways of overcoming social constraints—but my view is that whatever the strengths and weaknesses of any particular strategy, it will still always require a prior act of reflective subjectivity. In other words, whatever strategy one adopts, in order to go beyond existing limits, there is a logically prior point at which the act of subjectivity becomes quite fundamental. This is because, everything else being considered, it is only in thought that we can take the distance, or begin to take the distance, adopt a perspective, on each and every form of determined existence: on *what is*. Thought alone provokes a medium for self-determination and freedom. This means that the first stage for the cultivation of freedom has got to be in the mind: it cannot exist in a way that is external to it, and obviously the mind itself is very much influenced by social developments and social influences.

An act of subjectivity involves an element of imagination. Self-determination—which engages the individual in a project of testing the boundaries of necessity—has this kind of imaginative quality to it, and, an admittedly limited, although substantial, independence from the material and the relational conditions that partly determine it. It is in this sense that we can see reflexivity as a power, as a medium through which we can hope to create a space for the exercise of autonomy. That is what is fundamental to the process of self-reflection: it is an attempt to create a space in which we can determine for ourselves certain dimensions of our lives.

Of course, though, reflection can exist in both a passive and an active form: there are different ways of understanding it. So, the question about reflection that must be asked is whether it is intentional—is it voluntary—because it must be *intentional* self-reflection if it is to have any chance of acquiring a conscious and purposeful form. And it seems to me that the logical priority of self-directed and willed reflection is critical, but it does not mean that we can ignore the social and the relational dimensions. We always have to remember that when we talk about discovering our true selves, or we talk about reflecting on our real selves, the very attempt to grasp ourselves is influenced, not simply by our own imagination, but at the same time by preconceived and culturally framed ideas about the self and how the self needs to be understood. And I think that is the balance we need to put on this very important relationship.

That there are limits to the freedom of the reflective self was already intuitively grasped by the ancient Greeks: they understood that what can be gained in inner freedom is not always in lockstep with the workings out of actual life. That after all is the central message of Greek tragedy: human beings are involved in attempts to realise inner freedom, but in the process they often pay a serious price for those attempts. There is a long history of thinking about the self in which the question of the expansive freedom or socially and materially bounded character of the self is central. One recurring question is whether the self is innate or the product of external experience, to which John Locke famously answers that what we start with is a *tabula rasa*, an 'empty slate' to be shaped and formed by experience (See Locke 1998 [1690]). This inevitably drew Locke's ideas into conflict with those of the Church, which regarded the soul and the self as innate: as an original and originating gift of God. The idea that the self is fundamentally an achievement of society reaches its clearest elaboration in the writings of Émile Durkheim (see Durkheim 2002 [1897]). Durkheim claimed that the self had its roots in the social and goes so far as to argue that 'collective consciousness' is the highest form of social life (Martin and Barresi 2006: 481).

This is a very important question in itself but is also linked to a further question: which is whether or not the self is knowable through introspection, through self-reflection, or only becomes capable of being known through others in society who act as a mirror for us, allowing us to see ourselves. There is equally a history—perhaps best exemplified in modernity in the works of the Scottish moral philosophers—of inquiring as to whether or not the self is selfish, that is to say, greedy, or whether the self is oriented towards solidarity. In David Hume's thought, the self has a capacity for sympathy which can co-exist with self-love and provide a way of fusing together the idea of someone else's feeling with our own. The self, in this understanding, provides a vehicle for social interactions.[1]

Furthermore, we can ask if the self is rational or irrational. In the nineteenth century there are the beginnings of the development of irrationalism in European, specifically German, philosophy, seen to some extent in thinkers such as Fichte and Schelling in their challenges to Kantian dualism. Schelling questioned the rationality of the ego and in his reflections on this subject anticipated the subsequent deliberation on the unconscious in Freud. According to Lukács: Fichte purifies 'Kantian philosophy of its materialist fluctuations and creates a purely subjective idealism' while Schelling seeks to ground his 'objective idealism' in a semi-mystical 'intellectual intuition' over and above rational understanding (Lukács 1980: 217: 141). It is at this point that some of the most serious challenges to the idea of autonomy first emerge: asking what autonomy means at this particular stage in history.

* * *

Whatever questions are asked about the self, and almost *whenever* they are asked, there is one thing that must always be borne in mind: if we are to stand any chance of knowing what the self is really like, we need to remember that we find the self to be something that is true only in the course of having a conversation with ourselves. I think we often overlook the fact that all of us as human beings are continually having a conversation with ourselves, whether we know it or not: it is once that conversation stops that the possibility of very serious mental health problems occurs.

---

[1] Hume, of course, also creates problems for any straightforward understanding of the self, arguing that there is no one site or thing that the self is. See most obviously *An Essay Concerning Human Understanding* (1748).

Thinkers have debated whether the self comes first (e.g., as a soul in some sense) or whether the self is preceded by its empirical reality. They ask whether the self is already in existence before it is actually willed or acted upon, or is it only manifested or actualised as a result of action. Overall, I think there are two interesting questions that come out of these other bigger questions, or two important trends that are in competition with each other and which dominate our existence even today. I think that, on the one side, some believe in the importance of *self-authorisation*. For them, the authority of the self is seen as being crucial and anybody who takes self-determination and self-fashioning seriously will agree. The authority of the self was seen as almost absolute by Hegel who argued that through grasping the self we can actually understand the meaning of the age: the spirit of the age. He had an overwhelmingly positive attitude towards this idea of self-grasping. And, in Marx, as we saw above, we have the theory of self-creation which leads to ideas of self-emancipation.

But on the other hand, the other trend—and I think this comes increasingly to the fore post-war, in the twentieth century, and even more so today—is the *de-authorisation of the self*. From this perspective, in place of the self, particularly the self-determining self, we have an emphasis instead on the power of the unconscious. We have an emphasis on the fragility of the self; we talk about multiple selves and how the more multiple the self is, so the less fixed the self can ever become. As a result of the dominance of this trend, we now, very often, have a much-diminished version of the self in the twenty-first century than would have been the case in the Enlightenment, or even the immediate post-Enlightenment era.

* * *

I always go back to the Greeks because in many respects it is in the ancient world that a shift begins to occur whereby the self is taken seriously for the first time, and to some extent it is true to say the Greeks discovered the self. This process of self-discovery, if we can call it that, naturally took a very long time to unfold. In Homer, in the *Iliad* for example, all the epic heroes very seldom reflect on themselves: they have next to no interior life. As Bruno Snell put it:

2 The Emergence of the Self in History 21

> There are no divided feelings in Homer… no genuine reflexion, no dialogue of the soul with itself… Homer does not know genuine personal decisions; even where a hero is shown pondering two alternatives the intervention of the gods plays the key role… Mental and spiritual acts are due to the impact of external factors, and man is the open target of a great many forces which impinge upon him, and penetrate his very core. (Snell 1953: 19–20)

In fact, if one examines the way Homer writes about people, about his heroes, he tends to talk about their physicality and their bodily dimensions, rather than anything to do with their interiority (Snell 1953: 5–6). It is interesting to observe that there is no introspection within the Homeric hero at all. But no sooner has Homer written his poems than, bit by bit, the idea that somehow all human decisions and thoughts have a divine origin—which was the traditional idea—is gradually called into question and, little by little, we can trace the emergence of the interior processes of the self being intuited and taken seriously in Greek culture. What begins to happen with the Greeks is an intellectual leap, a revolution in fact, whereby, all of a sudden, they discover the human mind and the human self. It is not for nothing, after all, that Freud interprets the Oedipus tragedy in a psychological way: what he is really looking at are universal problems of the unconscious—very modern problems—but problems which are already immanent within the Greek tragedies themselves. What we have in the tragedy of Oedipus is really nothing other than the discovery of the self as being simultaneously both free and determined by fate. Oedipus is, on the one hand, the archetypal self-made man: becoming King of Thebes as reward for freeing it from the Sphinx. On the other hand, everything he does at the same time encompasses his doom. He exhibits self-capacity and moral freedom and the possibility of breaking with tradition, but also the terrible fate (self-inflicted blindness) which awaits those who do not really know themselves.

And by the time you get to Plato's Socratic dialogues, there is a much clearer understanding of self-reflection being promoted. With the Stoics too there are very exciting ideas put forward concerning the importance of the self: ideas of the possibility of changing yourself and being able to control your life through that whole process. So, I think, with the Greeks we can see a very interesting development whereby the self is discovered in terms of what both Plato and Aristotle understand as the *soul*, and it thenceforward becomes the intellectual, theoretical, centre of selfhood and, in a sense, becomes the very principle of life and thought.

In the Christian middle ages, according to Wiley: the 'Christian doctrine of the soul—its sacredness, immortality, and freedom—bolstered the self.' Augustine, for example, in his *Confessions*, demonstrates 'the vast interiority that could be explored with these ideas.' However what Christianity does, in a sense, is also diminish the self from its classical highpoint: 'The interaction of the soul with God and divine grace made it extremely porous and nonrational. Both freedom and cognition lost some of the autonomy they had achieved in the classical, Greek self.' So, what happens in Christian Europe is that both freedom and cognition lose some of the autonomy—because of the interaction with God—that had been achieved in the classical Greek self (Wiley 1994: 536).

Wiley's conclusion is that we are left by the Christian tradition with an ambiguous understanding of the self. On the one hand the 'idea of the immortal soul increased the importance of the self in ways that would have long-term consequences' for European civilisation and European ideas. But at the same time 'the idea of God submerged the self under a higher semiotic level, itself, as Feuerbach saw it, modelled after that which was submerged' (Wiley 1994: 537).

What makes the figure of Martin Luther so important in the development of thinking about the self is that he did not simply claim the authority of individual conscience on his own behalf, but instead put forward an argument that more or less negated the capacity of external authority to exercise power over the inner lives of people. The reason that this is an epochal step forward is that, in refusing to allow external authority to have any power over people's inner lives, Luther created the foundation for the self as a self-authorising self. However, in the very act of endowing the self with authority, he fundamentally undermined all forms of external authority. Marx says of Luther that he 'negated the idea of priests as something separate and apart from the layman by transferring the priest into the heart of the layman' (Marx 1988: xxxvi): after which point the meaning of authority is perpetually called into question.

2 The Emergence of the Self in History 23

Thus, from Luther we inherit a newly liberated concept of the self which is also a concept of the self that is in crisis. From Luther forwards—through the Reformation onwards, all through the eighteenth, nineteenth, and twentieth centuries, this aspiration to authorise the self and to limit external influences becomes one of the core themes within Western political theory, and within Western philosophy and social thought. This is the aspiration to a form of autonomous selfhood no longer dominated by external authority. In that sense, I think what we have is a very important transformation occurring, but a deeply contradictory one, at the same time.

I think this contradictory relationship that Luther initiates is never resolved. It creates a powerful anti-authoritarian tendency which is a positive development: the refusal to take authority on face value, the idea that authority now must be earned. There is also, I would argue, an important liberating impulse. While Luther himself was no liberal or supporter of a right to rebel (see: *Against the Murderous, Thieving Hordes of Peasants* [1525]), his ideas start to take on a life of their own: it is very often the case that ideas pushed to a certain point start to rise and bring to light contradictory elements which evolve and develop in directions their original author never could have entertained.

So, it is that this fundamental blow to authority then leads to the ascendancy of the idea of the *self-authorisation of the self*. In the present moment—and by present moment I mean recent history, the last 40, 50, 60 years—a new kind of contradiction emerges which is still with us all the time, and which haunts many aspects of the world that we live in. One of the things that occurs at the very moment the authority of the self gains cultural power and validation is that it inevitably becomes, simultaneously, *de-centred*. The more we have a sense of our selves, the more the process of focusing on our selves gains so much momentum and speed, that, in that moment, the self becomes so fluid and so difficult to imagine that it becomes de-centred. It is in the act of becoming de-centred—the result of the victory if you like of the authority of the self—that the self becomes uncomfortably aware of its own fragility. This fragility is often understood to be the product of a world that is increasingly unpredictable and fast changing. However, I have come to believe that this oversimplifies the situation. The self's fragility is not just the result of being in a fast-changing, unpredictable world that we cannot really direct, where our fate becomes subject to so many heterogeneous and complex influences (a world in which 'complexity' is used to explain anything that we do not understand, in which complexity breeds more complexity). To an important degree we perceive the world in this way, at least indirectly, *because* of the fragility of the self, so that the perceptions that we have of our own inner life, of our own inner world, are sublimated through an idea of an external complicated reality that we simply cannot possibly master which we posit to explain away, and thus permit ourselves to reconcile ourselves to our fragility. It is in our own sense of fragility that the determination of external reality as complex and unpredictable is to be found.

As a result, there are very unfortunate but understandable developments which mean the contemporary self is continually involved in making demands for protection for itself against external forces that are felt to be threatening to overwhelm and destroy it. The self, especially in the Anglo-American context, in the act of demanding to be protected from these dangerous and risky forces, actually begins to revel in its own weakness and fragility. It is as if the fragile, de-centred, multiple self, saturated in powerlessness and in weakness, becomes a cultural trope we come to *celebrate*: to the point at which so many films and so many novels in popular culture present this kind of self, this sensitive self, and by what they mean by sensitivity is a self that is extremely sensitive to its own weakness and its own self-imposed, almost imprisoned or locked-in, way of perceiving itself.

* * *

Under these circumstances it was more or less inevitable that the self's weakness and fragility and its demand to be protected from external forces would become politicised. In these circumstances, the self finds it very difficult to do politics *outside* of the self. Instead we have the demand which was coined in 1969—'the personal is political'—which ultimately becomes 'the self is political,' which reframes the self in a quasi-political form, and leads to a journey that invariably hits the dead end of identity politics.

The problem is not identity per se: we all need identity. Nor is the problem the fact that we aspire to cultivate our identity because, as we saw above, Marx himself said, we have to change ourselves to be genuinely human. No, I think the problem occurs when identity, the politicised self, acquires this almost self-propelled dimension in which it effectively pleads for protection, pleads that its weakness should be recognised, and when this self-proclaimed weakness starts to be seen as its defining feature. This amounts to a complete reversal of the trajectory of self-determination as we have known it since early modernity, and it appears that the fragile self is in practice more than happy to trade in its claim to autonomy for the mandatory provision of respect and esteem.

To conclude, the very project of the self-authorisation of the self, in the conditions of the last 40 or 50 years, leads to the ultimate de-authorisation of the self. As soon as we allow external forces to guide us, to provide assistance on what should be one's own road, the effect is that autonomy, one's capacity for self-determination, becomes a commodity which is willingly traded-in in return for protection. It is this psychological dynamic that underpins the idea that freedom can be traded-in for security (see in particular, Furedi 2007: 172–173). This is why we live in a world where what counts is no longer self-determination or autonomy, but instead a self that is addicted to validation and respect. In terms of contemporary political theory, it is the politics of recognition that appears progressive, as the ultimately civilised way of respecting one another in the twenty-first century. This approach renders the self passive. From this perspective, the flourishing of the self depends far more now upon external validation than on the act of self-creation.

References

Durkheim, E. (2002 [1897]). *Suicide: A study in sociology*. London: Routledge Classics.
Furedi, F. (2007). *Invitation to terror: The expanding empire of the unknown*. London: Continuum.
Furedi, F. (2011). *On tolerance: A defence of moral independence*. London: Continuum.

Furedi, F. (2013). *Authority: A sociological history*. Cambridge: Cambridge University Press.

Locke, J. (1998 [1690]). *An essay concerning human understanding*. London: Penguin Classics.

Lukács, G. (1980). *The destruction of reason* (P. Palmer, Trans). London: Merlin Press.

Martin, R., & Barresi, J. (2006). *The rise and fall of soul and self*. New York: Columbia University Press.

Marx, K. (1985). *The German ideology*. London: Lawrence and Wishart.

Marx, K. (1988). *Economic and philosophical manuscripts of 1844*. London: Prometheus Books.

Seigel, J. (2007). *The idea of the self: Thought and experience in Western Europe since the seventeenth century*. Cambridge: Cambridge University Press.

Snell, B. (1953). *The discovery of the mind: The Greek origins of European thought*. New York: Harper Torchbooks.

Wiley, N. (1994, Winter). History of the self: From primates to present. *Sociological Perspectives, 37*(4), 527–545.

3

In Praise of Selfish Individualism

Jamie Whyte

Introduction

Critics of capitalism often complain that it is based on selfish individualism. The idea is so widespread, in fact, that even the former Conservative Prime Minister Theresa May believes it. In a speech during the United Kingdom's 2017 general election campaign she told her audience that 'We do not believe in untrammelled free markets … We reject the cult of selfish individualism'.[1]

Theresa May and her ideological ilk are right. Capitalism is indeed based on selfish individualism. But they are wrong to complain about it. Selfishness is an unavoidable feature of the human condition. We do not face a choice between selfish individualism and selfless collectivism. We face a choice between selfish individualism and selfish collectivism—and,

---

[1] Speech in Halifax, 25 May 2017, quoted in the *Financial Times* (25 May 2018).

J. Whyte (✉)
London, UK

for that matter, selfish theocracy, selfish monarchy, selfish militarism. There is no selfless option.

Which is precisely the virtue of individualism. It constrains the harm that unavoidable human selfishness would otherwise do. That is why people who live in capitalist countries are freer and richer than people living in countries that reject selfish individualism.

Most of the work needed to show that this is true lies in explaining what it means. What is individualism? In what sense are humans unavoidably selfish? And how does selfish individualism, properly understood, relate to capitalism? Once these questions are answered, the historically astonishing success of capitalist societies will be entirely unsurprising.

Methodological Individualism

In the sense relevant to capitalism, individualism is an idea about who should make which decisions. It is the idea that Jack should decide what Jack does, and Jill should decide what Jill does. No one's actions should be coerced by anyone else. I will need to explain what coercion means, and why slight exceptions to the general individualist rule may be needed. But first I need to motivate that general rule.

It is founded on two other theses that are themselves individualistic.[2] The first is *methodological individualism*, the view that nothing acts except individual humans (and animals too, but set that aside since it is irrelevant here). When someone says, 'Germany invaded Poland in 1939', this is merely shorthand for saying that a lot of individual men from Germany invaded Poland, ordered to do so by another individual German. 'The Bank of England has raised interest rates' means that the majority of individuals on the monetary policy committee have done this. Even such 'collective decisions' are nothing but individual decisions and a rule about how they are to be combined into a final decision.

---

[2] When I say, 'it is founded on …', I do not mean that everyone who believes the principle has derived it from the more fundamental individualist theses I am about to explain. In other words, I do not mean that *belief* in it is founded on these theses. I mean to explain why the principle is correct, not why people believe it.

Political commentators occasionally forget this and analyse the result of elections as if a collective entity—the electorate—allocated its many votes so as to communicate a subtle message to politicians. For example, following the failure of the Conservatives to win a majority in the June 2017 general election, the journalist Matthew d'Ancona said that '… the voters have made clear … that their anger outweighs their yearning for calm surfaces and smooth transitions'.[3]

But 'the voters' doesn't refer to something that can have the feeling that d'Ancona alleged explains the distribution of votes in the 2017 election. There were millions of individual voters, each of whom voted for a particular candidate in her constituency. Some who voted for non-Conservative candidates may have been more angry than concerned about smooth transitions. But those who voted for Conservatives presumably were not that angry. Voters almost certainly had a great variety of opinions about the government.

Imagine a two-party competition in which the governing party wins by 51% to 49%. Each voter in the 51% who voted for the government may believe it to be brilliant. And each in the 49% may believe the opposition to be obviously superior. No one believes that the governing party is just a little better than the opposition. But that is how a commentator who sees the electorate as a collective entity with a collective opinion would be inclined to interpret the result.

The reason only individuals can act is that actions are caused by beliefs and desires. You go to the fridge because you want milk and believe there is some in it. You take an umbrella when you leave the house because you believe it is raining and want to keep dry. And so on and on, for everything you do. The only way someone else's beliefs and desires can make you do something is by causing you to have certain beliefs or desires of your own. You make me join the army and invade Poland by making me believe that if I don't, you will imprison or shoot me. Or by making me believe that I will earn a salary if I do. Or making me believe that …

Concepts such as Karl Jung's 'collective consciousness' may have merit as ways of drawing attention to the pervasive and subtle ways in which we

---

[3] Matthew d'Ancona. 'The best leaving present Theresa May can give us is a route to stability'. *Evening Standard*, 9 June 2017.

influence each other's thoughts. But they are metaphorical (let us hope). There is no collective mind. Nor, therefore, are there collective actions.

Preference Utilitarianism

All actions may be performed by individuals, but why should these individuals decide for themselves what they will do? Why shouldn't they be coerced? In other words, how do we get from methodological individualism to the individualist doctrine relevant to capitalism?

Some individualists do not take this question seriously. It is simply obvious to them that actions should not be coerced, that each individual should decide for herself what she does. But it isn't obvious. No one believes that young children should make all decisions for themselves. Far from acting wrongly, a parent who did not occasionally coerce his children would be negligent.

If it is sometimes okay to coerce children when it would not be okay to coerce an adult—about what they will eat for dinner, for example, or when they go to bed—then there must be some difference between children and adults that explains this difference in how they should be treated. But then the wrongness of coercion is not 'just obvious' or a simple fact of human existence. It depends in some way on the relevant difference between adults and children. What is that difference, and why is it relevant?

The answer is not to be found in 'natural rights' theories, such as those promoted by seventeenth- and eighteenth-century liberals (such as Locke 1689; Paine 1791) and, in the twentieth century, by Robert Nozick (1974). The idea that God or nature has bestowed certain rights on humans is not only mysterious; it doesn't explain why children should lack the protection against coercion that, so we individualists say, should be enjoyed by adults. Perhaps God or nature bestows the gift of rights only on those over 18 years of age. But it looks arbitrary. And good theories do not include arbitrary elements.

Never mind. The answer to our question is provided quite naturally from a less mysterious notion than natural rights. Utilitarianism is the idea that an outcome is better or worse insofar as it increases or decreases utility. Without some more precise definition, 'utility' simply means 'personal welfare' or what is good for you. In other words, without some more precise definition of utility, utilitarianism is vacuous; it is the triviality that you are better off if you get more of what is good for you.

Jeremy Bentham (1781), the first official utilitarian, thought of utility as pleasure and pain (disutility). But many things can be better than their alternatives without being any more pleasurable. Pleasure and pain are the effects of only a portion of the things that can be better or worse for us. And some people *like* pain, at least under special circumstances.

The fashionable idea that utility is happiness (see Layard 2005) faces the same objection. Some things are better for me than others even though they make no difference to my happiness. If happiness means something other than 'whatever I prefer' (which it must to distinguish it from the theory I favour—see below), then many alternatives that increase my utility, such as merlot over pinot noir, make no difference to my happiness.[4]

Preference utilitarianism avoids this problem. According to preference utilitarianism, something is good or bad for someone insofar as it satisfies his preferences. If you prefer apples to oranges, then eating an apple makes you better off than eating an orange. If you prefer boys to girls, you are better off kissing a boy than a girl. If you prefer Beyoncé to Mozart, you are better off listening to Beyoncé … and so on, for any preferences you can think of.[5]

Individualism follows immediately from this understanding of personal welfare. If our preferences both cause our actions and measure their success, then people will be better off if left alone to act as they choose.

That is too quick. I seem to have committed myself to the idea that, left to their own devices, people can never do something that is bad for them. If you choose A rather than B, that is because you prefer A to B. And if you prefer A to B, then A is better for you than B is. So, whatever you do, it is the best thing for you.

---

[4] See Whyte (2013, ch. 4) where I develop this argument.

[5] Philosophers associate preference utilitarianism with the Australian philosopher Peter Singer (see, for example, his 1993 study). This is peculiar, even though Singer is indeed a preference utilitarian. It is peculiar because preference utilitarianism is a foundational assumption of welfare economics. Singer's allegedly controversial position would strike most welfare economists as little more than obvious.

If you spend five pounds on a Big Mac Meal rather than a bowl of lentil soup, that shows you prefer the Big Mac Meal to the lentil soup. So the Big Mac Meal was better for you than the bowl of lentil soup. No one ever eats the wrong food! If you could have married George Clooney but you chose Brad Pitt, this shows you prefer Brad Pitt to George Clooney. So Brad Pitt is better for you than George Clooney. No one ever marries the wrong person! And the same will automatically go for everything else. No matter what you do, you can never go wrong.

Of course, it isn't true. We often voluntarily do things that are bad for us, for the simple reason that we do not know what all of the effects of our actions will be, including how much we will like them. You might prefer a Big Mac to lentil soup only because you don't understand the different effects they will have on your health. If you did, you would prefer the lentil soup. You might prefer Brad Pitt to George Clooney only because you don't know what Brad is like after a long flight and a few too many drinks. If you did, you would prefer George.

And herein lies the different attitude we rightly take to the coercion of adults and of children. Whether or not an action is the right one (for the agent) depends on the preferences of the agent and the effects the action will have. This gives an adult agent a massive advantage over any third party in making the right decisions for himself. He has an unbeatable knowledge of his own preferences and of his particular circumstances, which are crucial for knowing the effects of any action he might perform.

Being omniscient, God could help an adult by pushing him around. But the humans who might take our decisions for us are not omniscient. The idea that a politician or other remote authority might know better than the agent which action will best satisfy his preferences is fanciful. The agent does not know everything relevant to making his decision, but the third party knows almost nothing relevant.

By contrast, I do understand my 11-year-old daughter's circumstances better than she does. I know pretty well the alternatives she faces and the likely effects of her actions, and she does not. Admittedly, I do not know my daughter's preferences better than she does. But I can still know them well because I live with her, because I am not a stranger. A politician can only suppose I have the preferences characteristic of my kind of human being. I can observe the particular dispositions of my daughter, including her tastes and preferences. In fact, I play an unavoidable role in forming them.

Given my good knowledge of my daughter's preferences and my vastly superior understanding of her circumstances, I can help her by pushing her around. As she grows up, she will come to understand her circumstances better than I do and her dispositions will not be mine to influence. I will no longer be able to help her by commanding her. Good parents are bullies when their children are young, deciding even when and what they eat. But they back off as their children grow up.

In short, adults should be left to their own devices because they will be better off if they are. This follows from the preference utilitarian theory of what 'better off' means and from the fact that each individual knows better than others his own preferences and circumstances. The reason individuals should be allowed to 'go to hell their own way' is that this allowance will reduce the number who end up going to hell.

There may be occasions when the individualistic principle doesn't hold, when coercion makes adults better off. We will come to them later. But the justification of these exceptions can be understood only if we understand the basic utilitarian case for individualism.

Human Selfishness

That is the case for individualism. But what about the case for *selfish* individualism?

As mentioned, all that is required is to show that selfishness is inevitable. Making the case for selfish individualism is like making the case for disappointing individualism or temporary individualism. Because selfishness, disappointment, and the end of human life are each inevitable, every arrangement of human affairs will be selfish, disappointing, and temporary.

This section is therefore devoted to looking at the senses in which human selfishness is inevitable. But it provides more than this basic requirement of my argument. Because, as it turns out, selfishness itself provides an argument for political individualism. Selfishness isn't merely an unavoidable part of any arrangement of human affairs; it is a reason to favour individualism.

Trivial Interpretations

Two trivial selfishness hypotheses must be set side before we get to the real thing. The first is that people are selfish because the preferences they act on are their own. I choose an orange rather than an apple because *I* prefer oranges to apples. This is silly. Whether someone acts selfishly depends on the content of his motive, not its location. Being mental states of agents, motives are always located in the agent—inside their heads, as it happens. But they might nevertheless be selfless motives. Your desire to help an old woman cross the street is located in you. That doesn't make it selfish.

The second quick but wrong way of arriving at a thesis of universal selfishness starts with the observation that acting selflessly typically makes the benefactor feel good about herself. Apparently selfless actions are in fact selfish actions aimed at enjoying this feeling.

It is a bad inference. I burn calories when I dance, and I know it. It doesn't mean that my real motivation for dancing is to burn calories. Similarly, even if I know I will feel good about myself if I act kindly, it does not mean that this is what motivates me—it doesn't follow that I wouldn't act kindly if I didn't think I would get the reward of feeling good. Indeed, there are obvious counterexamples. Atheists sometimes sacrifice their lives for others. They know that, being dead, they won't get any emotional reward.

The emotional reward we receive from altruistic behaviour may help to explain altruism. But that wouldn't show altruism to be an illusion. Consider another human inclination and alleged explanation. Some evolutionary psychologists think that many men in their 50s become strongly attracted to much younger women (when they weren't attracted to them ten years earlier), because the mother of their children has become infertile and sex with young women will increase their chance of having more children. The genes of men who do this are passed on in greater numbers than the genes of men who don't. Hence the observable tendency in the population. If true, this would not show that men in their 50s do not really fancy 20-year-old women. It would not show that, really, they just want to have more children. It would explain why they are inclined to fancy much younger women. When you explain something—be it cross-generational lust or altruism—you do not thereby show it to be non-existent.

Real Selfishness

Selfishness is a matter of the content of motives, not their location or cause. You are selfish if you value your own welfare higher than other people's. I find a £20 note on the ground. I know someone who would get more benefit from it than I will. Yet I keep it for myself. That is indeed selfish.

But it is not *wickedly* selfish. We reserve 'selfish' in the pejorative sense for those whose over-weighting of their own welfare is unusually great, or who violate norms concerning altruism toward kith and kin. This is evidence that selfishness, defined as above, is part of the human condition. No one blames me for keeping that £20 despite my knowing a more needy person—it is only human.

Adam Smith's 'little finger' parable gives the flavour of the extra value we give to our own welfare:

> If he was to lose his little finger to-morrow, he would not sleep to-night; but, provided he never saw them, he will snore with the most profound security over the ruin of a hundred millions of his brethren, and the destruction of that immense multitude seems plainly an object less interesting to him, than this paltry misfortune of his own. (Smith 1759, Pt III, ch. 1)

There are exceptions, of course. Parents generally value their children's welfare almost as high as their own, sometimes higher. We also tend to favour other family members over strangers. As with quintagenarian lust, evolutionary psychology (or sociobiology) offers an explanation. Relatives who behave altruistically to each other increase the chance of passing on their related genes. So familial altruism is favoured by natural selection (Hamilton 1964). For the same reason, how much we are willing to sacrifice for our kin varies with the closeness of the relationship—more for a sister than a first cousin, more for a first cousin than second cousin once removed.

Such sociobiological explanations of human behaviour remain controversial. They suggest a genetic basis for dispositions that many people, especially Marxists, believe to be the result of economic or other social factors. Selfishness is not part of human nature, they claim. If social structures differed in the right ways, people would no longer put their own welfare ahead of others.

Economic and cultural arrangements surely do influence selfishness. They must influence whose welfare, besides our own, we care about and how much. How much people care about extended family members seems to vary culturally, as do patriotism and other feelings of affiliation. The economics of tribal hunter-gather societies, for example, seem to promote a high willingness to make sacrifices for members of your own tribe, and a low willingness to make sacrifices for members of other tribes. Hence 'tribal' as a description of people with such tendencies regarding other affiliations, such as to football clubs.

Yet such variations do not show that selfishness, in the sense relevant here, is totally culturally variable. In no society in history have people valued every other human's welfare as highly as their own, for the simple reason that you couldn't get through the week if you did.

Imagine how you would feel if you were today diagnosed with a terminal illness that will kill you within the month. If you are anything like me, you would have a bad day, overwhelmed with feelings of loss and dread. Well, several people really were diagnosed with a terminal disease today, and you know it (even if you don't know who they are). If you cared about them as much as you do about yourself, you would now be crippled by dread. And you would be ecstatically happy, because someone whom you care about as much as yourself has just won millions in a lottery. And you would be nervous, because someone you care about as much as yourself is about to sit an important exam. And so on and on … Not caring very much about strangers is necessary for functioning humans.

Why Selfishness Calls for Individualism

You are out at night in Camden. You want to eat. Who should decide which restaurant you go to? If God existed, He should. He knows you better than you know yourself and He loves his creatures more than they love themselves. But set God aside. Even if He exists, standard theology says He is reluctant to direct our actions in this way (Plantinga 1977). Let us restrict ourselves to the human alternatives.

Maybe Jack, the proprietor of Jack's Burger Joint, should decide. He is a decent man: married with kids, kind to dogs, helps old women across the street, never had a speeding ticket, and so on. Alas, he is selfish, in the unavoidable sense described. He will be strongly inclined to think that you should go to Jack's Burger Joint, even if you shouldn't, even if Jill's Vegetable Village would suit you better.

Substituting Jill for Jack will not improve matters, because Jill will be selfish too. She may think she wants to make the best decision for you and not just for her. Nevertheless, she will be motivated to arrive at the conclusion that you will be best off if you go to Jill's Vegetable Village, even if it is untrue, even if Jack's Burger Joint would suit you better. People can benefit from their interactions with others. If someone gets to decide what those other people will do, he will be all too likely to make them do what benefits himself, not them.

But what about a third party? Perhaps an expert restaurant chooser—appointed by a duly elected government, let us suppose—should decide where you eat. You inform him by text that you intend to eat in Camden and he texts back the restaurant you must go to (on threat of some penalty if you disobey).

I have already dealt with the problem of the ignorance of such strangers. Expert or not, this third-party decider cannot know your preferences and your circumstances, such as what you ate for lunch (and, hence, what you feel like now) and what else you hope to do on your evening out, which will affect both what you want to eat and how much you want to spend.

Yet the problem is not merely his ignorance but his selfishness. He is likely to suffer from a common human defect which is especially strong in do-gooders. He may think that you would benefit most by acting as if you shared his preferences, even though you don't share them. Suppose he is like most modern politicians and thinks that health is much more important than pleasure. Then he will command you to go to Jill's Vegetable Village even though you might value pleasure ahead of health and just love Jack's Burgers. Third-party deciders can benefit at your expense by making you act against your interests; they get a world that more closely resembles their vision of how it should be, and they get the gratification of having 'saved' you.

There is another reason third-party deciders are likely to harm those for whom they decide. Return to the restaurant decider. Hardly a moment after he takes up the position, he will receive a phone call from the owner of a restaurant chain seeking a meeting at which she will explain why he should direct people to her chain. The decider will be bribed or mislead or flattered into favouring the restaurant chain at the expense of the population, whom he will coerce into favouring his new friend. The power to make decisions for third parties is an invitation to cronyism.

As noted, people often go wrong when they make decisions for themselves. Ignorance and irrationality make error inevitable. But empowering a supposedly superior few to make decisions for fallible individuals makes matters worse. Not only must those superiors be far more ignorant of the relevant facts than the individuals concerned, but the superiors are inevitably selfish. The power to make decisions for others will be used to exploit them.

Individualism insists that interactions be voluntary. If I buy your house for £500,000, we both benefit if the transaction was voluntary. You must have valued the house less than £500,000, and I must have valued it more. Otherwise we would not have voluntarily done the deal. This is a general feature of voluntary interactions; they take place only when both parties benefit from them. Not so when individualism does not reign. Not so when decisions are coerced. Then, I might get your house for £500,000 even though you value it more than that, even though you think it a bad deal.

Using Coercion to Minimise Coercion

Individualism reigns when no actions are coerced.

To see what this means, we need to be clear about what coercion is. It is not just any kind of influence on action. When I induce my local shopkeeper to hand over a pint of milk by giving him £2, I have not coerced him. When I convince my wife to go on holiday in Portugal rather than Blackpool by showing her pictures of both, I have not coerced her. If I induce my local shopkeeper to hand over a pint of milk by threatening to shoot him if he doesn't, then I have coerced him. If I induce my wife to pick Portugal by pulling the face that indicates she is in for weeks of nagging, I have coerced her.

In the voluntary cases, I convince the other party that they will be better off by doing what I want. In the coercive cases, I convince the other party that they will be worse off if they don't do what I want. In the voluntary case, I promise a benefit; in the coercive case, I threaten a cost. An individualistic society is not one in which no one's decisions are influenced by other people; it is one in which no decisions are brought about by the threat of costs for refusing to do another person's bidding.[6]

Of course, even on this understanding of coercion, a society perfectly free from coercion is practically impossible. Two human imperfections mean that we will always be stuck with a degree of coercion.

The first is the common willingness to use coercion to get the better of others. To minimise this, we threaten force against those who would coerce others, and often use it when nevertheless they do coerce others. Enslave someone, take possessions at gunpoint or rape someone and you will be put in prison, whether or not you agree to be imprisoned. The laws against coercion entail some coercion of would-be and actual coercers.

---

[6] Freedom of action in this sense has no connection with the doctrine of 'free will', the idea that humans are not mere automata and may properly be held responsible for their actions. In this 'free will' sense, I act freely when I hand over $100 to a man who is holding a gun to my head. I could, after all, choose to instead be shot in the head. People with free will can still be coerced. And, even if free will is an illusion, as some argue, because all our actions have causes that ultimately lie outside of us, we can still distinguish between coercive and non-coercive influences of other people—the former involving threats of costs and the latter promises of benefits.

And even with such laws, we will still have coercion beyond the laws themselves, not only because laws are always imperfectly enforced but because using law to rule out all forms of coercion would be worse than letting some of it go. When I nag my wife into taking a holiday in Portugal, I have coerced her ('anything to shut him up!'). Should the law rule out matrimonial nagging? The intrusions required to rule out such house-and-garden coercion, the kind that arises in the everyday muddling along of people who nevertheless choose to associate with each other, would be far worse than the harm caused by these petty coercions.

The second defect that makes the total elimination of coercion unlikely is the common desire to 'free ride' on the efforts of others. Who will pay for the production and enforcement of the laws that protect us from coercion? We all have an interest in such laws, but that doesn't mean we will all willingly pay for them. If *someone* pays for them, everyone gets the benefit of them. Law and order is a 'non-excludable' good, as economists put it. If it exists, everyone gets the benefit of it whether they paid for it or not. So, many people will not pay for it, hoping to free ride on those who do pay for it. If too many people think this way, then law and order will not be supplied at all (or not sufficiently). Hence, it may be necessary to force people to pay for it by taxing them.[7] Again, therefore, minimising coercion may positively require some coercion—this time, in the form of taxation.

So let us say that individualism reigns, not when coercion is eliminated, but when it is minimised.

Individualism and Capitalism

I began this article by agreeing with the common idea that capitalism is based on selfish individualism. This needs some qualification. What I will call 'free market capitalism' is based on selfish individualism, because free markets are. Markets are free when exchange is voluntary and when there

---

[7] This is the standard 'public good' argument for tax funding the supply of law and order. The idea that law and order is non-excludable and wouldn't be adequately supplied unless tax-funded is disputed by anarcho-capitalists, such as David Friedman (1973). I have some sympathy with Friedman's arguments but cannot explore them here.

is 'freedom of contract': that is, when the terms of contracts are decided by the transacting parties alone, rather than being dictated or constrained by outside parties. In other words, markets are free when individuals decide for themselves, when actions are not coerced. Free markets are simply individualism applied to economic affairs (Smith 1776).

But you can have capitalism without free markets and free markets without capitalism. To see why, capitalism must be properly understood. An economic arrangement is capitalist if it promotes the creation and use of capital. Capital goods are goods that are not consumed but are used in the production of other goods. In stone-age societies, there were few capital goods beyond a few simple tools and weapons crafted from wood, natural fibres, and stone. Today, the variety and sophistication of capital goods is astonishing—computers, robots, cranes, oil drills, power plants, bulldozers, electronic looms, combine harvesters, fishing trawlers, … and so on and on.

Humans have always created some capital goods. But the great explosion in their creation, which accounts for our modern prosperity, began with the industrial revolution of the late eighteenth century. Hence the emergence of the notion of capitalism in the nineteenth century.

As a matter of historical fact, markets in the nineteenth century were reasonably free in the United Kingdom and the United States (at least, once slavery was abolished and mercantilism abandoned). But capitalism need not be combined with free markets. For example, the Soviet Union was more capitalist than the feudal Tsarist society it replaced, its economic planners having decided to invest heavily in new forms of mechanised production.

Similarly, free markets do not require capitalism. Farmers with little in the way of capital can still trade with each other, unmolested by third parties. And they will still benefit from it. If you have two chickens and I have 20 potatoes, and we have typical preferences, we will both be better off if we swap one of your chickens for 10 of my potatoes. The 'market economy' long predates capitalism. It emerged at least 4000 years ago in ancient Babylonia and Assyria (Sanandaji 2018).

Though separable, capitalism and free markets do work best when combined. Then, the creation, preservation, and replacement of capital goods are determined, not by the diktat of people with coercive power, but by investors who will profit if they offer what consumers want, and who will make losses if they do not.

Economic individualism thus makes capital serve the interests of the people, rewarding those who do it well and punishing those who do not. Economic planners face no such direct rewards or punishments. And even if, miraculously, they were just as keen to please consumers in the absence of these incentives, without the signal provided by profit, they could not know if they were succeeding (Mises 1920). That is why the state-directed capitalism of the Soviet Union and China were far less successful than the (relatively) free-market capitalism of the United States in providing citizens with what they wanted.

* * *

Contemporary Western capitalism is far from the individualistic, free-market ideal. Freedom of contract has been severely restricted by the torrents of regulation that flow from legislatures and regulatory agencies. And much exchange is not voluntary. By providing tax-funded healthcare, education, pensions, and unemployment insurance, governments compel us to purchase them whether we want them or not.

The free-market ideal was more closely approximated in the late nineteenth century—at least, in the United Kingdom and the United States. Though more individualistic in this sense, these societies were far less individualistic in the 'atomised' sense of the word. Voluntary association flourished. Pre-industrial associations, such as guilds, were being replaced by associations adapted to the new economic arrangements: trades unions, friendly societies, and recreational clubs made possible by the increased leisure time brought about by capitalism.

Such associations have been in decline over the last century, as the state has played a larger and larger role in economic decision making. It is not a mere coincidence. How can friendly societies survive when the government forces people to contribute to its own income insurance scheme? What need have workers of trades unions when working conditions and minimum wages are regulated by the government? Even family bonds are weakened by compulsory contributions to income insurance. When your family is no longer your ultimate 'backstop', an important reason for maintaining good relations has been removed.

Where selfish individualism reigns, I need to cooperate with others. I cannot get what I want from them without winning them over. We must 'get along'. When they can be compelled to provide me with what I want, I needn't get along with them. I need only win favour with those who wield the power to coerce. Selfish individualism is not only the foundation of economic prosperity. It is the foundation of a decent society.

References

Bentham, J. (1781). *The principles of morals and legislation*. Reprinted by Prometheus Books, 2012.
Friedman, D. (1973). *The machinery of freedom*. New York: Open Court.
Hamilton, W. D. (1964). The genetic evolution of social behaviour. *Journal of Theoretical Biology*, 7, 1–16.
Layard, R. (2005). *Happiness: Lessons from a new science*. London: Penguin.
Locke, J. (1689). *Two treatises of government*. Republished by the Law Book Exchange in 2010.
Mises, L. (1920). Economic calculation in the socialist commonwealth. Reprinted in F. Hayek (ed.), *Collective economic planning*. New Jersey: Kelley Publishing, 1975.
Nozick, R. (1974). *Anarchy, state and utopia*. New York: Basic Books.
Paine, T. (1791). *The rights of man*. Republished by Musicum Books in 2016.
Plantinga, A. (1977). *God, freedom and evil*. Grand Rapids, MI: Eerdmans.
Sanandaji, N. (2018). *The birthplace of capitalism*. Sweden: Timbro.
Singer, P. (1993). *Practical ethics*. Cambridge: Cambridge University Press.
Smith, A. (1759). *The theory of moral sentiments*. Republished by Penguin, London, 2010.
Smith, A. (1776). *The wealth of nations*. London: Strahen and Cadell.
Whyte, J. (2013). *Quack policy: Abusing science in the cause of paternalism*. London: IEA.

4

Self-Enlightenment

Angus Kennedy

Introduction

This chapter will touch on three areas:

1. With the weakening of the authority of Christianity in late Feudal and Renaissance Europe there was a reaction against an ideal of the self as identified with the immortal soul. In its extreme form, this reaction argued that the self was entirely material. In such views, the self (and society) was seen as Natural. Scientific or early Enlightenment theorists of the self and society struggled, however, to reconcile their lived experience of human subjectivity as freedom with their intellectual belief in material and social determination.
2. The effect of the weakening of the authority of monarchy on conceptions of the self is exemplified in the work of Rousseau. Society is rejected as being the proper ground of the self. In fact, society is viewed as corrupting of the self: the authentic self is rather to be found in the

A. Kennedy (✉)
West Sussex, UK

withdrawal from, or in the remaking of, society. This two-fold distancing of the self from God and from society as it is leaves the self standing alone, with nothing to obey but the promptings of its own conscience. The self though cannot rely on itself alone to be a reliable guide to action since it is riven by internal contradiction: torn between passion and reason, reliant on both the thought and the felt in order to come to understanding. Man may be more than a machine. But what then *is* he?

3. If the self can be fully explained in terms of neither nature nor society, then the self must find its explanation in something that precedes both: namely freedom. In the later works of Kant, in particular in *What is Enlightenment*, we see him drawing out the implications of his understanding of the self as being defined in terms of freedom and the capacity for reason. The self is seen as caught up in an ongoing and unresolvable (albeit productive) tension between itself and other selves, that is to say, between the self and other selves in society at large. Although the self is grounded in nothing else other than its own freedom, it, by virtue of being free, has the capacity to self-determine and to set its own limits. *Argue… but obey!* Man must discipline himself, obey his conscience, or risk sliding into a fruitless and destructive search for authenticity.

What I want to try and explore here then is the difficulty that is made plain in Enlightenment thinking about the self: the tensions that threaten to pull our understanding of the self apart.

On the one hand, there are strands of thought putting forward a broadly materialist, scientific view of the self: trying to reduce man to the physical foundation of *what is*, but always struggling to account for the fact that each of us *appears* unique to ourselves, in a way that our flesh and blood commonality does not seem to be adequate to explain. We might be intellectually convinced we are nothing but atoms and fully subject to the physical laws of cause and effect, but there is at least sometimes a feeling that our actions are not determined in advance. Instead, the actions of the self can present themselves to us as choices for which we will be held responsible. We cannot escape the phenomenology of self-consciousness as freedom. We can, after all, always turn our thoughts upon our own selves, we can self-reflect, we can disagree with ourselves, we can be split, be apart from our own self. All of this speaks to the possibility that the self is not wholly determined by its materiality: if it was, it would be wholly predictable. At the very least, this idea of consciousness as resting on a fold or internal division is problematic for materialist theories, which claim that we just *are* our brains: the brain, after all, being matter, could not easily stand apart from itself without not being itself.

Yet, as selves, we do appear to stand apart from both nature and from the human social world rather than to be just a part of it. There is something about being us which means that we just do not *fit in*. In other words, we appear to ourselves as a question, almost a dilemma or a problem: as alienated beings, somehow offset, at one remove from the world. How can it be that we are simultaneously a material object in the world—a thing that can be acted on and subjected to external forces—but also an active subject, a participant in the creation of that same world? We stand apart from the animal world because, being conscious of our own mortality, we are not part of a species.[1] We are individuals who will come to an end: genetic survival brings no continuity for *me*. It is knowing this that endows me with a sense of purpose: a drive to make that inevitable ending *my* ending stamped with the historical imprint of *my* projects and the ends *I* pursued. And that makes us—each of us—unique: fully explicable neither in terms of nature nor in terms of society.

The Enlightenment as a whole can well be seen as a contested ground for ideas of selfhood: partly played out along a contradiction between materialist and idealist conceptions of the self against a backdrop of increased agency of individuals in society. But there is equally a contradiction here between two views of the relationship of self to society. In one view, individual self-interest works to the benefit of society and society is harmoniously ordered for the benefit of those who live in it. Some of this thinking, for example, is to be found in Adam Smith's notion of the 'invisible hand' of providence.

---

[1] For a fuller discussion of this, see Arendt (2006: 42ff). '[I]t was mortality which became the hallmark of human existence. Men are the "mortals", the only mortal things there are, for animals exist only as members of their species and not as individuals.'

But the other view, maybe most associated with Rousseau, is that society corrupts the individual: that moral liberty and civil liberty are distinct, if not actually at odds. If the laws of society will overlook or condone the *moral* transgressions of its members (their greed, vanity, pride, and so on) as they do, how can man ever be what he ought to be without first breaking free of society? The idea develops that we are autonomous only insofar as we are autonomous with respect to society. This stress on the moral responsibility of the individual to free himself and to remake society anew appears to be a concern that Kant also shares in his writings on the progress of human history: based on the possibility of self-improvement through the public use of reason. What in Kant is discussed in terms of man's capacity for reason as the basis for morality is underpinned in Rousseau's thought by the faculty of conscience: a faculty only developed once people have become conscious of themselves as social—rather than natural—beings.

Kant, however, does admit to the situation being a bit more complex than that when he urges us—in the essay *What is Enlightenment?*—not only to argue, but also to obey. We will come back to this later: the idea that since we are free in virtue of the power of our reason to act *against* our instincts, then it follows too that freedom presents itself to us in the form of a demand, coming from outside oneself as it were, an imperative we have no choice but to (freely) obey.

But, given this, why is it that, today, the subject, largely freed by the advance of civilisation from the constraints of nature, suffers under the illusion that he can achieve full control over anything that restricts his freedom? What is it about man's self-understanding that leads him to try and reject the condition in which he finds himself and—in the process—reject himself and turn against his fellow man? I will argue, in conclusion, that it is at least partly due to a one-sided development of Kant's radical approach to freedom, his rooting of freedom in the individual (and abstract) self itself. But if man is freedom, then what is the foundation of freedom? Is it itself unrooted? Is there anything we must obey, or are we just free to do what(-ever) we will?

Before examining that question, however, it is necessary to go back and trace the development of these ideas as they played out alongside the crisis of authority ushered in by early modernity.

Scientific Materialism: The Self as Natural

The development of modern subjectivity can be usefully considered within the horizon of the question of authority in society. After all, the question concerning subjectivity is in large part a question of *who* should do the thinking. Should it be done for one by one's betters, or should one think for oneself? In its most extreme form, this is a question as to whether it is God who thinks best or mortal men. If God is identified with divine reason, as He is in the Western tradition of thought reaching back as far as Plato, then humanity is seen as rational thanks to the possession of an immortal soul, albeit only partially rational given its weighting down by fleshly clay. To the extent that I do manage to reason well, then, that is thanks to God. The real me is conceptualised, in this line of thought, as an ideal immortal-me—in Heaven—not this actual material-me on earth.

It is this question—of authority—that Luther's Reformation writ large. With the waning of religious authority in late-medieval, early modern, Europe, so too came the creation of a relatively enlarged space for the exercise of individual conscience in matters of morality. Luther refers to *himself* when in doubt: and not to the authority of the established church. Or, more accurately, he refers to himself in the sense that his reading of scripture is not necessarily worse than that of the Pope. Only scripture (*sola scriptura*) has authority: not its interpretation by secondary authorities such as the church and the priesthood. As Luther put it 'a simple layman armed with Scripture is greater than the mightiest pope without it'. With the advance of the Protestant reformation all established institutions became open to the possibility of being reformed on the basis of being re-read: everyone was now a critic, every re-reading a potential transformation if not a revolution. Reason[2] in the Protestant and Baptist interpretation takes centre stage with a diminished role for tradition and experience.[3]

---

[2] Even if 'reason' is understood in a Lutheran sense as being the personal witness of the Holy Spirit in each individual.

[3] Although to a lesser degree in the Anglican and Methodist church.

The version of subjectivity that emerges, however, is not a radically self-determining one. Absolute authority rests with scripture, not with men: scripture *is* the word of God, and it reveals itself unambiguously to the rational reader (a process helped immensely by the translation of the Bible into the vernacular). The readers of scripture can see for themselves the truth that is written there, yes, but it is The Truth that is written there, not a matter of interpretation or debate. Luther portrays himself as having no choice *because* of his choice: he must be obedient to what he has himself chosen. It is here I stand. I can do nothing otherwise. Luther's subjectivity is truly a very *determined* subjectivity.

Nevertheless, despite his intentions, Luther had submitted authority to the question and the attempts of the Counter-Reformation to put the genie back in the bottle, by asserting the material reality of scripture,[4] were to no ultimate avail (except maybe, and ironically, to hasten the understanding of man as being material). By the end of the seventeenth, and start of the eighteenth century, thinkers were looking elsewhere than just scripture to find the rules that governed man. Some Enlightenment writers sought to find these in physics and in the iron laws of man's material nature. Man was re-imagined as a clockwork automaton,[5] but remained a mystery to himself. Condillac (in his *Traite des Sensations*, 1754) tried to ground reflection and introspection in sensation: in smell, sight, and touch. But Condillac still could not explain a certain necessary gap or leap: 'I see myself, I touch myself, in one word, I experience myself, but I do not know what I am' (Outram 2006: 188).

Others tried to overcome this problem by simply denying the existence of both the soul and the self. Julien Offroy de La Mettrie's *L'Homme Machine* (1748) argued man was a form of automaton, while Baron Paul d'Holbach's *Système de la Nature* (1770) was burnt by the public hangman in Paris for its argument that the human body is entirely made up of matter: since everything is matter, with no gaps, there is just no room in a body for a soul, it is packed out. For D'Holbach, man was simply a material thing: his moral dimension nothing more than his physical exis-

---

[4] Consider the hyper-realist statues of martyrs like that of St Bartholomew in the Duomo of Milan: depicted holding his flayed skin.
[5] If the early Enlightenment, in its rejection of man's immortality, sought to see him as a machine, then it is suggestive that today's rejection of man's freedom is inclined to see him as merely programmed, as a robot.

tence considered '*sous un certain point de vue, c'est-à-dire relativement à quelques-unes de ses façons d'agir*'. Man is driven by nothing more than instinctual self-preservation; let him 'submit in silence to laws from whose binding force nothing can remove him' (Taylor 1989: 326).

The response to the loss of the authority of the church is thus an attempt to assert the authority of science and, in terms of society, the authority of the way things are. It seems a stretch given the self-conception of the early Enlightenment as a progressive struggle against the dictates of religion—foregrounding natural man as God recedes from view—but one can also read the period as an attempt to put social authority on a new footing by stressing the contingency and relative weakness of man against the laws of both physics and society.

But in eighteenth-century France in particular this view started to give way to a form of pessimism—helped along by the great Lisbon earthquake of 1755, which shook any Panglossian belief in divine providence—a pessimism that society was maybe not ordered for the best: reason alone was maybe not enough to change society for the better. And that progress was maybe not inevitable nor necessarily always for the good. The problem was to be found at least in part in the way we were: in our selves. Men did evil things and suffered as a result.

To sum up, I cannot be wholly explained by my material self because I am, at bottom, conscious of my own freedom. And that freedom, as often as not, is a freedom to do wrong. The understanding of the self took one step away from its material and social aspects. Distanced itself in short from what was and took a step towards imagining itself as it should or could be.

Rousseau: The Self as Anti-Social

Jean-Jacques Rousseau's autobiography, published after his death, was designed to be the truest, most authentic, portrait of a man ever written. The *Confessions* (1782–1789) are—he tells us—the story of an enterprise without precedent, and beyond imitation:

> My purpose is to display to my kind a portrait in every way true to nature, and the man I shall portray will be myself.

> Simply myself (*Moi, seul*). I know my own heart and understand my fellow man. But I am made unlike anyone I have ever met; I will even venture to say that I am like no one in the whole world. I may be no better, but at least I am different (*au moins je suis autre*). (Rousseau 1970: 17)

His declaration that he is 'made unlike anyone I have ever met' might be lacking in humility but it is honest. We all feel it. Our selves are our own—individual and unique—not communal. Rousseau set out to tell everything, to try and relate the infinite chaos of subjectivity in its raw experiential form, to confess the good, the bad, the ugly: everything.

And confess he does to an increasingly shocking series of failings ranging from stealing, first an apple, then asparagus, then graduating to theft of a theatre ticket, down the slippery slope to consorting with prostitutes, and culminating in abandoning his five illegitimate children to a foundling hospital, where they were sure to die.

In Rousseau's account of his life there is no narrative arc, no story of redemption, no social or moral order in this catalogue of sentiment. Except that is the order and the centre provided by himself. The world throws events at him: he survives. The world changes and moves on. His consciousness floats above it. Certain of being right, certain that everyone else is out to get him, certain of his superiority and difference.

The end of the *Confessions* draws a stark portrait of a man alone, withdrawn from and shunned by society, unable even to provoke a reaction from the audience of society ladies to whom he is reading his own memoir:

> Thus I concluded my reading, and everyone was silent. Mme d'Egmont was the only person who seemed moved. She trembled visibly but quickly controlled herself, and remained quiet, as did the rest of the company. (Rousseau 1970: 606)

If there was ever a man who did not fit in it was Rousseau. Why? Society was to blame.

At the age of 37 Rousseau had what he called an 'illumination' while walking to Vincennes to visit Diderot, who had been imprisoned there because of his irreligious writings. The daily walk was six miles and the summer was excessively hot:

In order to slacken my pace, I thought of taking a book with me. One day I took the *Mercure de France* and, glancing through it as I walked, I came upon this question propounded by the Dijon Academy for the next year's prize: Has the progress of the sciences and arts done more to corrupt morals or improve them?

The moment I read this I beheld another universe and became another man. (Rousseau 1970: 327)

The resulting, and winning, essay was the first discourse, *Le Discours sur les sciences et les arts* (1750), which argues that increasing civilisation walked hand in hand with man's moral decay. Man—good by nature—is corrupted by the advance of society.

Rousseau's argument is not really a primitivist one as it is so often caricatured. He draws the picture of the noble savage to make the argument that, in himself, man is good. Man left alone is independent and—therefore—free. He relies on himself alone and is subject only to the laws of his own making. He has an instinctual drive to self-preservation, which Rousseau calls *amour de soi* (self-love), and which consists in using reason to tend to one's own needs.

Man in the company of others—however—becomes prey to what Rousseau calls *amour propre* ('love of self' but in English 'pride' or 'vanity') as he compares his situation to that of his fellows, especially in terms of his attractiveness as a mate to the other sex. This self-interested drive concerns one's relative success or failure as a social being: it is related to a demand for recognition and respect for what one has achieved, often relative to what others have achieved.

As society develops further man becomes increasingly prone to giving and receiving flattery and to misrepresentation of his own beliefs and desires (what one really wants) in order to attain *socially* valued ends: the result is frustration and self-alienation.

We should understand of course that this has always been the case.[6] Man has always been in society. Rousseau has, though, found a way to explain to us the problem that we represent for each other in society: if

---

[6] Larry Siedentop, for example, argues that the humanist 'cult of individuality' in the Renaissance presented social institutions 'as a threat to the self': a victim 'of social pressures' (Siedentop 2014: 337).

we all act independently then society is not harmonious and we—lacking a whole of which we are a well-fitted part—are unsettled and disturbed, in continual conflict both with our better natures and each other. Was there any way to resolve this?

* * *

The publication of Rousseau's sentimental novel *Julie, ou la nouvelle Héloïse* in 1761 made him a—the first—literary superstar. The publication of *The Social Contract* and *Emile* in 1762 forced him to flee France or face arrest for his challenges to religious orthodoxy. Quite apart from the offense caused, the opening of *The Social Contract* posed a shattering paradox:

> Man is born free, and everywhere he is in chains. Many a man believes himself to be the master of others who is, no less than they, a slave. (Rousseau 1960: 169)

How could men be free (i.e. if they were really slaves)? How could the tension between the freedom of the individual and the authority of the state and society ever be reconciled? Only, or so Rousseau thought, if civil society could be based on a genuine contract based on the general will. Since this was clearly not the case then it had to be made the case through revolution.

People would have to sacrifice some of their independence—in order to generalise it—but in return they would gain *republican* liberty. This liberty would be based on obedience to a self-imposed law. The general will is the source of law and is willed by each and every citizen. In obeying the law each citizen is thus subject to his or her own will, and consequently, according to Rousseau, remains free.

The problem is of course that this general will is artificial and exists nowhere. It is a mechanism imposed to deny the legitimacy of the conflicts of interest between those who live in a given society. The paradox is best expressed by Rousseau's argument that man must be *forced* to be free… that is the law that makes him, coerces him to, realise his true interests. Rousseau argues in short that good laws make good citizens.

However, the citizens we actually have back in this society live under bad laws, and therefore cannot be relied upon to draft good laws. This calls for something of a deus ex machina and so enters the figure of the Legislator (who plays a role much like the Tutor in *Emile*) who will persuade the citizens through non-rational means to legislate in their own interest. The Legislator must be possessed 'of a superior intelligence which can survey all the passions of mankind, though itself exposed to none'. This Legislator cannot, 'in speaking to the vulgar herd', make use of reason since 'excessive generalisations and long-range views are… beyond the comprehension of the average man'. Instead the Legislator must—since he can use neither force nor argument—have recourse to

> authority of a different kind which can lead without violence and persuade without convincing. (Rousseau 1960: 208)

Now, one may bristle at his contemptuous dismissal of the vulgar and the average, but Rousseau is simply restating a problem as old as Plato: just what is the foundation from which society, its laws and institutions, draws its authority? Not from any one individual (in this, he is right, we are not up to that) nor from any force that compels an individual. The authority must just be there. Plato and Rousseau appeal to 'non-rational' means: to myth or to godlike intelligence to underpin authority in society.

Rousseau is of course right to see that there is a need for something more than individual reason. The problem is not in the vulgarity of the herd but built-in to the nature of man: we are not perfectly rational. We are limited and historical. We are mortal. But we are also born into society and that allows for the possibility of institutions and ways of living surviving after us. Which can be a basis for authority.

Late Enlightenment thinkers, such as Rousseau of course, as well as David Hume,[7] but also many artists and writers (see Hewitt 2017), become relatively more interested in emotion than mechanical reason: they acknowledge the importance of what we feel, of sympathy and sentiment. In Hume though we also see an effort to find a standard that is not fully reducible to sentiment. As human nature develops more complex

---

[7] 'Reason Is and Ought Only to Be the Slave of the Passions'.

forms of social organisation, so too does it create 'some steady and general points of view' (Hume 1975, III.3.1 581–582). Conventions grow up slowly over time as a way of mediating conflicting desires and increasing the chance of individual ends being realised.

This general point of view (most fully developed by Hume in his essay 'Of the Standard of Taste') allows for reasoned aesthetic judgments—even in questions of taste, apparently so subjective—that are not completely free of the feelings we experience in looking at a work of art or hearing a poem, nor yet completely determined by our passions. Looking at things in this way starts to allow for some recognition of the power of ideas independent of experience. Hume does not hold that there is a simple causal relationship between what happens—experience—and what we think. Indeed, he takes rather a strong view of the incommensurability of ideas and matters of fact. Seeing no way to derive what *ought* to be from what *is*, Hume expressed scepticism about the very possibility of moral knowledge.

It was this scepticism (notably about the relationship of cause and effect) that awoke Kant from his 'dogmatic slumber'. What has been called 'Hume's fork' placed ideas on one tine of the fork (as being abstract, necessary, a priori, analytic) with concrete existence on the other tine (as being contingent, a posteriori, synthetic). Kant was to respond to this from the standpoint of reason: arguing it is the *same* reason that allows moral knowledge as affords knowledge of what is. Kant allowed reason to be a cause of experience rather than just something affected by experience. It is reason, in fact, which supplies the concepts of space and time without which sense impressions would be random and meaningless.

This response to Hume, by stressing the idealist side of man as well as the material, moved the human subject into a different—and more active—relationship to the world in which he found himself. Some later thinkers (such as Fichte and Hegel) end up moving a very long way towards a subjectivist account of the world: placing man, and freedom, fully at its centre. Some anticipate and prefigure some of the themes of later essays in this collection: relativism, the importance of the figure of the other, as well as questions of identity and authenticity.

Kant: The Self as Freedom

But first, we need to examine how Kant developed his thinking: in reaction to both Hume's fork and Rousseau. It is said that, on reading his *Emile*, Kant was so struck by the idea of human nature being basically good that he was put off his daily walk for several days, struggling to reconcile the idea that man was simultaneously object *and* subject, animal *and* person:

> Two things fill the mind with ever new and increasing admiration and reverence, the more often and more steadily one reflects on them: *the starry heavens above me and the moral law within me*. I do not need to search for them and merely conjecture them as though they were veiled in obscurity or in the transcendent region beyond my horizon; I see them before me and connect them immediately with the consciousness of my existence. (Kant 1999: 269)

Kant was attempting to resolve the tension that exists between what is 'out-there' (the starry heavens, the cold, distant, and objective world of nature and science) and the 'in-here' (the moral law in my heart, my own feeling of what is right and what is wrong directly available to me through introspection). The world out-there is vast and 'annihilates, as it were, my importance as an *animal creature*... a mere speck in the universe' (ibid.). The world in-here 'infinitely raises my worth as an *intelligence* by my personality, in which the moral law reveals to me a life independent of animality and even of the whole sensible world' (Kant 1999: 269–270).

His intent is to provide a way out of the opposition between seeing man as narrowly natural or seeing man as exclusively social. Between the material and the ideal: between what is determined and what is free. He does this by taking a step away both from what is and what should be to afford him (or his reason) the distance and perspective necessary to 'see them before me'. He has taken a step into the position of an independent observer with almost divine powers: nothing is 'beyond the horizon of my vision'.

Kant makes his appeal to a faculty for reason inherent in us all which allows us to act freely: *against* natural instinct. If we acknowledge our ability to act against instinct, even if only sometimes, then it follows that reason is not *fully* reducible to nature but is in some sense ideal, supra- or anti-natural, and, to that extent, free. Freedom is the power to will an end of action for myself without reference to my desires. After all, if I only did what I desired to do, what I *wanted* to do, then my actions would be determined by my desires. Freedom is most clearly understood then, paradoxically, as a capacity to be able to do what I *don't* want to do. Autonomy relies on our ability to ignore the promptings of self-interest and desire where they conflict with reason. This is the causality of freedom as opposed to the causality of nature.

Kant's idea of the self has become a strange one. It is a self that demonstrates its freedom by doing what it does not desire, and it is a self that stands apart from both the objective world out-there and the subjective world in-here: connecting them with 'the consciousness of my existence'. Where then *am* I? Where is this self-reflexivity one step removed from the self on which it reflects? Who is this I that asks myself what I think? For Kant these questions are not mysteries but something built-in as it were to the business, or the grammar, of being an I, a first-person subject. Part of what it means to be an I is to possess immunity to certain types of epistemological error. There can never be any doubt that my point of view is mine. *My* knowledge of *my* experiences cannot be mistaken about, in the end, at least one thing: that they are *my* experiences. As the philosopher Roger Scruton explains it:

> I know that I am a single and unified subject of experience… I know this on no basis, without having to carry out any kind of check, and, indeed, without the use of criteria of any kind—this is what (or what ought to be) meant by the term 'transcendental'. (Scruton 2014: 72)

In other words, logically, I come before the world: the unity of my self-consciousness is not something given to me by or through experience of the world. It is 'on no basis': it is groundless, undetermined. It is instead a presupposition of experience itself. We are able to think about the world—it is thinkable—only because we are already thinkers: that is to say a thinking being needs to be pre-armed with concepts—such as those of substance, causality, temporality—in order to think in the first place.

This is where the empiricists are mistaken: we do not receive these concepts from the world but use them to understand the world.

This understanding of who I am is equally the possibility of a 'You'. Understanding myself as a perspective from which the question 'how should I act' can be asked (a question which operates on the assumption of my freedom) is also to recognise the existence of a different perspective (a *You* we could call it), from which an answer may come. I have to address myself as an Other, see myself from another's point of view, in order to reason about what is best for me. This different perspective allows me to see myself differently and can afford me a picture of what I am not yet but could become: a different me, an-other self. My reason becomes the possibility of my escape from my self.

It is this possibility of escape from the prison of the self that Kant defined as Enlightenment: 'man's emergence from his self-incurred immaturity' through 'the courage to use your *own* understanding' (Kant 2009: 1). It is all too *convenient* to allow others to do one's thinking for one: 'a doctor to judge my diet for me, and so on' (Kant 2009: 1). Instead Kant encourages us to be bold and to be brave: to recognise that our immaturity is self-imposed and therefore to set out on a project of self-overcoming through making use of the ability to self-reflect: to turn's one's reason on one's self. The self becomes a self by a process of overcoming its own self. Kant expresses this casting off of immaturity as a coming-out (*Ausgang*), a becoming-adult, an awakening from childhood. A process of self-education and self-improvement (*Bildung*) appropriate for a self that needs to overcome its own self in order to become its *real* self. This is the working out of autonomy and authenticity. One can, in this view, look on oneself and shape oneself towards the vision one has for oneself.

Rousseau seemed to be saying that man's dependence on others—on society in other words—is in inverse relationship to his freedom and, therefore, his goodness: 'the distinction of vice and virtue... has been aligned with the distinction between dependence on self and dependence on others. Goodness is identified with freedom, with finding the motives for one's actions within oneself' (Taylor 1989: 361). Society suppresses and distorts the individual. Revolution is necessary to remake society through the free willing of all: the general will. Kant, however, writing in between the American and French revolutions, thinks that although a public—be it just 'left in freedom'—has more chance of enlightening itself than individuals on their own, it will not happen quickly:

> a public can only achieve enlightenment slowly. A revolution may well put an end to autocratic despotism and to rapacious or power-seeking oppression, but it will never produce a true reform in ways of thinking. Instead, new prejudices, like the ones they replaced, will serve as a leash to control the great unthinking mass. (Kant 2009: 2–3)

Although the exceptional individual may reason his way free from the prejudices of society, it is a difficult or impossible task for most people. Best that the greatest possible latitude be afforded all people in order to maximise the possibility of progress towards enlightenment. Not through revolution, but through the public use of reason to see through the prejudices of the past:

> One age cannot enter into an alliance on oath to put the next age in a position where it would be impossible for it to extend and correct its knowledge, particularly on such important matters, or to make any progress [*weiterzuschreiten*] whatsoever in enlightenment. This would be a crime against human nature, whose original destiny [*Bestimmung*] lies precisely in such progress [*Fortschreiten*]. Later generations are thus perfectly entitled to dismiss these agreements as unauthorized and criminal. (Kant 2009: 6)

The Self in Society: Freedom *and* Authority

Kant draws a compelling picture of the central role of human (inter-)subjectivity in constructing the world in which it finds itself. It is open, however, to one-sided interpretations which take the idea that subjectivity exists 'on no basis' as license to justify as valid whatever response the self gives itself when asking 'what should I do?' The self in this reading becomes self-justifying and sees whatever is most authentic in terms it gives itself: accounting what is most *self*-ish as what is morally right. This authentic self, finding its justification in itself, is, of course, tempted to be intolerant of the judgements others may make of it. This is really best understood as the *subjectivity of identity*: I am what I am, rather than what I could become; hyper-sensitive to the imagined gaze of others, rather than imagining myself in the shoes of others in order to better judge myself.

Kant responded rightly to Hume's empirical scepticism but opened the door too widely to radical ungrounded subjectivity through the idealism of his response. Thinking may indeed be logically prior to the world. But only *logically*. Practically, if we did not feel, sense, and experience the world, then there would be nothing to think about. Intuition and prejudice (at least in the sense of ready-made judgements) are as necessary as reason in order to act in the world. And I must act in order to know myself and that knowledge—achieved through action—is limited in that it is practical and not theoretical knowledge. I can know myself through the exercise of my freedom. But that activity takes place in the world and is, therefore, limited and relative. Relative to the freedom of others and to the limits imposed by the world and by—do not forget—my (natural) self:

> I am governed by a law of freedom, which compels my actions, and a law of nature, which binds me in the web of organic life. I am a free subject and a determined object: but I am not *two* things, a determined body with a free soul rattling inside. (Scruton 2014: 40)

It is these laws which constrain us: without them people's 'unruly impulses would destroy the possibility of common life' (Seigel 2007: 324).

Remember Kant's strange conception of freedom as autonomy: the self's ability to act towards the good and *against* those ends it desires? Properly understood, autonomy is not the freedom of the self to do whatever it wants, although that is the popular understanding. The consensus view today says that an 'act is considered to be good if it allows the individual to fulfil himself' (Delsol 2003: 65). This understanding comes about because the fact that subjectivity is a perspective on the world exposes us to a constant temptation to imagine the world as if seen from no point of view at all: through God's microscope as it were. In this way we can escape judgement by arguing that my viewpoint is the only point of view and it is also *THE* point of view. This complacent ethics of self-satisfaction imagines itself as tolerant and open-minded (viz., it is up to you alone to become the real you) but in reality, by denying the possibility of judgement, becomes profoundly intolerant to any form of criticism or question raised from the perspective of the Other. When I overreach myself and make judgements as if from no point of view (claiming the authority of the scientist or expert or indeed that of God), I overlook the fact that you and you and you also have perspectives and, in overlooking all of you, I deny you your freedom. What is overlooked or disregarded here is in fact the judgements that go to make up a society of Is and of Yous. The accumulated judgements of society—its traditions, customs, settled ways of life—should be something that binds us together into a community of mutual recognition of each other's freedom. As individuals we are essentially limited: our reason is testament to our ability to represent a perspective on the world, but it is only a single perspective; and our mortality means that 'man's existence is always more limited than his thoughts, which very naturally strain against their limits, as they forever look beyond for an invisible horizon' (Delsol 2003: 177).

The very nature of thought is to strain towards the transcendence of limits: this means a struggle to overcome one's own laziness and self-imposed immaturity, but it also tends towards a rejection of the authority of past judgements as the individual searching for enlightenment comes into conflict with his fellows, and with society and its accumulated prejudices. Human beings, however, live in particular societies which they inherit pre-constituted, already bound together by ties of duty and reciprocal obligation. These cannot be lightly cast aside. Kant in his essay *Conjectures on the Beginning of Human History* argues that we cannot treat the society we inherit as the result of the mistaken reasoning of those who came before us.[8] Instead he says everyone has 'every justification for acknowledging the actions of his first ancestors as his own' (Kant 2009: 105).

This may seem in almost direct contradiction with the passage quoted above in which Kant stated it was the destiny of human nature to make

---

[8] Overwhelmingly the attitude of the 'woke' generation today to the 'sleepers' who preceded them: all too happy to put the past on trial for its failure to adhere to the standards of the present.

progress in enlightenment by dismissing the errors of the past as a crime. It is, I think, only an apparent contradiction. Kant is saying that when we ask ourselves what we should do—what is right—we can do so only by taking a perspective on ourselves: the perspective of a disinterested judge; the perspective of a You. Society has been made by the cumulative judgements of Yous and so it follows that I cannot dismiss your reasoning lightly. In fact, my duty is to put myself in your shoes: to acknowledge your actions as my own.

Yet there is a real issue here too: in 'a world that is neither structured by authority nor held together by tradition' (Arendt 2006: 191), the imperative of autonomy and the desire for authenticity start to diverge. As Frank Furedi argues in his earlier essay in this collection, this contradiction between the aspiration for individual liberty and the imperative of order in public life remains unresolved, centuries after the Reformation. Kant saw the contradiction as one which posed two irreconcilable choices: argue or obey. Put every prejudice, custom, and tradition to the questioning of reason. Or simply obey and conform to the way things are: stay in our self-imposed immaturity. His way of resolving this antinomy drew on the underlying nature of the contradiction itself. We can both argue and obey. We argue in that we have a particular and unique perspective. And we obey in recognition of the particular and unique perspective of others: past, present, and future. We can find the right answer by asking ourselves how others have, do, and will act. We draw, in short, on the customs and traditions of the society we live in: confident that the reason the customs and traditions have survived from generation to generation has something to do with them being *reasonable* customs and traditions. There is a possibility of judgements made according to standards external to me: the insights of hindsight.

Kant ends his famous essay *What is Enlightenment?* in just this way. He points up a paradox:

> A high degree of civil freedom seems advantageous to a people's *intellectual* freedom, yet it also sets up insuperable barriers to it. Conversely, a lesser degree of civil freedom gives intellectual freedom enough room to expand to its fullest extent. (Kant 2009: 10)

Once this ability to act freely has developed—within the security of what Kant calls the hard shell of protection afforded man's inclination to *think freely*—only then may governments:

> find that they can themselves profit by treating man, who is *more than a machine*, in a manner appropriate to his dignity. (Kant 2009: 11)

So, while enlightenment is man's emergence from his self-imposed immaturity—his willing dependence on the guidance of another rather than the courage to use his own understanding—it depends, it turns out, on having an enlightened ruler who has 'a well-disciplined and numerous army to guarantee public security' and can therefore say

> what no republic would dare to say: *Argue as much as you like and about whatever you like, but obey!* (Kant 2009: 10)

The point here is that we should have complete freedom to argue in public. But as private individuals we should do our duty. Society would fall apart if the soldier did not obey orders, and if the citizen refused to pay his taxes. As Kant argues 'all this means restrictions on freedom everywhere' (Kant 2009: 3).

But since for enlightenment all that is needed is the public use of man's reason, it is quite compatible with the restricted use of reason in private. Pay your taxes and then make your argument as to why they are unjust by all means. But pay your taxes. Freedom is not only compatible with doing one's duty: Kant would also argue that it is our duty to be free.

Conclusion: The Temptation of Transcendence and the Need for Restraint

Rousseau's *Emile* begins: 'Everything is good as it leaves the hands of the Author of things; everything degenerates in the hands of man' (Rousseau 1991: 37). Society is corruptive of the individual. Education must be put into the hands of experts in order to socialise man without destroying his goodness. And this naturally leads to the idea that society needs to be remade so people can be made good (again). A self-defeating idea as it can only make the individual subject to the demands of society whereas individual freedom must properly be at the heart of society. It is individuals who give life to the institutions of society. Society works when individuals fit in and find no contradiction in fitting in. They have to find their own way to do so however rather than be forced; but it is possible to find such a way or accommodation because the inheritance of tradition serves them as a guide and means we do not need to always start out from first principles.

This is what I read Kant to mean by the 'hard shell of protection'. Not so much the armed body of the state (though that is necessary too) but more the support and protection provided by tradition and custom: themselves based on the working out of reason through history. It turns out then that 'argue' (freedom) and 'obey' (determination) can be usefully considered as twin aspects of reason. Kant's idea of providence is something that prefigures Hegel's cunning of reason: it speaks to the working out of human reason and freedom in the world behind men's backs allowing human affairs to 'develop gradually from the worse to the better' (Kant 2009: 105), rather than to degenerate from a primal good.

This is not to say that customs should be unquestioningly accepted. It is however to say that they should be accepted questioningly as befits something that has managed to stand the test of time. If we respect nothing traditional—if we question everything and hold nothing sacred—then nothing makes sense: in the absence of tradition there would in fact be no questioning of tradition.

Kantian theory worked as a lever between self and society given the importance he attached to reason. Unlike Rousseau, he did not believe that society could constrain personhood:

> because reason defined being human from the very start, so that even infants who had not yet learned to say 'I' still possessed the innate intelligence that would bring them to it. In an essay on the 'Conjectural Beginning of Human History' (1786), Kant located the separation of reason from instinct inside the garden of Eden, at the point where the possibility of eating as-yet untried foods (the apple!) made the first humans aware of their ability to exercise free choice, and thus to rise above mere

nature; from this arose the need to understand things in the world, and to control one's own conduct. (Seigel 2007: 325)

Because human nature was defined by dualism at its root (between object and subject, nature and culture) it could never be fully shaped by culture, by society. The self comes first no matter how much Kant exhorts us to obey.

The temptation that Kant revealed is that the validation of self-choosing as the highest and only good leads inexorably to the present moment: when it is the choosing that is validated and the self becomes the object of choice raised to a level of unassailable purity. In response we must stress the importance of individual conscience. Of doing the right thing because, when we look inside, we find the moral law within and—on asking why we should obey it—find the same law inscribed in *your* heart. And in the hearts of our parents and our children. We should pay our obligations to their perspective because it is our perspective too, and in recognising it as such we meet ourselves reflected back in their eyes. And in the eyes of all those who go to make up our society.

References

Arendt, H. (2006). *Between past and future*. London: Penguin.
Delsol, C. (2003). *Icarus fallen: The search for meaning in an uncertain world*. Wilmington, DE: ISI Books.
Hewitt, R. (2017). *A revolution of feeling: The decade that forged the modern mind*. London: Granta Books.
Hume, D. (1975). *A treatise of human nature* (L. A. Selby-Bigge, Ed., P. H. Nidditch, Rev.). Oxford: Clarendon Press.
Kant, I. (1999). *Practical philosophy* (M. J. Gregor, Ed. and Trans.). Cambridge: Cambridge University Press.
Kant, I. (2009). *An answer to the question: 'What is enlightenment?'*. London: Penguin.
Outram, D. (2006). *Panorama of the enlightenment*. London: Thames & Hudson.
Rousseau, J. J. (1960). *The social contract*. Oxford: Oxford University Press.
Rousseau, J. J. (1970). *The confessions* (J. M. Cohen, Trans.). London: Penguin.
Rousseau, J. J. (1991). *Emile or on education* (A. Bloom, Trans.). London: Penguin.

Scruton, R. (2014). *The soul of the world*. Oxford: Princeton University Press.
Seigel, J. (2007). *The idea of the self: Thought and experience in Western Europe since the seventeenth century*. Cambridge: Cambridge University Press.
Siedentop, L. (2014). *Inventing the individual: The origins of Western liberalism*. London: Allen Lane.
Taylor, C. (1989). *Sources of the self: The making of modern identity*. Cambridge, MA: Harvard University Press.

5

'Of Individuality, as One of the Elements of Wellbeing.' J.S. Mill and the Nineteenth-Century Liberal Individual

James Panton

The liberal model of society that first emerged more than three and a half centuries ago is organised around a particular understanding of what it is to be an individual. In opposition to a society cohered around hierarchy, privilege, and superstition, a range of thinkers contributed to a model of society that would instead enshrine rights and freedoms, equality and universalism, a suspicion of power, rational enquiry, and a fundamental belief in the rational agency of the individual, as the core principles around which society should be organised. When Thomas Hobbes (*Leviathan*, 1651), then John Locke (*Two Treatises of Government*, 1689), developed theories of the state as being the product of a more or less explicit agreement or contract between individuals, they drew on a particular understanding of the individual *qua* rationally self-interested agent as the foundation upon which state power could be justified and limited. (In the following century Jean-Jacques Rousseau (*The Social Contract*, 1762) would go on to develop a still more complicated theory of both the individual and his relationship with the state in which the

J. Panton (✉)
Magdalen College School, Oxford, UK

autonomy of the individual is preserved in a state whose constitution derives from the will of each and every individual.)[1] When Thomas Jefferson (1776), in justifying a revolutionary war against tyranny, outlined the 'self-evident' truths that 'all men are created equal' and 'endowed by their Creator with certain unalienable Rights', he made a claim to the universal moral equality of all individuals against which his own and later societies would rightly be measured, and often found wanting. When Immanuel Kant wrote that one must 'always treat humanity, whether in your own person or the person of another, always at the same time as an end and never simply as a means' (1785 [2012]), he pushed that ethical universalism further, asserting a rational necessity to the recognition of other individuals as (like me) free and autonomous beings with their own purposes: purposes I ought to respect as part of my respect for the humanity we share in common.

This starts to outline a model of what it is to be a human individual: a creature capable of rational thought, with the potential for autonomy and self-development; a bearer of rights, and someone who shares in a universal condition of being human. The idea that individuals are capable of reason, and thus capable of making rational sense of the world around them, and then choosing their course of action in the world, poses a radical challenge to authoritarian and paternalistic states, just as much as it challenges us all, as individuals, to work out what we think is right in order that we might live accordingly. The implication of this belief in reason is a demand, on the one hand, for individual freedom—the freedom to develop myself as an individual, to live the life I want to live, and to live it as *my* life based upon the values I believe in and the judgements I make—and on the other hand, an imperative that I am tolerant of the decisions and judgements and lifestyles of other people, however far removed from or contradictory to my own values and priorities they may be.

This model of the individual that can be traced through a number of key thinkers in the emerging tradition of liberal thought reaches its apotheosis in the work of John Stuart Mill. Mill was an essayist, a political campaigner, a civil servant, and sometime Member of Parliament, who

---

[1] See Chap. 7 of this book, Tim Black, 'Autonomy and the birth of authenticity', for a longer discussion.

made significant contributions to social theory, ethics, logic, economics and, of course, politics. According to one recent account he was 'the most influential English language philosopher of the nineteenth century' (Mcleod 2018). Indeed, it is remarkable the extent to which some of Mill's core ideas continue to have purchase today; and to which certain of his arguments, built as they are around a particular understanding of what it is to be an individual, have maintained their radical and progressive implications more than a century and a half after they were written. This relevance is particularly so in the context of contemporary political discourse in which the possibility—much less, the desirability—of individual autonomy is questioned, and the model of robust, rational individualism that Mill and other early liberals championed is often disparaged.

Everyone with a cursory acquaintance with philosophy knows how Mill's *Utilitarianism* (1863 [1987]) took the already radical reformist ideas of Jeremy Bentham, whose 'fundamental axiom' was that 'the greatest happiness of the greatest number that is the measure of right and wrong' (1776 [1977]), and raised this code to a more sophisticated level.[2] Debate on Mill's theory and, not least, the role of the individual within that theory, continue to be a staple of any introduction to philosophical ethics (and one which I will touch on below). In *Considerations on Representative Government* (1861), Mill argued for liberal democracy as the most ideal form of government; he called for a radical extension of the franchise and the reform of the electoral system into one organised around proportional representation. He was elected as MP for the City of Westminster in 1865 on a platform which included votes for women. In 1866 he presented a petition to the House of Commons in favour of women's suffrage and tabled an amendment to the Second Reform Bill demanding the enfranchisement of all households, regardless of sex. The amendment was defeated, but it can be credited with bringing the emergent campaign for the enfranchisement of women to wider political attention: numerous further bills for the extension of the franchise were presented to Parliament in the following decades until the eventual codification of voting equality in 1928. After losing his seat in 1868, Mill

---

[2] See Chap. 3 of this book, Jamie Whyte, 'In Praise of Selfish Individualism'.

went on to publish *On the Subjection of Women* (1869), which argued for the full recognition of legal equality between men and women, including voting rights and equality in divorce law. As with other areas of his thought, Mill saw legal equality and the equal capacity for self-development as a condition necessary not only to the well-being of the individual, but also to social progress generally: 'The legal subordination of one sex to another' he argued, 'is wrong in itself, and now one of the chief hindrances to human improvement' (1869: 1).

In what follows I want to focus my interpretation, for the most part, on one of Mill's other significant contributions to the liberal cannon, his essay *On Liberty* (1859). Amongst other things, I want to demonstrate the extent to which the model of individualism around which Mill builds his polemic is deeply socially engaged, dynamic, and robust. This model stands in stark contrast to the quite diminished model of the individual which underpins much contemporary discussion. While it is not necessary to be a committed utilitarian to appreciate the power of Mill's argument for individual and social freedom in *On Liberty*, the debate on the relationship between individual freedom and the ethical theory of utilitarianism is a helpful place to begin to unpack Mill's account of what it is to be an individual.

* * *

Mill famously begins *On Liberty* with a 'very simple principle'—the fundamental axiom around which a free society should be organised:

> The sole end for which mankind are warranted, individually or collectively, in interfering with the liberty of action of any of their number, is self-protection… [T]he only purpose for which power can be rightfully exercised over any member of a civilised community, against his will, is to prevent harm to others. (1859 [1991]: 30)

This 'harm principle' establishes individual freedom as the key principle of social organisation. Individual freedom, it seems, should trump other values or priorities in society: this freedom can only be limited in so far as the actions of one individual will result in harm to others. Mill goes on to make the case yet more explicit. 'His own good, either physical or moral, is not a sufficient warrant' to interfere with the liberty of the individual:

> He cannot rightfully be compelled to do or forbear because it will be better for him to do so, because it will make him happier, because, in the opinions of others, to do so would be wise, or even right. (1859 [1991]: 30)

Commentators over the years have noted the extent to which this prioritisation of individual liberty seems to contradict the ethical core of the utilitarian philosophy which Mill espoused. In *Utilitarianism*, first published as a series of articles two years after *On Liberty*, and soon thereafter as a single book, Mill argues that 'happiness is desirable, and the only thing desirable, as an end; all other things being only desirable as means to that end' (1863 [1987]: 36). It should seem obvious here that prioritising happiness, even the happiness of the individual, might lead us to want to restrict the freedom to make the kinds of mistakes in life that can result in misery and suffering. The core explanation for interventions which limit the freedom of the individual in Mill's time, much as in our own, was the attempt to prevent the harm that individuals inflict upon themselves or upon others: think about restrictions on drugs or alcohol, or newly introduced taxes on the individual's consumption choices such as sugar and fat taxes, as well as codes of conduct around speech and behaviour. We need not go as far as the standard tropes or moral dilemmas in Ethics 101 classes—that as good utilitarians we should sacrifice the freedom of the individual if that sacrifice could lead to greater aggregate happiness—in order to recognise that the freedom of the individual, and the principle of individualism itself, may not at all times achieve maximum utility. The greatest happiness does not seem to be a necessary consequence of the maximisation of individual liberty; Mill cannot maintain his commitment to liberty and his commitment to utilitarianism, on this account.

The emphasis on utilitarian ethics is not, though, the result of a change of heart between the publication of *On Liberty* and *Utilitarianism*. In the former Mill already made clear an explicit appeal to utilitarianism.

Expanding upon what he proposes as the limits to the sanction of the individual by either state or society at large, he states:

> .... the only part of the conduct of any one, for which he is amenable to society, is that which concerns others. In the part which concerns himself, his independence (of choice) is, of right, absolute. (1859 [1991]: 31)

Yet, he continues to say such ethical considerations are not grounded in any standard classically liberal account of the natural rights of the individual (which Bentham had famously derided as 'nonsense upon stilts'[3]):

> I forgo any advantage which could be derived to my argument from the idea of abstract right, as a thing independent of utility. I regard utility as the ultimate appeal on all ethical questions.... (1859 [1991]: 31)

Mill's account of individual freedom is firmly grounded in an appeal to utility.

The solution to the apparent conflict between the end of individual liberty and the end of maximum utility is to be found in Mill's understanding of what it is to be an individual.[4] In Chapter 3 of *On Liberty*, 'Of Individuality, as One of the Elements of Wellbeing', Mill raises his concern that the biggest problem in maintaining liberty as the key principle of social organisation is a generalised indifference in society towards the end of living freely. '[I]ndividual spontaneity', complains Mill, 'is hardly recognised' as having 'any intrinsic worth'. To this problem he responds:

> If it were felt that the free development of individuality is one of the leading essentials of well-being; that it is not only a co-ordinate element with all that is designated by the terms civilization, instruction, education, culture, but is itself a necessary part and condition of all those things; there would be no danger that liberty should be undervalued, and the adjustment

---

[3] 'That which has no existence cannot be destroyed—that which cannot be destroyed cannot require anything to preserve it from destruction. Natural rights is simple nonsense: natural and imprescriptible rights, rhetorical nonsense—nonsense upon stilts.' (Bentham 2002)

[4] I am grateful to Michael Freeden for this insight: according to my tutorial notes, it was he who suggested this resolution to the conflict between liberty and utility.

of the boundaries between it and social control would present no extraordinary difficulty. (1859 [1991]: 73)

Mill means that to live a good life involves not only living freely, but also, it seems, continuously working upon oneself as an individual in a project of growth and self-development. Having reached the maturity of our faculties—that is, as adults—we are individuals who must struggle to discover what is valuable in life, and who must struggle to create our own lives for ourselves. Liberty is thus not simply a means to any one of a number of extrinsic values or virtues—civilisation, education, culture, development—that we might consider constituent parts of living the good life. On the contrary, liberty is both a necessary condition and an essential component of the achievement of each of these things. Liberty is necessary to, and an essential part of, the pursuit of our humanity in the modern world—of what it is to discover and live at the height of our powers. On this reading it can be argued that for Mill, maximising 'utility'—which he otherwise refers to in *On Liberty* as 'well-being'—means maximising the scope for individuals to live freely and to develop themselves. Liberty is not a means towards the good life, but rather a necessary constituent part of it.

Here we begin to see how Mill understands what it is to be an individual. One is, or ought to be, engaged in the development of the self. As we will see below, this also quite likely means one ought also to be engaged in the development of others and in society as a whole. The free development of individuality which is fundamental to our well-being requires that we ourselves engage in, or at the very least that in society we are tolerant and supportive of what Mill calls 'experiments in living', because the only way to work out how best to live the good life is to be open to the many different ways in which life can be lived. Mill is, of course, aware that the individual's pursuit of their own way of living in the world does not exist in isolation from other people. When I imagine the individual as conceived by early liberals such as Locke, I imagine an individual frontiersman: pursuing his life in a battle against nature: if not in isolation from others, at least potentially self-sufficient. With Mill, however, the individual he imagines seems to be far more fundamentally, and perhaps essentially, socially engaged. The 'harm principle' is fundamental because my actions as an individual have direct and inevitable consequences for other individuals in society, and their actions have direct consequences upon me.

However, my own and other peoples' individuality is a great deal more robust, and thus a lot less susceptible to harm, than the individual as conceived of in much contemporary discourse. Mill certainly does not consider the notion that difficult or dangerous or challenging ideas could be the cause of harm to other people: causing offence, for Mill, is not a harm. On the one hand we might imagine that causing offence is simply an inevitable consequence of the existence of individuals who are pushing against the limits of social norms and seeking to live their lives freely. On the other hand, however, it seems likely that in a society that understands itself to be organised around the pursuit and development of individual freedom, individuals would be much less likely to take offence at the actions or ideas of others. In pursuing our individual freedom, we will inevitably rub up against each other in more or less problematic ways; but that such experiences of social engagement can be at times positive, at other times negative, is simply part of what it is to live in a world populated by other individuals with their own ends. Note also that argument and disagreement between individuals with different ideas of how one ought to live seem fundamental to Mill's understanding of how we ought to behave in society. While the harm principle dictates that the individual 'cannot rightfully be *compelled* to do or forbear because it will be better for him to do so, because it will make him happier, because, in the opinions of others, to do so would be wise, or even right', Mill suggests that an individual's belief about what is in the best interests of another individual are nonetheless 'good reasons for remonstrating with him, or reasoning with him, or persuading him, or entreating him' (1859 [1991]: 30). The argument for liberty is not an argument for individuals to disengage from one another or from society at large; on the contrary, Mill seems to think we ought to be engaged with one another through arguments and remonstrations and attempts to persuade.

The utility that Mill argues should be 'the ultimate appeal on all ethical questions' has to be understood not in terms of immediate experiences of happiness or dissatisfaction, but rather, Mill argues: 'it must be utility in the largest sense, grounded on the permanent interests of man as a progressive being...' (1859 [1991]: 31). A key part of what it is to be a human being is to have the capacity to strive and seek and develop ourselves. A significant threat to us achieving our humanity is the limits placed upon our freedom to develop as individuals in the world and to take control of our own lives. The 'permanent interests of mankind as a progressive being' draw together an understanding of the individual as inherently capable of living freely and developing as an individual, with a recognition of the relationship between the individual and the social world whereby the individual's project of self-development contributes to the development of society as a whole. This relationship between individual and society explains the importance Mill places upon freedom of speech and argument.

* * *

Mill argues that freedom of speech and debate, and the constant contestation of ideas, is essential not just to individual development and wellbeing, but to the possibility of social development, progress, and the achievement of the good society. A society that does not guarantee or cultivate a culture in which people think and speak freely and challenge received opinion, a society that is nervous about allowing individuals to say things that are controversial or offensive, or too insecure to allow individuals to live their lives differently, does not just place unacceptable limits on individual freedom, but it limits itself as a society and does itself some very fundamental harm. Mill claims that in the censoring of individuals who challenge the norms or question accepted wisdom:

> The greatest harm done is to those who are not heretics, whose whole mental development is cramped, and their reason cowed, by the fear of heresy. Who can compute what the world loses in the multitude of promising intellects combined with timid characters, who dare not follow out any bold, vigorous, independent train of thought, lest it should land them in something which would admit of being considered irreligious or immoral? (1859 [1991]: 52)

Kant famously argued that 'Enlightenment is man's emergence from self-imposed nonage', a condition of heteronomy which takes significant intellectual and moral courage to overturn. '*Dare to know! (Sapere aude.)* "Have the courage to use your own understanding," is therefore the motto of Enlightenment' (1784). Mill similarly sees the pursuit of knowledge and understanding as a project requiring intellectual and moral courage, and the social consequence of limiting humanity's ability to develop its understanding, is severe. 'The price paid for this sort of intellectual pacification is the sacrifice of the entire moral courage of the human mind' (1859 [1991]: 51).

Mill argues that during those periods when society has been confident enough to hold in check its fear of heresy and controversy, in which 'the yoke of authority' has been broken and 'mental despotism' discarded, we see humanity making great intellectual, scientific, moral, and political leaps forward. At other times ideas do still develop and knowledge can grow, but its progress is stultified and retarded. We might take the example of scientific and technological progress in our own age. We live in a culture that feels uneasy about the extent of scientific knowledge and human intervention in nature—when ideas of uncertainty and risk dominate narratives around what developments are possible or desirable. But nonetheless, scientists continue working, and discoveries are made. The difficulty is that development is slow, and breakthroughs are exceptions made against the odds. To challenge the consensus in times of conformity takes exceptional courage. Mill uses the examples of Socrates and Jesus: two heretics who made and lived by great intellectual and moral discoveries which challenged the societies in which they were born; and suffered the severest of consequences. While the ideas of both live on, and the world would be a worse place without their ideas, Mill asks us to consider how many other heretics of their times, and since, were silenced, their reason cowed, or their ideas suppressed? Only in a society that nurtures freedom of thought and experiment, as well as constant criticism and interrogation, can we expect the pursuit of truth to be properly unleashed, and that the resultant discoveries made by those prepared to think seriously will translate into progressive and consistent social development.

Here we can see the extent to which Mill's understanding of robust and dynamic individualism is not that of an individual disengaged from society at large; quite the contrary, the individual Mill celebrates is an individual whose contrariness and heresy contribute to the betterment of our shared existence. A society that does not allow the full and free development of individuals will much inhibit, perhaps entirely suppress, the possibility and rate of a broader collective social development.

Mill's understanding of the role of contest and argument in the development of understanding is not based upon a relativist account of truth. The pursuit of truth is the most vital concern for human civilisation because it enables the development of knowledge and understanding about the world that allows us to develop as both individuals and as a society. However, Mill seems to be acutely aware that *truth* as we discover it is necessarily provisional: neither as individuals nor as a society overall do we ever reach a point of complete certainty that we have got it all right. One of Mill's points here is that silencing dissent from received opinion, or from what he calls 'socially useful ideas', while it might seem to come from a position of certainty about what is right and wrong, is actually a result of our intellectual *insecurity*. If our beliefs are that true, if we are as confident in them as we suggest we are, they ought to be able to stand up to whatever challenges come along. In contemporary discourse this insecurity might be most clearly expressed in the tendency to want to close down certain areas of debate as beyond dispute (as in 'the science is settled'). From scientific arguments around climate change to moral and political arguments around identarian rights and freedoms, there is a tendency to reject debate.[5] While the ideas that dominate in the present may be different in content, Mill seems to be attuned to a very similar tendency in his own day. Describing his age as one which is 'destitute of faith, but terrified at scepticism', Mill argues:

> people feel sure, not so much that their opinions are true, as that they should not know what to do without them—the claims of an opinion to be protected from public attack are rested not so much on its truth, as on its importance to society. There are, it is alleged, certain beliefs so useful, not to say indispensable, to well-being that it is as much the duty of governments to uphold those beliefs, as to protect any other of the interests of society. (1859 [1991]: 41–42)

---

[5] In 2018, to take one example of many, BBC *Woman's Hour* presenter Jenni Murray pulled out of a talk at Oxford University after LGBTQ+ students argued that allowing airtime to 'publicly transphobic speakers' risked doing harm to the welfare of trans students and staff.

The closing down of such areas for discussion and contestation results from apparently good intentions:

> It is also often argued, and still oftener thought, that none but bad men would desire to weaken these salutary beliefs; and there can be nothing wrong, it is thought, in restraining bad men, and prohibiting what only such men would wish to practice. (1859 [1991]: 42)

The inclination to attribute malign intent to those who challenge dominant ideas, and to seek to uncover the vested interests that lie behind beliefs which surely could not otherwise be sincerely held or argued, is a dominant tendency in our own time.

In a rebuttal to the prevailing culture of his—and our own age—Mill argues that only in a society that tolerates and encourages absolute freedom of thought and speech, and which allows people to live their lives in different ways in accordance with their beliefs, can we have the possibility of developing a real understanding of the world we live in. First, the free flow of argument and ideas is necessary in order that we can work out what we think is true. Without diversity of opinion and ideas we are necessarily restricted in our choice of what path to follow and of what answers we think are the right answers. Second, this freedom must not be restricted to the set of things that we already accept are matters of dispute. It is just as important that 'extreme' ideas are freely expressed—because the best test of extreme ideas is that they are subject to scrutiny and debate. Third, it is further important that those things that we *know* to be true are also subjected to question and challenge—because it is all too easy for these 'certainties' to become 'dead dogmas'. Mill says:

> not only the grounds of the opinion are forgotten in the absence of discussion, but too often the meaning of the opinion itself .... Instead of a vivid conception and a living belief, there remain only a few phrases retained by rote .... Ninety-nine in a hundred of what are called educated men are in this condition; even of those who can argue fluently for their opinions. Their conclusion may be true, but it might be false for anything they know: .... they do not, in any proper sense of the word, know the doctrine which they themselves profess. (1859 [1991]: 57)

5 'Of Individuality, as One of the Elements of Wellbeing.'...

Mill seems to be very much aware that the complexity of the world and the questions we ask of it means that, as often as not, real truth is discovered to lie somewhere between a host of competing conceptions and ideas. When that is the case, a free flow of ideas is necessary for truth to be uncovered; when that is not the case, the conflict of ideas can only contribute to our understanding of the truths of which we are certain.

It is important to note that Mill does not believe that *all* debate is objective and rational:

> I acknowledge that the tendency of all opinions to become sectarian is not cured by the freest discussion, but is often heightened and exacerbated thereby; the truth which ought to have been, but was not, seen, being rejected all the more violently because proclaimed by persons regarded as opponents. (1859 [1991]: 69)

Nor does he think that from all debate *the truth will always out*. Quite the contrary, he recognises that not infrequently in human history truth has been overwhelmed by untruth, and progressive ideas by superstition. But only in a society that is confident enough to accept a continuous conflict of ideas and opinions do we have any real confidence for the belief that truths will be discovered, and that suppressed ideas will eventually find their way to the light. The danger, for Mill, does not lie in the exposure of people to ideas that are wrong or preposterous, but in the 'quiet suppression of half of it':

> there is always hope when people are forced to listen to both sides; it is when they attend only to one that errors harden into prejudices, and truth itself ceases to have the effect of truth, by being exaggerated into falsehood. (1859 [1991]: 69)

The freedom of the individual is thus necessary not only for the free development of individuality in order that the individual can realise themselves *qua* individual, but also in order that society can progress, and knowledge can develop.

* * *

Mill, following Tocqueville, takes the earlier liberal concern about the propensity of the state to undermine individual freedom into a more socialised understanding of the relationship between individualism, individual freedom, society, and culture. That which threatens freedom and undermines individualism the most is not the coercive power of state regulation, but the cultural constraints we place upon ourselves in a society that fails or refuses or is too uncertain of itself to really push back the limits of individual and social freedom. The point here is not that state regulation, intervention, and coercion should not be resisted. Mill is in general just as concerned about this aspect of modern society as we ought to be ourselves. We might well note that the extent of regulatory, statutory, and bureaucratic legislation under which we live our lives is beyond any possible imagining for a nineteenth-century liberal like Mill. Still, however problematical the juridical restriction of freedom is, regulations can always be flouted, and unfree laws and oppressive governments can always be overthrown. But what if we come to no longer value our freedom? What if we fail to recognise when it is being undermined? What if we live in a culture whose very norms and socialisation processes encourage conformism and discourage the development of critical thought and the freedom to experiment with how we want to live our lives? These, it seems to me, are the profound questions about culture that Mill's *On Liberty* raises for us. Individuals who aspire to freedom can tame and direct the overwhelming stigma of unreflective opinion, the overwhelming desire not to offend, the ill-considered acceptance of social norms, and the official sanctioning of 'socially useful ideas' that serves to silence dissent. But the absence of a belief amongst citizens in the importance of their own freedom breeds conformity and, in the context of an acquiescence to authority and an acceptance of the status quo, these cultural pressures can become overwhelming. They can undermine individuals' belief in their capacity to navigate their lives, to reason for themselves. They can encourage the acceptance of received wisdom as if it were truth—and as such—risk losing the vitality of even those beliefs we might hold which happen to be true. They disguise our intellectual and moral uncertainty, our existential insecurity, behind an often absolutist certainty in good and evil, truth and lies.

In the second chapter of *On Liberty* Mill makes comment on three historical periods (the Reformation, the late Enlightenment, and the Germany of Goethe and Fichte) that he thinks have come closest to the spirit of human freedom and the pursuit of truth:

> These periods differed widely in the particular opinions which they developed; but were alike in this, that during all three the yoke of authority was broken. In each, an old mental despotism had been thrown off, and no new one had yet taken its place. The impulse given at these three periods has made Europe what it now is. Every single improvement which has taken place either in the human mind or in institutions, may be traced distinctly to one or other of them. Appearances have for some time indicated that all three impulses are well nigh spent; and we can expect no fresh start until we again assert our mental freedom. (1859 [1991]: 53)

Mill's clarion call for society to recognise the fundamental importance of the free development of individuality to the well-being of individuals, and to the possibility of social development, seems to me to be as important today as it was when Mill first wrote it. A society that values reason, freedom, and tolerance places certain demands on all of us as individuals: that we should be capable of arguing about what we think is right and robust enough to accept that not everyone will agree with us. It proposes a certain model of what we are capable of as individuals and of the potential value to rational argument with one another about our common interests. That we share enough in common to constructively disagree; that we can disagree fundamentally with each other without undermining the value that we each hold as human beings.

References

Bentham, J. (1776 [1977]). A comment on the commentaries and fragment on government. In J. H. Burns & H. L. A. Hart (Eds.), *The collected works of Jeremy Bentham*. Oxford: Oxford University Press.
Bentham, J. (2002). Nonsense upon stilts, or Pandora's box opened, or the French Declaration of Rights. In C. Pease-Watkin, C. Blamres, & P. Schofield (Eds.), *The collected works of Jeremy Bentham: Rights, representation and reform:*

Nonsense upon stilts and other writings on the French Revolution. Oxford: Oxford University Press.

Jefferson, T. (1776). Declaration of independence: A transcription. *National Archives*. Retrieved December 12, 2018, from https://www.archives.gov/founding-docs/declaration-transcript.

Kant, I. (1784 [2009]). *An answer to the question: What is enlightenment?* London: Penguin.

Kant, I. (1785 [2012]). The groundwork for a metaphysics of morals. In *Kant: Groundwork for the metaphysics of morals* (Rev. ed.). Revised by J. Timmerman and Translated by M. Gregor. Cambridge: Cambridge University Press.

Mcleod, C. (2018). John Stuart Mill. In *Stanford Encyclopaedia* (Fall ed.). Retrieved June 5, 2018, from https://plato.stanford.edu/archives/fall2018/entries/mill/.

Mill, J. S. (1859 [1991]). On liberty. In J. Gray & G. W. Smith (Eds.), *J.S. Mill on liberty in focus*. London: Routledge.

Mill, J. S. (1861). *Considerations on representative government*. London: Parker, Son, & Bourn.

Mill, J. S. (1863 [1987]). Utilitarianism. In J. S. Mill & J. Bentham (Eds.), *Utilitarianism and other essays*. London: Penguin Books.

Mill, J. S. (1869). *The subjection of women*. London: Longmans, Green, Reader, & Dyer.

6

The Rise and Fall of the Rule of Law

Jon Holbrook

The expression 'the rule of law' is seen as a timeless and essential hallmark of liberal democracy. But it is 'an exceedingly elusive notion' which gives rise to contrasting convictions save that 'everyone is for it' (Tamanaha 2004: 3). This failure to define the rule of law's essential quality whilst portraying it as an enduring feature of Western liberalism does much to give the phrase its hallowed status. Yet, if we define 'the rule of law', as Francis Fukuyama does, to mean 'a set of rules of behaviour, reflecting a broad consensus within the society' (Fukuyama 2015: 24) that is binding on all, then we can see that the notion has been anything but an enduring feature of British liberalism.

This essay argues that the rule of law's essential quality—namely laws that reflect a broad consensus within society—has rarely been a reality for Britain. Over the last 200 years the rule of law has been a reality for the 50-year period between about 1930 and 1980 when law was based on reasonableness and common sense. Before then the law was too distant

J. Holbrook (✉)
London, UK

and antagonistic towards its people to be able to reflect a broad consensus. Moreover, in the current era that started to develop in the 1970s, the law has once again become antagonistic towards its people, motored as it is by a rights-based concept of law. But whereas that nineteenth-century antagonism was accompanied with legal weakness (and political strength), today's antagonistic relationship between law and society is accompanied with legal strength (and political weakness). In the nineteenth century the relationship between law and politics was captured in Dicey's view that 'the legislative supremacy of Parliament is the very keystone of the law of the constitution' (Dicey 1982: 25). Whereas, in 2018 the UK's top judge, Lady Hale, could argue without protest that moral and political issues are matters 'the courts are as well qualified to judge as is the legislature'. In fact, she claimed that 'the courts may be thought better qualified' to rule on such issues (Hale 2018: §38). Whereas the rule of law was traditionally subject to political oversight, many today see the rule of law as a means of curtailing the political sphere. This has damaging consequences for liberal democracy, which a complacent attitude towards 'the rule of law' does much to mask. For in the absence of a broad consensus within society about rights-based law the rule of law has morphed into the rule *by* law. Instead of the law enabling personal autonomy to flourish, the law now restricts it.

The Slow Development of the Rule of Law

For much of the nineteenth century English law had a distant and antagonistic relationship with British society. It was short on any theory or principle that could engage or connect with society. The political philosophy of laissez-faire, that emphasised the importance of private and property rights, combined with a religious outlook, that man should prove his worth in God's eyes by hard work and earthly gain, worked well when delivered from Parliament or the pulpit (Griffith and Street 1952: 1). But it could scarcely provide remedies for the poor, the sick or the injured who might have sought redress against an employer or anyone else worth suing (nobody sues a man of straw). This did not much matter in an era of liberalism, rather than of liberal democracy, when people were descriptively *subjects* rather than *citizens*. The law did not need principles that could connect with people and—in place of principles—it drew its authority from precedents developed in a pre-industrial age that it applied to suit the interests of an industrial class.

The law's mid-nineteenth century shortcomings were captured by Charles Dickens, who, having started his career as a court reporter, knew whereof he spoke (Slater 2009: 340–358). His novel *Bleak House*, published in 1852–1853, begins with this apposite description of law as an advert for its avoidance:

> On such an afternoon some score of members of the High Court of Chancery bar ought to be … mistily engaged in one of the ten thousand stages of an endless cause, tripping one another up on slippery precedents, groping knee-deep in technicalities, running their goat-hair and horsehair warded heads against walls of words and making a pretence of equity with serious faces, as players might. … This is the Court of Chancery, … which gives to monied might the means abundantly of wearing out the right, which so exhausts finances, patience, courage, hope, so overthrows the brain and breaks the heart, that there is not an honourable man among its practitioners who would not give … the warning, 'Suffer any wrong that can be done you rather than come here!'

Dickens' colourful portrayal of mid-nineteenth century law captures its essential problem: it was governed by 'slippery precedents' and served the interests of 'monied might' but most of all it was so dire that it encouraged potential litigants to avoid it. This was a law that related to the people by warning them that it was better to 'suffer any wrong' than seek redress in court. The 'slippery precedents' were, throughout the nineteenth century, a hallmark of a law that served its essential purpose of making itself largely impenetrable and irrelevant to society. The extent of the problem was evident in the first edition of Thomas Beven's *Principles of the Law of Negligence* (1889) that devoted 700 pages to the subject of negligence in order to cover what Dickens called the 'slippery precedents' and which a legal commentator described as a 'wilderness of single instances', rather than a coherent framework delineated by principles.[1]

---

[1] *The Duty of Care towards One's Neighbour* (1883) 18 *Law Journal* 618, p. 619.

In the nineteenth century there was a gulf between the interests of a minority, anxious to develop an industrial free-market economy, and the majority, that was keen to protect itself from the negative consequences of that economy. Law at the time sided with the minority by embracing the political philosophy of laissez-faire but it preferred not to say so. Telling the working man that his industrial injury, for example, was a price he needed to pay in pursuit of a free market would have brought the law into disrepute. But telling the working man that his legal claim for redress failed because the judge's hands were tied by precedent avoided this problem.

Precedents were a brake on the expansion of negligence as a tort that would otherwise have hampered risk-taking and industrial development. Consider the seminal case of *Winterbottom v Wright*[2] in which the claimant was ruled unable to sue. He was a mail-coach driver who was thrown from his seat and made lame for life when a wheel flew off the coach he was driving. But because there was no precedent for such a claim to succeed it was dismissed, even though, as a matter of principle, it was difficult to see why the claimant should not succeed if the defendant had failed to construct the mail-coach with reasonable skill and care.[3] Precedents drawn from a pre-industrial era enabled judges to apply rules that served 'monied might' or as David Ibbetson put it: 'the court was transparently concerned not to allow an action that might cast what they perceived as an unreasonable burden on manufacturers. Consequently, judge-made rules, stemming from transparent judicial preferences, meant that negligent manufacturers largely escaped liability for damage caused by their goods' (Ibbetson 1999: 174).

For most of the nineteenth century the law succeeded in avoiding too much of a relationship with British society. This was evidenced by the fact that in the mid-nineteenth century 'the entire judiciary of England and Wales sitting in courts of general jurisdiction numbered just fifteen' and they sat individually to hear cases, either in London or major provincial towns (the assizes), for just two four-week terms a year (Ferguson 2014: 92).

---

[2] *Winterbottom v Wright* (1842) 10 M & W 109.
[3] Lord Abinger, CB, had no qualms about ossifying the law when he dismissed the claim after noting that: 'If there had been any ground for such an action, there certainly would have been some precedent of it', p. 114.

But, try as it might, avoidance was not always possible and when law met society its impact was often negative. Nineteenth-century Britain was a nation of interests shaped by class, and even those with monied might experienced the law negatively. Railways, the single most important sector of the Victorian Industrial Revolution, experienced the 'English common law [as one of] profound and largely negative impact'. Solicitors were notorious as speculative railway-share promoters, judges were publicly accused of favouritism, and the Parliamentary Bar ran a nice little racket: effectively selling statutory approval for new railway lines (Kostal 1994).

It was the interests of trade unions that fared worst at law's hands, particularly around the turn of the century. The High Court judges of the day were, says Professor Heuston, 'not on the whole notable for progressive views on social or industrial matters'.[4] The judges' anti-trade union views came to a head in 1901 when the House of Lords unanimously held, contrary to what was generally assumed,[5] that trade unions could be sued, in effect, for losses sustained by employers as a consequence of strike action. This decision in favour of the Taff Vale Railway Company[6] left 'a legacy of suspicion and mistrust ... to poison relations between the courts and the unions for many years'.[7] Indeed, the decision was so unpopular that it was reversed when Parliament passed the Trades Disputes Act in 1906.

In the nineteenth century and the early part of the twentieth, law's relationship with society varied between the abstinent and the antagonistic. Monied might occasionally got its way but the Dickensian view of law, scornfully described in *Bleak House*, as an institution to be avoided was one shared by a majority of wealthy and poor alike. The law in this era was too weak, distant and antagonistic, to constitute the rule of law.

---

[4] R. F. V. Heuston, *The Lives of the Lord Chancellors 1885–1940* (Oxford, 1964), pp. 119–120.
[5] J. A. G. Griffith, *The Politics of the Judiciary* (Fontana, 1997), p. 66: 'because of their large and fluctuating membership and because of certain provisions in the Trade Union Act 1871, it was assumed that it was impracticable to bring actions against [trade unions] so as to make their funds liable.'
[6] *Taff Vale Railway Co v Amalgamated Society of Railway Servants* [1901] AC 426, HL.
[7] Heuston, *op cit*, p. 76.

The Rule of Law and the Mid-Twentieth Century

Law's largely absent and antagonistic relationship with society could not last for ever. Whether it is called industrial, free market, capitalist or great, the society that was developing during the nineteenth and early twentieth centuries needed law to play a greater role. For as society developed it became impersonal and brought more men into contact with other men and their machines. Traditional codes of behaviour that had come from family, community and church needed bolstering with normative principles, which could address the new challenges. Necessity is often the mother of invention and society's need for new normative principles found a home in the law. But first, the multiplicity of 'slippery' legal precedents that caused the law so much ridicule had to be organised around or replaced with unifying principles that could serve society's interests. Over a period of about 100 years from the mid-nineteenth to the mid-twentieth century the common law, with occasional assistance from Parliament, set about the task: so that precedents became the servants of principles, rather than a 'wilderness of single instances'.[8] This done, Roger Scruton, an admirer of the common law, was able to describe this 'great society' as one 'composed of millions of cooperating strangers under a single rule of law' (Scruton 2017: 3). An era in which the law either abstained from or challenged the people slowly gave way to an era in which the law became sufficiently relevant and authoritative to give rise to what could properly be described as the rule of law.

Central to the project of connecting law with society was the notion of reasonableness, which, over time, the law came increasingly to rely on as the arbiter of legal rules and standards. The point about reasonableness is that it is rooted in a cultural, social and political norm. A legal rule or standard that is reasonable is one that, if determined by society, accords with common sense. An issue of reasonableness is often described as a jury question in the sense that it is one that is not determined by the law.[9] John Gardner describes a test of reasonableness as one that allows the

---

[8] *The Duty of Care towards One's Neighbour* (1883) 18 *Law Journal* 618, p. 619.
[9] *Glasgow Corporation v Muir* [1943] AC 448, Lord Thankerton, p. 454.

judge 'to pass the buck to the finder of fact, who is invited to use extra-legal standards'.[10] Gardner is correct about the use of 'extra-legal standards'. But what he describes as 'passing the buck' is rather the essential means by which the law is able to give effect to the views of ordinary people: of individual subjects. The quality of reasonableness became a hallmark of law in the rule of law era.

In order to give effect to the notion of reasonableness as being rooted in the views of ordinary people, the law has often personified the concept into the test of 'the reasonable man'. He has been described as 'the greatest concept that the common law has given to systems of law'.[11] Some judges of this era, of which Lord Denning was the most celebrated, used to deploy 'the man on the Clapham omnibus' to refer to the ordinary man of common sense.[12] The concept of reasonableness has usually been personified when it is helpful to visualise a particular decision taker such as when a judge is directing a jury to consider the issue from the perspective of a reasonable man. This tendency to personify a concept has caused the common law to create many other fictional characters who embody reasonable standards, albeit in particular circumstances. The 'ordinary prudent man of business' sets reasonable standards in a business context, the 'officious bystander' sets them in the context of contracts, the 'fair-minded and informed observer' determines allegations of bias[13] and the 'reasonable man properly directed' sets them when sitting as a juror. As Lord Hope pointed out this 'select group of personalities who inhabit our legal village are available to be called upon when a problem arises that needs to be solved objectively'.[14] The reasonable man is the longest established inhabitant of this legal village but all the villagers share the characteristic of personifying a concept of setting rules and standards that are rooted in the views of ordinary people.

---

[10] John Gardner, *The Many Faces of the Reasonable Person*, Law Quarterly Review, 131 (Oct), pp. 563–584.
[11] *DPP v Camplin* [1978] AC 705, HL, Counsel for the Crown, p. 710.
[12] Lord Denning (1899–1999) would frequently refer to this hypothetical reasonable person in his judgments, although the phrase was first used in a legal judgment in *McQuire v Western Morning News* [1903] 2KB 100, Collins MR p. 109. Lord Denning sat as a judge between 1944 and 1982 and was Master of the Rolls, the senior civil judge, between 1962 and 1982.
[13] *Porter v Magill* [2001] UKHL 67.
[14] *Helow v Advocate General* [2008] UKHL 62, Lord Hope §1.

The concept of reasonableness as a basis for setting legal rules and standards developed during the nineteenth century. In civil cases as early as 1871 a reasonable man test was applied to decide the standards for the formation of a contract.[15] More recently the reasonable man has been deployed to interpret the meaning and terms of contracts.[16]

But it is with the development of the law of negligence that the reasonable man concept came to play its most significant role. Reasonableness as a hallmark of negligence law was first expressed in 1837 when the court held that 'Every man ought to take reasonable care that he does not injure his neighbour'.[17] And in 1856 a court described negligence as 'the omission to do something which a reasonable man, guided upon those considerations which ordinarily regulate the conduct of human affairs, would do, or doing something which a prudent and reasonable man would not do'.[18] But it was not until 1932 with the House of Lord's landmark case of *Donoghue v Stevenson*[19] that negligence law was finally put on a principled basis with rules and standards determined on the basis of reasonableness. This legal authority swept away the need to consider slippery precedents in favour of a test rooted in the views of ordinary people or as Lord Atkin put it, a tort 'based upon a general public sentiment' and developed from the rule that 'you are to love your neighbour'. This passage from Lord Atkin is one of the most quoted of legal passages, possibly because it captured the spirit of an era in which law walked in step with its people:

> At present I content myself with pointing out that in English law there must be, and is, some general conception of relations giving rise to a duty of care, of which the particular cases found in the books are but instances.

---

[15] *Smith v Hughes* (1871) LR 6 QB 597, Blackburn J, p. 607: 'If, whatever a man's real intention may be, he so conducts himself that a *reasonable man* would believe that he was assenting to the terms proposed by the other party, and that other party upon that belief enters into the contract with him, the man thus conducting himself would be equally bound as if he had intended to agree to the other party's terms.'

[16] *Investors Compensation Scheme Ltd v West Bromwich Building Society* [1998] 1 WLR 896, Lord Hoffmann, pp. 912–913.

[17] *Vaughan v Menlove* (1837) 3 Bing NC 468.

[18] *Blyth v Birmingham Waterworks* (1856) 11 Ex 781, Anderson B, p. 784.

[19] *Donoghue v Stevenson* [1932] AC 562, HL.

The liability for negligence, whether you style it such or treat it as in other systems as a species of 'culpa', is no doubt based upon a general public sentiment of moral wrongdoing for which the offender must pay. But acts or omissions which any moral code would censure cannot in a practical world be treated so as to give a right to every person injured by them to demand relief. In this way rules of law arise which limit the range of complainants and the extent of their remedy. The rule that you are to love your neighbour becomes in law, you must not injure your neighbour; and the lawyer's question, Who is my neighbour? receives a restricted reply. You must take reasonable care to avoid acts or omissions which you can reasonably foresee would be likely to injure your neighbour. Who, then, in law is my neighbour? The answer seems to be—persons who are so closely and directly affected by my act that I ought reasonably to have them in contemplation as being so affected when I am directing my mind to the acts or omissions which are called in question.[20]

Lord Macmillan in the same case also based his test on ordinary human experience and made specific reference to the reasonable man as the arbiter of whether a duty of care was owed and if it was, what the standard was:

What, then, are the circumstances which give rise to this duty to take care? In the daily contacts of social and business life human beings are thrown into, or place themselves in, an infinite variety of relations with their fellows; and the law can refer only to the standards of the *reasonable man* in order to determine whether any particular relation gives rise to a duty to take care as between those who stand in that relation to each other.[21]

In criminal law the judiciary and Parliament empowered jurors to decide the reasonable man's standards particularly on issues such as whether a defendant could rely on the defences of self-defence,[22] necessity,[23] duress[24] and provocation.[25] With the defence of provocation,

---

[20] Ibid., Lord Atkin, p. 580.
[21] Ibid., Lord Macmillan, p. 619.
[22] *Attorney General for Northern Ireland's Reference (No. 1 of 1975)* [1977] AC 105, Lord Diplock, p. 138.
[23] *In re F* [1990] 2 AC 1, Lord Goff @75.
[24] *R v Graham* [1982] 1 WLR 294, Lord Lane CJ, p. 300.
[25] Homicide Act 1957, s3.

for example, in the nineteenth-century judges strove to develop a general principle for its determination with a standard determined by reasonableness. In 1837 Coleridge J directed a jury that: 'though the law condescends to human frailty, it will not indulge human ferocity. It considers man to be a rational being, and requires that he should exercise a reasonable controul [sic] over his passions'.[26]

But, as with the reasonable man's role in negligence, it was not until much later that this reasonableness test was personified into a general reasonable man (or person) test for setting the standard of whether a conviction for murder should be reduced to manslaughter on account of provocation. In 1949 Devlin J established that a jury should be directed to consider a simple test:

> Provocation is some act, or series of acts, done by the dead man to the accused, which would cause in *any reasonable person*, and actually causes in the accused, a sudden and temporary loss of self-control, rendering the accused so subject to passion as to make him or her for the moment not master of his mind.[27]

As the twentieth century opened, the law, reeling from the fallout over its *Taff Vale* decision, reminded itself that it should leave contentious public policy issues to Parliament. Public policy was, said the House of Lords in 1902, 'a very unstable and dangerous foundation on which to build until made safe by decision'.[28] And 'by decision' the court had in mind a public policy that had 'been either enacted or assumed to be by the common law unlawful, and not because a judge or Court have a right to declare that such and such things are in his or their view contrary to

---

[26] *R v Welsh* (1869) 11 Cox CC 336, Keating J, p. 339.

[27] *R v Duffy (Note)* [1949] 1 All ER 932. With the Homicide Act 1957 Parliament made modest adjustments to this direction but retained the central importance of the reasonable man test:

> Where on a charge of murder there is evidence on which the jury can find that the person charged was provoked (whether by things done or by things said or by both together) to lose his self-control, the question whether the provocation was enough to make a reasonable man do as he did shall be left to be determined by the jury; and in determining that question the jury shall take into account everything both done and said according to the effect which, in their opinion, it would have on a reasonable man.

[28] *Janson v Driefontein Consolidated Mines Ltd*, [1902] AC 484, HL, Lord Lindley, p. 507.

public policy'.[29] After a brief foray into the fraught issue of industrial relations the law reminded itself of a dictum set out in 1824 that public policy was 'a very unruly horse which may carry its rider he knows not where'.[30] In short, the law was realising that contested issues of public policy were political issues for Parliament and the law should concern itself with uncontroversial issues where it could lay down rules that chimed with common sense.

After a slow development the law became grounded on a legal subject who was reasonable and autonomous. His reasonableness defined legal norms not because the law wanted to pass the buck but because the law, by giving legal effect to individual reasonableness, wanted to entrench and reinforce this notion of autonomy. Every time a negligence claim was decided by a standard of care determined by the reasonable man and every time a jury considered provocation on the basis of how the reasonable man would have responded, the law was celebrating the standards of its ordinary law-abiding citizens. Only those who strayed beyond the bounds of reasonableness felt a legal sanction. During this period that lasted for about 50 years between 1930 and 1980 the law walked in step with the individual and enabled personal autonomy to flourish. By doing what was reasonable the ordinary person was a law-abiding person who would have little reason to be challenged by the law. Law challenged the unreasonable but left the reasonable to determine their own lives.

It is no coincidence that the development of a consensual relationship between society and the law happened alongside the expansion of the electoral franchise, which began with the Great Reform Act of 1832 and concluded with universal suffrage for men and women in 1928. As democracy became the norm for politics, so consensus became an organising principle for law. Each development took a century to unfold fully. The result for law was an era based on principles that the people readily understood and instinctively found to be fair and necessary. The laws of contract, tort, crime and so on were consonant with the standards and norms of a broad consensus within society. For a period of about 50 years in the middle of the twentieth century the laws of the land were based on

---

[29] Lord Chancellor Lord Halsbury, *op cit*, p. 492.
[30] *Richardson v Mellish* (1824) 2 Bing, p. 252, Burrough J.

common sense and reflected a broad social consensus. In this era the rule of law was a reality.

From the Rule *of* Law to the Rule *by* Law

The rule of law era did not last. Starting in the 1970s[31] but continuing apace with the passing of the Human Rights Act 1998, the reasonable man found himself increasingly outflanked by the man of rights. This newest member of the legal village has, in the space of a few decades, established himself as its most influential inhabitant. The reasonable man and the man of rights are unhappy neighbours because they have contrasting views of the law. The reasonable man bases law on what society regards as reasonable and his objective is to ensure that the law has a consensual relationship with society. Law based on the reasonable man does not interfere with the ordinary citizen's autonomy. The man of rights, however, bases law on what various charters of rights regard as necessary. His objective is to ensure that the law accords not with society but with a body of rights-based law. And when the law of rights disagrees with the popular view then it is rights-based law that must prevail. Law based on the man of rights regularly interferes with the ordinary citizen's autonomy.

Consider a case that came before the House of Lords in 2004. The issue was whether a man, whose gay partner had died, could succeed to the deceased man's tenancy. Parliament had legislated for successions and limited the full right to a person who had been living with the tenant 'as his or her wife or husband'. As a matter of ordinary law it was clear—in a case decided ten years before gay marriage was legally possible—that

---

[31] The European Court of Human Rights made a number of influential decisions against the UK government during this decade: *East African Asians v UK* (1973) 3 EHRR 76 (discrimination against the wives of immigrants); *Golder v UK* (1975) 1 EHRR 524 (breach of prisoners' rights); *Ireland v UK* (1978) 2 EHRR 25 (British interrogation techniques constituted inhuman and degrading treatment); *Tyrer v UK* (1978) 2 EHRR 1 (birching on the Isle of Man was inhuman and degrading treatment); *X v UK* (1978) 3 EHRR 63 (laws against homosexuality came within the scope of articles 8 and 14); *Sunday Times v UK* (1979) 2 EHRR 245 (injunction breached freedom of expression); *Young v UK* (1979) 3 EHRR 20 (employee's dismissal for refusing to join a trade union under a closed shop agreement breached freedom of assembly).

the applicant could not exercise this right because he had not lived with his partner as a 'wife or husband', terms that applied only to heterosexual couples. Yet the House of Lords did not subject this case to ordinary law; they subjected it to rights-based law, which they concluded enabled them to give a meaning to Parliament's words that was abnormal rather than reasonable. As Lord Millett, who was outvoted by four to one, put it: 'Couples of the same sex can no more live together as husband and wife than they can live together as brother and sister'.[32]

Lord Millett sought to resolve the case by applying traditional legal norms drawn from an era when law reflected a broad social consensus. First, he concluded that 'questions of social policy ... ought properly to be left to Parliament and not decided by the judges'.[33] From this perspective the only question for the court was what Parliament meant when it gave a full right of succession to a person who had been living with a tenant 'as his or her wife or husband'. Secondly, by any reasonable standard of legal interpretation those words clearly excluded a gay partner. But the House of Lords resolved the case on a rights-based approach, which means that issues of social policy do not have to be left to Parliament and reasonable standards of legal interpretation do not apply. Indeed, because a rights-based approach obliges judges to uphold rights, they have an interpretative role that can give an artificial meaning to statutory provisions even where Parliament's language is unambiguous.

The underlying rationale for the House of Lords' decision was given by Lady Hale. She drew attention to law's new role as guardians of rights, even when these court-determined rights are at odds with the views expressed by Parliament or a majority of the population. Her point was made by elevating a political argument, equal treatment, into a legal point of principle that stands above democracy:

> Such a guarantee of equal treatment is also essential to democracy. Democracy is founded on the principle that each individual has equal value. Treating some as automatically having less value than others not only causes pain and distress to that person but also violates his or her dignity as

---

[32] *Ghaidan v Godin-Mendoza* [2004] UKHL 30, Lord Millett, §95.
[33] Lord Millett, ibid., §65.

a human being. The essence of the [European Convention on Human Rights], as has often been said, is respect for human dignity and human freedom …. Second, such treatment is damaging to society as a whole. Wrongly to assume that some people have talent and others do not is a huge waste of human resources. It also damages social cohesion, creating not only an underclass, but an under-class with a rational grievance. Third, it is the reverse of the rational behaviour we now expect of government and the state. Power must not be exercised arbitrarily. If distinctions are to be drawn, particularly upon a group basis, it is an important discipline to look for a rational basis for those distinctions. Finally, it is a purpose of all human rights instruments to secure the protection of the essential rights of members of minority groups, even when they are unpopular with the majority. Democracy values everyone equally even if the majority does not.[34]

This passage shows how the rights-based approach to law differs from the broad social consensus approach that it now challenges. First, the division of responsibility between law and politics has broken down. The social consensus approach to law eschewed controversial issues, which it saw as belonging in the political sphere. But the rights-based approach sees it as law's responsibility to resolve controversial issues, hence in Lady Hale's passage above there is no clear divide between law and politics. Issues that would previously have been resolved in the political sphere are now regularly contested in the legal sphere. As we saw in the introduction to this essay Lady Hale, now the UK's President of the Supreme Court, has recently argued that courts may be better qualified to rule on issues of law and politics than the legislature.

Secondly, 'equal treatment' as a legal doctrine is unobjectionable in the sense that like cases should be treated alike by the courts. But when the man of rights talks of 'equal treatment' he is using it as a political concept to trump the judgement of a reasonable man. Thus, the reasonable man may want to give outcomes to a heterosexual couple that are not extended to a gay couple just as he may think abortion on demand is or is not a good outcome. More generally, he may prefer outcome X to outcome Y. These are political issues that ought to be contested in the political sphere. But by making 'equal treatment' a legal doctrine that stands over

---

[34] *Ghaidan v Godin-Mendoza* [2004] UKHL 30, Lady Hale, §132.

politics, then all possible outcomes become subject to a legal filter. The reasonable man may contend for outcome X in the political sphere but be told that, applying the legal filter of equal treatment, it is off the table.

Thirdly, the law no longer draws its principles and standards from the reasonable man or the man on the Clapham Omnibus. Such principles may well be at odds with what is required from a rights-based framework. A rights-based approach will often require the court to direct itself to consider 'broadmindedness' as a means of distinguishing its views from those of ordinary people. For example, when the court decided that Parliament's approach to convicted prisoners being disenfranchised was unlawful it professed to be making a decision that was based on 'broadmindedness'.[35] Courts have adopted a similar approach, for example, to break down distinctions between homosexuality and heterosexuality[36] and to secure childcare leave for female prisoners even though 'public opinion' sees the issue differently.[37] Similarly, the rights-based approach requires the court to consider what is proportional, rather than reasonable. Proportionality enables the man of rights to decide what latitude is lawful when an individual right is interfered with. This is a process that need have little or no regard to the views of the reasonable man. The expansive nature of law and its antagonistic relationship with society means that the rule *of* law now exists alongside what is best described as rule *by* law.

Conclusion

The rule of law, properly understood as existing when law reflects a broad social consensus, bolsters democracy. In part this is because consensual law strives to express values and norms held by the majority. But it is also because under the rule of law the separation of law from politics enables politics, which is a dialogue between politicians and society, to resolve contentious issues. Rights-based law adopts a different perspective. As Lady Hale's quote shows, a rights-based approach does not view majority

---

[35] *Hirst v United Kingdom (No 2)* (2006) 42 EHRR 41, ECHR, §70.
[36] *Lustig-Prean v United Kingdom* (1999) 29 EHRR 548, ECHR, §§71, 76, 80.
[37] *R (MP) v Secretary of State for Justice* [2012] EWHC 214 (Admin), §154.

opinion as essential to democracy. When she claims that 'democracy values everyone equally even if the majority does not' she is elevating rights above majority opinion. Or to put it another way she is elevating elite opinion, determined by judges, above majority opinion, determined by the people. Majority opinion is, despite Lady Hale's claims to the contrary, the best way of treating every person's opinion equally. For example, in the *Ghaidan* case it was clear that Parliament, when expressing majority opinion, had not legislated to give gay partners the same succession rights as straight partners. In a democracy issues of this nature should be resolved in the political sphere by a dialogue between society and Parliament. But for Lady Hale, and the majority of the House of Lords, the differential treatment of gay and straight partners was not an outcome that was acceptable and hence the rule of rights-based law had to prevail. Moreover, by giving legal effect to this principle it cannot be confined to issues of gay rights and social equality because rights-based law can be applied to most political issues from abortion to prisoner votes.

Despite the distance that has opened up between society and rights-based law there has been little academic discussion of the problem. In part this reflects the strength of law as compared to the weakness of politics. But from time to time the problem tends to erupt into expressions of dissatisfaction, particularly from tabloid newspapers. A recent example came in response to the Brexit litigation. The narrow legal issue of whether Parliament or the Executive could trigger the UK's withdrawal from the European Union, pursuant to a referendum, was resolved on a rights-based basis. The rights of a citizen of the European Union (Gina Miller) were central to conclusions in the High Court[38] and Supreme Court[39] that the Executive (which had for centuries had the right to enter into and withdraw from international treaties) could not trigger the UK's withdrawal from the EU. In response to the High Court's decision the *Daily Mail* front page called the three judges 'Enemies of the people'.[40] The *Daily Telegraph* front page was 'The judges versus the people'.[41]

---

[38] *R (Gina Miller) v Secretary of State for Exiting the European Union* [2016] EWHC 2768 (Admin).
[39] *R (Gina Miller) v Secretary of State for Exiting the European Union* [2017] UKSC 5.
[40] Daily Mail, 4 November 2016.
[41] Daily Telegraph, 4 November 2016.

Rule by law is taking Britain into unknown territory. For whilst the law of the nineteenth and early part of the twentieth century did not express a social consensus, it was not a significant social force. Moreover, the law was developing towards having a consensual relationship with society, assisted by nudges here and there from the political sphere. The problem today is that the law is expansive, is developing in an increasingly elitist direction, and the political sphere appears powerless to apply a brake and corrective steer. This is not good for law, politics or democracy. It is time for the rule of law to make a comeback.

References

Dicey, A. V. (1982). *Introduction to the study of the law of the constitution.* Indianapolis: Liberty Fund.
Ferguson, N. (2014). *The great degeneration: How institutions decay and economies die.* London: Penguin Books.
Fukuyama, F. (2015). *Political order and political decay: From the industrial revolution to the globalisation of democracy.* London: Profile Books.
Griffith, J. A. G. (1997). *The politics of the judiciary.* Fontana.
Griffith, J. A. G., & Street, H. (1952). *Principles of administrative law.* London: Pitman Publishing.
Hale, L. (2018). *An application by the Northern Ireland Human Rights Commission for Judicial Review.* UKSC 27.
Ibbetson, D. (1999). *A historical introduction to the law of obligations.* Oxford: Oxford University Press.
Kostal, R. W. (1994). *Law and English railway capitalism, 1825–1875.* Oxford: Clarendon Press.
Scruton, R. (2017). *Conservatism.* London: Profile Books.
Slater, M. (2009). *Dickens: A life defined by writing.* New Haven, CT: Yale University Press.
Tamanaha, B. Z. (2004). *On the rule of law.* Cambridge: Cambridge University Press.

Part II

7

Autonomy and the Birth of Authenticity

Tim Black

> *Even as the sun and planets stood, to salute one another on the day you entered the world—even so you began straightaway to grow and have continued to do so, according to the law that prevailed over your beginning. It is thus that you must be, you cannot escape yourself.*
>
> (Goethe, Dämon)

The ideal of authenticity—of being true to how 'you must be', as Goethe had it—has become the organising ethic of modern social and political life. It is the aspiration of public figures; it suffuses the commercial world as the promise to buy and partake in authentic self-expression and experience; and, most fundamental of all, it gives the idea of identity, of identity politics, its moral force, motivating individuals and groups, providing an ever unfolding answer to the existential question of how to live—that is, by being true to one's self, one's feelings; by cultivating an inner essence; by expressing it, even modifying one's own body to do so.

T. Black (✉)
London, UK

The centrality of authenticity to Western social and political life has long been coming. In his 1970 lecture series, published as *Sincerity and Authenticity* in 1972, Lionel Trilling characterised authenticity as 'part of the moral slang of our day' (Trilling 1972: 93). As well he would. The idea reeked of the countercultural moment, only just receding *as a moment* in Trilling's rear-view mirror. It spoke of getting in touch with one's socially suppressed feelings, of finding one's inner child and of even seeking out some pharmaceutically-aided mode of spontaneous self-revelation. It seemed of a piece with what the social theorist, Theodore Roszak, in his 1968 article 'Youth and the Great Refusal', called the effort to forge 'new personal identities on the far side of power politics, the bourgeois home, and the Protestant work ethic' (cited in Hartman 2015: 14). To be oneself, to cultivate one's personal identity, was not a tautology here; it was seen as a political act. It was presented as a challenge to the prevailing social form in which one precisely could not be one's self, in which one's true self was stifled and suffocated. As Marshall Berman pointed out in *The Politics of Authenticity*, published in 1971: 'The search for authenticity, nearly everywhere we find it in modern times, is bound up with a radical rejection of things as they are'. The politicised charge of the idea of authenticity, Berman added, was likely to be the New Left's 'lasting cultural achievement' (Berman 1971: xvii). For good or ill, Berman may have been right.

Yet as voguish as talk of being authentic was during the 1960s, it was not a product *of* the 1960s. For a start, it drew deep on the Existentialist currents coursing through the New Left and the counterculture more broadly, with Albert Camus' *The Outsider* (1942), a staple of Roszak's youthful refuseniks' reading, and Jean Paul Sartre's *Being and Nothingness* (1943), a no doubt unread staple of their book shelves. And in its debt to the French Left Bank it reached further back, as an articulated idea, to Martin Heidegger (whose lectures Sartre attended) and his 1927 opus *Being and Time*, a work premised on the conviction that we have forgotten what it is to be, that the *Seinsfrage*, the question of being, has been obscured by Western civilisation's 'traditional way of interpreting itself', a self-understanding 'thoroughly coloured by the anthropology of Christianity and the ancient world' and effaced in our everyday social existence by the extent to which we lead the life of *das Man* ('the one' or 'the they') (Heidegger 2000: 74). To be authentic, countered Heidegger, was to cast off the weight of this accumulated inauthenticity, to be no longer as 'one is', but as 'I am'. Or at least that was the Existential reading.

And it was not just *Being and Time*, having emerged from the war-ravaged Europe of the 1920s, that now resonated with the affluent society of the 1960s, through Sartre, Camus and former Heidegger student Herbert Marcuse, with his sallies against one-dimensional man, and his idea of 'the great refusal' as being a refusal to conform to societal mores and demands (Marcuse 2002: 63). Sigmund Freud, with his more openly philosophical work *Civilisation and Its Discontents* to the fore, also struck a nerve, by seemingly pulling the rug out from under the moral verities and rectitude of bourgeois life. The truth of one's self lay less in one's conscious sense of what one ought to be, the respectable husband or dutiful wife, than in that great reservoir of unconscious feelings and impulses that lay repressed and distorted beneath the conscious surface.

As an explicit idea, then, indeed as a conscious aspiration, authenticity is largely a product of the interwar wars. But even that, as Trilling shows by locating its emergence in the mid-eighteenth century, is to misapprehend the depth of its roots. For in its almost pre-conceptual form, as a socio-cultural impulse, authenticity is best thought of as a constantly developing product of modernity itself. That interwar articulation can therefore be understood as the culmination, or better still, the explosion, of a longstanding discontent, indeed, a restless engagement, with the trajectory of modernity, and, perhaps most important of all, as a constantly evolving response to the promise—and the problem—of that great Enlightenment principle: individual autonomy.

This principle was itself the product of the great transformations that shaped modernity. The Reformation emancipated morality, in the form of the individual's conscience, from theology; 'the civilised victory of movable property' (Marx 1961: 91), as the young Karl Marx described emerging capitalism, emancipated economic relations from feudal political structures; and the revolutions in the Netherlands in the sixteenth century, and later, England in the seventeenth, began the explicit emancipation of the individual from his monarchic subjecthood. Early Enlightenment thought and culture thus drew deep on a growing sense of freedom, a freedom from feudal hierarchies, from church authorities, and, with it, a growing sense of the possibility of self-determination and of the necessity of relying on one's reason alone. 'On the word of no one' was the motto of the Royal Society, established in 1660, but it could just as well have been the slogan for all early Enlightenment thinkers, from Descartes to Locke.

Yet, by the mid-eighteenth century, that emancipation—or the 'great disembedding' as Charles Taylor, following Karl Polanyi, calls it (Taylor 2007: 146–158)—seems to have been simultaneously experienced by some as a loss. A loss, obviously, of the external authorities, from church to feudal custom, by which one had been guided. But with that, a loss, too, of meaning, of a ground for one's moral life, of a foundation for one's newfound sense of oneself as an individual. In other words, autonomy, this great promise of Enlightenment thought, this great product of the emancipating energy of modernity, was simultaneously beginning to be experienced as a problem. A problem for individuals, largely in the high-cultural fields, for whom freedom from traditional sources of authority was experienced, like Wordsworth's Leech-gatherer, as a source of solitude and madness. And a problem for societies in which self-governance was as much a threat to the absolutist status quo as a promise.

This is why it is at this moment, at the seeming height of the Enlightenment in the mid-eighteenth century, that a sense of what will later become the idea of authenticity first begins to emerge. Not as a principle of and in itself, but as the shadow cast by autonomy, as a way to reckon with the problem of being free. So, in what follows, I will explore the emergence of authenticity in the work of that most complex of Enlightenment figures, Jean-Jacques Rousseau (1712–1778), and show how it grows out of and is entwined around the roots of the promise of autonomy, self-determination, of governing oneself according to laws (of one's own) reason. I will show that authenticity is both closely related to autonomy but is also a response to what is felt to be its inadequacy, this sense that one's reason alone does not provide a sufficient ground for one's decisions and judgements. I will argue that the call to be true to one's self, to be true to one's nature, provides the individual with an emotional, sentimental direction, indeed a purpose, a trajectory of becoming, that the Enlightenment focus on the sovereignty of reason seems to lack. The problem of self-authorisation, therefore, is met with the seeming solution of self-authentication, or to put it another way, authenticity emerges as a closely related *alternative* to the idea of autonomy.

Rousseau and the Enlightenment

Rousseau was of the Enlightenment. He fraternised with the original self-styled *lumieres*, the *philosophes*—indeed, as a caustic, eloquent multi-talented thirty-something in the Paris of the 1750s, earning a living copying music, penning essays and poetry, and forging a reputation as a composer, he was considered one of their number, even contributing entries to that grand testament to Enlightenment learning, the *Encyclopédie*. He was a close friend of Diderot; he was close in spite of himself to Baron D'Holbach, whose rebarbative materialism was anathema to him; and he was a close enemy of the aristocratic Voltaire, with whom he indulged in vituperative exchanges for much of his life.

And yet what marks Rousseau out is that he also seems to swim against the Enlightenment mainstream. Not because he really was the primitivist of 'noble savage' myth.[1] But because he draws on the radical promise of Enlightenment to denounce the supposedly Enlightening world. That is, he draws on the promise of autonomy to denounce the nascent modernity that denies it. Much is made of Rousseau's use of paradox on stylistic grounds. But it is on social grounds that it makes sense; Rousseau used paradox because his reality was paradoxical. 'Man is born free', runs the promise, 'and everywhere he is in chains', comes the rejoinder (Rousseau 1987: 141).

Rousseau's target here is just as much the world of his Enlightened peers—the world of Paris, of the salons in which intellect glitters, and wit sparkles; the world of commerce and celebrity; the world of industrialising production methods and private property; the world of cities and

---

[1] The term 'noble savage' was used long before Rousseau, most prominently by poet and playwright John Dryden. But it was not until the mid-nineteenth century that it gained wider currency, thanks mainly to British anthropologists like John Crawfurd who, writing in ideological support of British colonialism, falsely attributed the idea to Rousseau to give the idea intellectual weight. From that point on, the assumption that the idea was Rousseau's entered anthropological and ethnological discourse, and was taken as truth (see Ellingson 2001).

crowds—as it is the bondage of a still semi-feudal France, labouring under monarchic absolutism. Because, as Rousseau discerned, the newly Enlightened world, the world of *the bourgeois*, was in the revolutionary ascendant, despite regal appearances to the contrary. 'We are approaching a state of crisis and the age of revolutions', he wrote in 1762, addressing an imaginary member of court. 'Who can answer for what will become of you then? All that men have made, men can destroy. The only ineffaceable characters are those printed by nature; and nature does not make princes, rich men, or lords' (Rousseau 1979: 194).

So, in 1755, when Rousseau sends his second discourse, the scabrous *Discourse on Inequality*, to Voltaire, the response is that of one who feels as if he is being attacked. 'I have received, Monsieur, your new book against the human race, and I thank you', writes Voltaire. 'No one has employed so much intelligence to turn us men into beasts. One starts wanting to walk on all fours after reading your book. However, in more than 60 years I have lost the habit' (Cited in Cranston 1991: 306).

Voltaire's chagrin was justified. The second discourse deepened and developed the cultural jeremiad of the first, the *Discourse on the Sciences and the Arts* (1750), counterposing the amoral, self-sufficient freedom of savage man to the immoral, other-dependent bondage of civil man. It really did look like an indictment of Voltaire's Enlightened now in the name of Rousseau's savage past. Yet it was more than that. Taken alongside two of Rousseau's other major works, *Emile, or on Education* and *The Social Contract* (both 1762), what emerges is, yes, a merciless critique of society, but alongside it a theory and assertion of moral autonomy, a vision (or visions) of a social form in which individual autonomy and social, civic life are reconciled, and, simmering away underneath it all, squats the spectre of authenticity.

Rousseau's Social Critique

Rousseau's critique of society does begin with a conception of pre-social man. He is an 'absolute', as Rousseau puts it in *Emile*—he relates only to himself, having 'no sort of intercourse among [other humans]' (Rousseau 1987: 55). Driving him, motivating him, is self-love, '*amour de soi* or *amour-propre* taken in its extended sense' (Rousseau 1979: 92–93)—which amounts to a concern for his own wellbeing. He does however have an innate capacity for pity, writes Rousseau, which is born of recognising in others like him his own self-love. In others' suffering, then, he recognises his own potential suffering.

So in this state he wants no more than he needs, and needs no more than he, as an individual, has the capacity to provide. He needs no one else and depends on no one else. For Rousseau, this constitutes natural man's freedom, a freedom, at this stage, that is inseparable from necessity, because natural man wants no more than he needs. He follows the law of nature—his human nature—because he has no desire or will not to. He experiences no contradiction between his passions—from the need for food and sleep to the desire to copulate—and his ability to sate those passions. There was no war of all against all in the state of nature, because savage man was not in a relationship with others. Contra Hobbes,[2] life was tranquil, innocent and no longer than necessary.

The key moment, the moment of man's Fall, is the moment he enters into association with others. Or, as Rousseau puts it in *Emile*, 'The more [men] come together, the more they are corrupted' (Rousseau 1979: 59). This is for two related reasons. Firstly, in coming into a relation with others, man develops new needs, and becomes dependent on others for the satisfaction of those needs, from the provision of cooked meals eaten with utensils (which were made by others) to the persistence of monogamous or polygamous relationships. This dependence, argues Rousseau in anticipation of the lord-bondsman dialectic of Hegel's *Phenomenology*, goes as much for the master, who cannot live freely without his slave, as it does for the slave who cannot live freely because of his master: 'rich, he needs their services; poor, he needs their help' (Rousseau 1987: 67).

And secondly, in coming together with others, savage man not only ceases to be independent, he also, more importantly, ceases to be absolute: he becomes relative. That is to say, in the state of nature, savage man is only in a relation to himself, and only understands himself in relation

---

[2] For Hobbes, 'war of every man against every man', prevailed in the state of nature. It was a perpetual and violent state of competition in which each individual asserts a natural right to everything, regardless of others. It made for a life that was famously, 'solitary, poor, nasty, brutish, and short'.

to himself. But, in coming together with others, he becomes relative to others; he compares and judges, and is compared with and judged by, others. Some are handsomer, some are stronger, some are faster. In response, others are envious, vain, contemptuous. And so on. In the instant of social intercourse, then, savage man's absolute care for himself, his undeveloped self-love, his *amour de soi*, inexorably acquires its extended form of *amour-propre* (Rousseau 1979: 92–93)—that is, a self-love that is no longer related only to the satisfaction of one's immediate needs, but to the satisfaction of needs generated by one's relation to others. This is the need to be esteemed by others, to be thought the fastest, strongest, indeed, the need to be thought physically attractive to others. The need, in short, to be *recognised* as first among men. These needs, these passions, develop as society develops, and so *amour-propre* is engorged and encouraged, too, as individuals seek the esteem and praise of others. '*Amour-propre*, which makes comparisons, is never content and never could be', notes Rousseau, 'because this sentiment, preferring ourselves to others, also demands others prefer us to themselves, which is impossible' (Rousseau 1979: 213–214).

Rousseau traces the development of man's social intercourse, and therefore the growth of his material and emotional dependence on others, through various phases. But the signal moment, as Rousseau sees it, comes with the institution of private property, and the relations of 'mine and thine' that flow from it. For on the basis of private-property relations, socially unequal relations of dependency are not only entrenched, but antagonised, pitting those with nothing to lose against those with everything already gained. Hobbes' 'war of all against all' did not pertain to the state of nature, therefore, but to the state of society, and the universal laws and justice instituted to protect property relations and protect the particular interests of the rich and powerful. Surveying the social relations of his time, Rousseau saw that the *de facto* inequality of nature, in which all are as equally free as nature allows, has been replaced by a *de jure* equality, in which all are as unequal and unfree as social relations dictate.

But Rousseau focuses his most trenchant critique of his Enlightened present on the extent to which man's interior world is enslaved. The individual is not only in thrall to property relations of dependency, 'work[ing] until he dies; run[ning] to his death in order to be in a position to live', he is also emotionally and psychologically in thrall to others, needing their approval and praise, flattering those on whom he depends for advancement or employment, and disdainful of those on whose debasement he depends for his own elevation (Rousseau 1987: 80). Everyone performs 'his step... in this beggars' pantomime', as Diderot had it in *Rameau's Nephew* (written 1761–1762) (Diderot 1976: 120). As the dependency deepens, as the individual's need of others' approval expands, as his thirst for rank, for prestige, for celebrity—for recognition— increases, so even his ideas, his opinions, cease to be his own. They become, or, better still, *conform* to, what others expect, what the fashion demands, what the ruling ideas suggest they ought to be. 'The savage lives in himself', explains Rousseau, while 'the man accustomed to the ways of society is always outside himself, and knows how to live only in the opinions of others. And it is, as it were, from their judgement alone that he draws the sentiment of his own existence' (Rousseau 1987: 80–81). That is, it is from the opinions of others that he develops a feeling for who he is, what he believes, what he thinks. *Rousseau's* portrait of Parisian high society in *Julie, or the New Heloise* (1761), especially in its intellectual pretension and pretended virtue, captures well this culture of conformism masquerading as Enlightened sophistication:

> [T]he men to whom you are speaking are not the ones with whom you converse; their sentiments do not emanate from the heart, their perceptions are not in their minds, their words do not represent their thoughts, all you see of them is their shape, and being in a gathering is like standing before a moving tableau, where the detached spectator is the only creature moving under his own power. (Rousseau 1997: 193)

And:

> If this people of followers were full of original characters it would be impossible to know about it; for no man dares be himself. One must do as others do, is the primary maxim of wisdom in this country. That is done, that is not done. This is the supreme pronouncement. (Rousseau 1997: 205)

This is Rousseau's vision of social existence, an existence in which material and psychological dependence has enfeebled the body and enslaved the mind. And this is the vision Immanuel Kant drew on in *What Is Enlightenment?* (1784), in which he defined pre-Enlightenment man as being caught under self-incurred tutelage, incapable of using his own understanding or reason, and dependent on others for his thoughts and actions, be it the pastor to act as his conscience or the physician to prescribe his diet.

Rousseau's Theory of Moral Autonomy

Emile, or On Education and *The Social Contract* were both published, banned and burned, in 1762—thanks, in the main, to a 40-page section in Book IV of *Emile* known as 'The Profession of Faith of a Savoyard Vicar'. This scandalised the *philosophes* by revealing Rousseau's deist faith and outraged the authorities by exposing the church's folly. Yet, as integral to *Emile* as 'the profession of faith' is, it is only a part of its main thrust. For *Emile*, as the 'education' of its title suggests, concentrates on how to cultivate individual autonomy—and *cultivate* is the correct verb for what is, in part, a *Bildungsroman*. Rousseau's central contention is that if we are to cultivate an independent, self-sufficient individual, able to reason and will for himself, we have to cultivate his inner nature. We have to let him grow and develop according to nature's law, not man's. *Rousseau* is attempting, then, to ground the individual's freedom on his nature.

What follows then in the first Books I-III of *Emile* is an imaginative reconstruction of what it would be like to bring a child up *as nature intended*. So as a baby and infant he should be given no more than he needs and allowed as much freedom as his physical strength permits. *Rousseau* advises, for instance, tying diapers loosely so as to allow a baby's limbs to move freely. And slowly, with the hidden care and oversight of his governor, the young infant, allowed to try to act for himself, is learning to live. He is not being pushed, argues Rousseau; he is learning to do what he can do, and no more. His needs and desires develop only in accord with the extent to which he himself can satisfy them. He is learning to judge and to act, to act and to judge. As Rousseau puts it, 'Acting always according to his own thought and not someone else's, he continually unites two operations; the more he makes himself strong and robust, the more he becomes sensible and judicious' (Rousseau 1979: 119).

And, the older he gets, he is learning, too. Not from books—Rousseau characterises books as a 'plague' inducing dependency on others' thoughts—but through practical experience, through sensual reason. 'Our first masters of philosophy are our feet, our hands, our eyes', writes Rousseau. 'To substitute books for all that is not to teach us reason. It is to teach us to use the reason of others. It is to teach us to believe much and never know anything' (Rousseau 1979: 125). Admittedly, there is one book that Rousseau does allow Emile, to read: *Robinson Crusoe*. But that is because Crusoe, living alone, is an archetype of self-sufficiency, a castaway forced to act on and understand the world around him for himself, and in terms of its utility. As Rousseau puts it, Crusoe will be Emile's entertainment and his heuristic, encouraging him 'to judge everything from the perspective most likely to yield the truth about the relations of things—the position of the isolated man—and to judge everything only in terms of its usefulness' (Rousseau 1979: 184–185).

Eventually, at the end of book three, we meet Emile aged 15. He knows little, concludes Rousseau, but what knowledge he does have is resolutely his own. He has needs, and passions, even a touch of *amour-propre*, but his passions rarely depend on anyone else for their fulfilment, and his self-love, lacking extensive comparison to others, is as little developed as his vanity or envy.

And it is at this point, in Books IV and V of *Emile*, that Rousseau turns the image of his work as an encomium to the savage, to the state of nature, inside out. Because it is here that *Emile*, now an adolescent, is allowed to develop deeper and more expansive relationships with others. *Rousseau* was therefore never interested in returning man to the state of nature (where he had been free). Rather, he wanted to return freedom to man's existence in society today. Or as he puts it, 'although I want to form the man of nature, the object is not, for all that, to make him a savage and to relegate him to the depths of the woods. It suffices that, enclosed in a social whirlpool, he not let himself get carried away by either the passions or opinions of men, that he see with his eyes, that he feel with his heart, that no authority governs him beyond that of his own reasons' (Rousseau 1979: 255).

But how is he to resist being 'carried away by either the passions or opinions of men'? Firstly, because of the way in which he has been brought up to think and act for himself. And secondly, and most importantly, because in his deepening engagement with others, his widening circle of relations, from his earliest relationship with his family (and his governor) to his friendships and his lovers, and from there, ultimately, to his country, his *patrie*, his autonomy develops its moral dimension. And it simultaneously develops its interior: the individual's conscience.

It is important to note that Rousseau roots this process of becoming ethical in nature, our human nature. That is, he is grounding our ethical capacity on nature, as something that can *naturally* develop. This draws on his initial contention that we naturally pity those around us as beings like us, with their own self-love, their own concern for their wellbeing, and, therefore, a capacity for suffering. So as our relationships with others develop, as our intercourse with family, friends, lovers and those in wider society, deepen, so this innate sentiment of pity, of self-love extended to others, develops, too. And as we mature, we develop *sentiments* of good and bad, of obligation and duty, of treating these others—our kith, kin and, ultimately, our kind—as we would want to be treated ourselves. We do not understand justice or goodness as, first, abstract words. Rather, we experience them first as concrete relations between ourselves and others.

Initially, suggests Rousseau, this natural moral education will take the form of sentiments of love and hate—felt responses to the behaviour of others—that we then extend to others, because they, like us, will hate, say, having the flowers they planted and nurtured destroyed, or love someone standing up for someone being picked on. And, as we grow to understand our sentiments of love and hate, establishing *reasons* for why this or that action or behaviour is loveable or hateful, so we develop ideas of goodness, of justice, and so on. And with this our most important inner sentiment—our conscience—is developing an ever more sonorous, reasoned voice. It is the inner voice that will tell Emile what he knows, through his reason, he *ought* to do. And it is in this ability to do what one ought to do, rather than what one merely desires to do, that man's freedom lies. For, as Kant was to develop the argument, it is the freedom to act according to one's own moral reason, rather than one's inclinations.

And here is the twist: man's social existence is not therefore antithetical to Rousseau's conception of freedom as moral autonomy. Man's social existence is in fact the very condition of morality's possibility. And because the possibility of acting according to what we deem to be the good, rather than according to our inclinations, is to be free, so society is the condition of possibility of individual freedom. Savagery was never noble in Rousseau, but society *is* ennobling. For it is only in society, in the civil state, that man can realise a higher form of individual freedom than he might have enjoyed in the 'natural state'. There he willed as he pleased—here, as a potentially autonomous citizen, he can will the good; there he was absolute—here he is relative; there, relating to no one but himself, he did what he wanted—here, thinking of others, he has to think of what he ought to do. He has to become autonomous. And as such, he is able to judge his prospective actions 'in the depths of [his] heart' (Rousseau 1979: 287), according to whether *all*, because they are like him, ought to will likewise. 'The good man orders himself in relation to the whole', explains the Savoyard vicar, 'and the wicked orders the whole in relation to himself' (Rousseau 1979: 290).

Rousseau did, as we have seen, criticise his society. Justice and law, dominated and divided by property relations of dependence, developing to serve the particular interests of particular property owners, betray their potential universality. And, keen to advance themselves in the opinion of others, individuals in this society turn virtue and goodness into mere means to win approval or, worse still, tributes to hypocrisy, be it the bourgeois, advocating equality under the law, while seeking to enrich only himself, or the *philosophe*, preaching morality in a Paris Salon, while desiring no more than his self-promotion. Yet as imperfect as society is, as betrayed in practice as the public good has been, it still provides a whole and a principle, even if only honoured in the breach, to which Emile can relate himself. 'The public good, which serves only as a pretext [for others]', writes Rousseau, 'is a real motive for [Emile]. He learns to struggle with himself, to conquer himself, to sacrifice his interest to the common interest... Human laws have taught him to reign over himself' (Rousseau 1979: 473).

'Human laws have taught him to reign over himself' is a line that could well have come from *The Social Contract*. In Rousseau, the possibility of individual freedom, in the form of moral autonomy, goes hand in hand with his ideal of the republic. If *Emile* is a vision of the morally autonomous individual, *The Social Contract* is a vision of a state and civil society composed of Emiles. It is, in short, a vision of civic freedom. The key to understanding this is the idea of the *general will*, which underpins, authorises and legitimates the republic as a self-determining body. The general will is best understood not as a proto-democratic popular will, but as an ethical will, a will that would form if each and every citizen, if and when legislating, adopted the point of view of the whole, or more accurately, the point of view of the rational being in its universal dimension, and one therefore willing according to the precepts of reason. This is why Rousseau distinguishes the general will from the will of all: 'The latter considers only the general interest, whereas the former considers private interest and is merely the sum of private wills' (Rousseau 1987: 155). It is because the general will legislates for itself much in the same way as Kant's morally autonomous agent does, in the form of a universal *ought*, that Rousseau can come up with what seems like a paradoxical and frightening authoritarianism: 'To avoid the social contract being "an empty formula", whoever refuses to obey the general will will be forced to do so by the entire body. This means merely that he will be "forced to be free"' (Rousseau 1987: 150). But this is really an extension of Rousseau's idea of moral autonomy. To be really free, to be autonomous, is not to act according to one's own private or particular interest. It is to act according to one's idea of what one *ought* to do, which is to act on that maxim or law that reason demonstrates should become a universal law. The general will is the universal law-making agent. To disobey it is to disavow one's own moral freedom to act according to it. As Rousseau puts it in *Emile*: 'In the republic all of the advantages of the natural state would be unified with those of the civil state, and freedom which keeps man exempt from vices would be joined to morality which raises him to virtue' (Rousseau 1979: 85).

Rousseau's contemporaries recognised the revolutionary implications of his arguments. The Jacobins, and Robespierre in particular, saw in this ethical freedom the society to be built. And, in Germany, Kant, whose otherwise spartan study contained a bust of Rousseau, set about honing an ethics that drew deep on *Emile* and *The Social Contract*. Hegel, in his *Lectures on the History of Philosophy*, captured his significance for those who came after him: 'The principle of freedom dawned on the world in Rousseau' (Hegel 1896: 402).

The Birth of Authenticity

Julie, or the New Heloise, published in 1761, proved a literary sensation. Countless editions were published to sate the public's appetite, but to no avail. Demand was too great. Readers queued desperately at book shops, and finding the shelves bare, began renting it out at an hourly rate. And Rousseau himself became a man almost as in demand as his books, claiming in his *Confessions* that there was not a female reader who wouldn't have given themselves to him had he asked (Rousseau 2008: 533). Jules Michelet, the nineteenth-century French historian, concluded that 'in all literary history, there had never been so great a success' (cited in Durant and Durant 1967: 43).

At first glance, *Julie* appears at one with Rousseau's philosophical and political vision. It tells the tale of two lovers, Julie and St Preux, her tutor, whose passionate relationship, consummated just once, and even then briefly and guiltily, is at odds with the extant social order, represented by Julie's father, Baron d'Etange. D'Etange wants Julie to marry someone of her station and does not want her ruined by St Preux. But St Preux is determined, telling Julie he is no 'vile seducer', but 'a simple and sensible man who readily displays what he feels and feels nothing for which he must be ashamed' (Rousseau 1997: 34). He issues many long entreaties to Julie, justifying their passion for one another on the grounds of nature and 'the heart', and imploring her to be with him in spite of her family, in defiance of social mores and in the face of the opinions of others.

Julie, however, is torn between her passions and inclinations, and her duty to her father. 'Obedience and faith dictate opposite duties to me', she writes to her cousin Claire. 'Shall I follow my heart's penchant? Who is to be preferred of a lover or father?' (Rousseau 1997: 164).

But Julie does make a choice. She resolves to do her duty: she marries her father's friend, Monsieur Wolmar, a rationalist and materialist, and does so because, in light of her growing faith, that is what she believes she ought to do. She therefore governs her own life according to a moral law.

In overcoming her passion, she becomes autonomous. In willing the good, she becomes virtuous, a beautiful soul. For Rousseau, what appears to be a form of self-denial is really a form of self-determination, a willingness to recognise and follow one's moral reason over and above desire and inclination.

St Preux, however, is recalcitrant. He strikes the pose of the Romantic hero, committed to a thwarted love and railing against the world that denies him. But Rousseau is not a Romantic before his time. He is an Enlightenment thinker ahead of his time. St Preux's grand passion, his *Sturm und Drang*, is portrayed as a weakness. He is trapped by his passion for Julie, not liberated by it. And as the years pass, as Julie becomes Madame Wolmar, St Preux's emotional commitment to Julie is a commitment to someone who has long since ceased to exist. His nostalgia is crippling. In *Emile*, Rousseau warns his charge not to fall prey precisely to those self-induced ills afflicting St Preux: 'those [ills] that render us victims of our passions', encouraging us to 'glorify ourselves for the tears at which we should have blushed' (Rousseau 1997: 445).

Thanks to the intervention of Wolmar—playing the same mediating role as the legislator in *The Social Contract*, and the governor in *Emile*—who invites St Preux to live at Julie's home of Clarens, an estate at the foot of the Alps, St Preux learns to subdue his passions and live once more in the present. 'Do not turn your entire life over to a long slumber of reason', Wolmar tells St Preux at the start of his stay at Clarens (Rousseau 1997: 429). Wolmar makes St Preux live with Julie the wife of Wolmar, Julie the mother, Julie the devout: Julie, that is, who is no longer Julie. He is also to fulfil his duty as a tutor to the Wolmars' children. And with that, with St Preux's subduing of his passion, he becomes free to will what he ought to will, free to act as conscience dictates, free to become virtuous. Not that it is straightforward. 'Virtue is a state of war', admits St Preux, 'living in it means one always has some battle to wage against oneself' (Rousseau 1997: 560). Yet it is always a possibility inherent in our nature because '[God/nature] has given us reason to discern what is good, conscience to love it, and freedom to choose it' (Rousseau 1997: 561).

But *Julie* is more than a simple tale of two beautiful souls becoming virtuous. It is also a novel in which the tension between passions, feeling and sentiment, and the social order, indeed the general interest, the universal law, that demands their repression, threatens to tear Rousseau's ethical edifice apart.

The form is important here. *Julie* is an epistolary novel, after the fashion of Samuel Richardson's enormously popular *Clarissa*. This was a form ideally suited to Rousseau's philosophical temper since it allowed his characters, in the course of their intimate exchanges, to unveil themselves, to give vent to their turbulent interiors. But the persistent self-revelation, the concentration on these interior lives troubled and warped by the often unjust demands of the exterior social order, simultaneously works against Rousseau's philosophical commitments. That is, it constantly points to the impossibility of reconciling the individual with the demands of the social world, one's duty to others, even morality itself. The sentimentalism of *Julie*, in the strong sense, was too much. It was excessive. It overflows. And this corrodes Rousseau's own emphasis on moral autonomy as the basis of freedom, civic or otherwise. Not perhaps from Rousseau's own perspective—after all, he concludes the novel with Julie's affirmation of virtue and faith at the moment of her death—but from that of those who read it and wept over the lovers' fate. But *Julie* escapes Rousseau. Because in *Julie*, the struggle to become virtuous, to live according to the idea of the good, seems to come at the cost, not of some obvious vice, but of love itself. Living according to the moral imperatives of reason seems to take away a reason for living. Towards the end of *Julie*, Julie gives voice to precisely this sentiment:

> All about me I see nothing but causes for contentment, and I am not content… A secret languor worms its way into my heart; I can feel how empty and oppressed it is… My attachment for all those I hold dear does not suffice to occupy it, it still has some useless strength which it knows not what to do. This affliction is peculiar, I concede, but it is not less real. Can you conceive of any remedy for this disaffection with wellbeing? For my part I confess to you that a sentiment that depends so little on reason has much diminished the value I placed on life, and I cannot imagine what sort of charm one can find in it that I lack or with which I should be satisfied… My friend I am too happy; I am weary of happiness… I live in it with a heart ill at ease, which does not know what it lacks; it desires without knowing what. (Rousseau 1997: 570)

Even as the novel nears its conclusion, Julie is still not really at home in the world. She is fragmented rather than free. She has all the outward signs of a content life: she has lived her life autonomously, governed by reason, not inclination, following her conscience, not her passion. And yet it is not enough. She is virtuous, but eviscerated. She is good, but hollow. Her self-mastery appears here as self-repression. Her striving for self-government has resulted in her self-alienation.

And here we approach the stirring of the idea of authenticity. As philosopher Alessandro Ferraro argues (Ferrara 1992: 103), Julie is autonomous, but she is not, crucially, authentic. Rousseau never uses the word 'authentic', but he captures its impulse. In becoming free, in Rousseau's sense, Julie has lost her self. She is true to her conscience, to what she reasons is the good, but in being so, she is not true to her feelings—she is not true to who she really is. Her autonomy is simultaneously the source of *in*authenticity, her good faith the source of her bad faith.

At the last, about to die, she denies the legitimacy of her sentiment for St Preux in favour of her fidelity to God. But, on Rousseau's part, it is a move that lacks conviction. Her love for St Preux, a union born of the heart, provides just as legitimate a ground for action, it seems, as her later love for God. And her heart, like St Preux's, speaks with a voice as compelling as that of one's conscience. It is as if Rousseau glimpsed the undermining of his ethical vision, in which man becomes free in the act of adopting the viewpoint of universal rationality and tried to contain it. Not that it affected the response of his readers. They responded to the story of Julie and St Preux as a tragedy, much as many were later to respond to Rousseau's social contract, and the demands of the general will, as the oppression of individual freedom.

Twenty years later, a far shorter epistolary novel by a young German writer surpassed *Julie* in impact, popularity and, most importantly, in its continuing resonance. Goethe's *The Sorrows of Young Werther* did what Rousseau's *Julie* shrank away from; it came down on the side of passion and sentiment *against* the morality of a Prussian society still yawning under the weight of tradition and caste. In *Julie*, St Preux is talked out of suicide; in *The Sorrows*, Werther talks himself into it. So, against Albert, the husband of Lotte, the object of Werther's passion, Werther makes the case for suicide, turning it into a 'great achievement', and rails against being the sterile respectability of society:

> Passion; inebriation; madness. You respectable ones stand there so calmly, without any sense of participation. Upbraid the drunkard, abhor the madman, pass them by like the priest and thank God like the Pharisees that He did not make you as one of these!... I have learned to understand that all exceptional people who created something great, something that seemed impossible, have to be decried as drunkards or madmen. And I find it intolerable, even in our daily life, to hear it said of almost everyone who manages to do something great, something that is free, noble and unexpected: He is a drunkard, he is a fool. They should be ashamed of themselves, all these sober people! And the wise ones! (Goethe 1962: 58)

Suicide here was no longer a mark of weakness or a sign of selfishness, as it had been in *Julie*; it was heroic, courageous, an indication of one's true individuality. Werther, in blowing his brains out, was acting according to his deepest feelings, his deepest passion. He had therefore been true to himself, and acted authentically.

Rousseau had done so much to substantiate a vision of moral autonomy, to ground individual (and collective) self-determination on man's inner nature, and therefore nature itself. He had seemingly successfully interiorised the moral law. He appeared to have ensured that one's ethics, the laws by which one lives, were no longer authorised from without, but from within, in the figure of the heart and that which grows out of the heart's 'movements' and 'affections' towards others; namely, the conscience. It was a radical move. It captured and developed the individuating tendency of modernity, the creation of individuals as individuals, and formulated what it meant to be free: which was synonymous with being a moral agent, acting according to the precepts of one's own reason, not one's inclination.

But there was a problem. And it was one of which Rousseau was already acutely aware. The social whole to which one was to relate oneself, the social precondition for moral freedom, was at odds with an actually existing society that seemed opposed to, even inimical, to the individual. In attempting to overcome the contradiction between the idea of an autonomous individual and society as it is (rather than as it ought to be), by 'forcing' man to be free in society, Rousseau's work constantly threatened to recreate this contradiction between the individual and society within the individual, within the moral interior. A torn individual, that is, in whom moral autonomy, as governing oneself according to what one reasoned was right because it was what ought to be willed by all, by the social whole, seemed internally antagonistic towards governing oneself according to what one felt was right, because it was what ought to be willed by every individual, by every authentic being. And this was expressed in the contradiction explored so powerfully in *Julie* between conscience and duty towards others, and feelings and passion towards others. Both exerted an *internalised* authority over the individual. One pointed towards the ethics of Kant and the dreams of civic freedom in the French Republic to be. And the other, through Romanticism, pointed towards something far more contemporary: namely, the politics of identity, of being true and loyal to who one feels one really is. Rousseau's legacy, caught between self-mastery and self-expression, is our present.

Mis-recognising Rousseau's Legacy

'[T]he lasting legacy of the New Left'. That was how Marshall Berman described the rediscovery of radicalism's Romantic roots (Berman 1971: viii). And in the ambiguous portrait of the repressed, frustrated desires of St Preux or Julie, or, more spectacularly, the heroic, suicidal audacity of Werther, and the general thrust of Romanticism's rejection of 'mind-forg'd manacles' (see 'London' (1794) by William Blake), and the economic instrumentalism of the 'cash nexus',[3] there was indeed something radical at work. Romantics, from Schiller to Keats, proffered a challenge to the world as it was, by finding in nature—its passions and desires—everything that society denied, including freedom: the freedom to pursue one's passion and one's love; the freedom, that is, to be oneself. 'The

---

[3] 'Cash nexus' was a phrase coined by Thomas Carlyle in his 1839 pamphlet, *Chartism*. It was then taken up and used frequently by Karl Marx and Friedrich Engels, particularly in the *Communist Manifesto* (1848). For all three, it served as a pejorative reference to the means-ends rationale of capitalism.

height of their claim, is the height of their despair', remarked Raymond Williams of the Romantics in *Culture and Society* (Williams 1958: 40).

Yet the New Left did not just revive this Romantic sensibility. Its proponents, from Marcuse to the Students for a Democratic Society, *politicised* authenticity. They turned it into a social aspiration, something that society was to value, even institutionalise. And in doing so, in politicising authenticity, they completely changed the meaning being true to nature, to one's feelings, had for its Enlightenment and Romantic progenitors.

For Rousseau and those who came immediately after him, what still united the law of the heart, passionate and desiring, with the moral law, reasoned and willed, was freedom. The freedom, that is, to pursue one's idea of the good. For the proto-authentic Julie, the idea of the good was a union of hearts with St Preux; for the autonomous Emile, the idea of the good was that which ought to be willed by all. The one was true to her love; the other was true to his conscience. In both cases, while the ground of freedom differed, it was still freedom that was important. And it was a freedom to be true to one's inner law *in spite* of what others thought and demanded. One had to raise oneself above society, stand in opposition to it, if one was to be free. Which is hardly surprising, given the nature of the social critique ventured by Rousseau: a critique taken up by Kant and adopted in modified form in the Existentialist tradition from Kierkegaard to Heidegger. For to be oneself, to be free to will one's idea of the good, was precisely *not* to think and act according to the thoughts and judgements of others. Rousseau called it 'the empire of opinion' (Rousseau 1979: 38), Heidegger 'publicness' (a species of inauthenticity) (Heidegger 2000: 165), and Sartre 'bad faith' (Sartre 2003: 112). In each, though, to be dependent on the opinions and judgements of others for one's sense of what one ought to do or be, for the law by which one lives, was to be unfree. It was to be living outside oneself, as an object of others' judgements and opinion.

So authenticity, in its inchoate Enlightenment and Romantic form, drew what political charge it had from being inexorably opposed to society. To be dependent on others' judgements was just as much a threat to authenticity as it was for moral autonomy. But something happens when authenticity shifts from being a principle born of opposition to social and political life, to being a principle installed at the centre of social and political life, as it was with the cultural ascendency of New Left-ish politics. As Charles Taylor notes, in his argument in favour of politicising authenticity, the idea of authenticity ceases to be monologic, and becomes dialogic (Gutmann and Taylor 1994: 34). Which is to say that authenticity ceases to be autonomous and absolute, and instead becomes dependent and relative. For the desire is no longer for freedom *from* the judgements of others; it is a desire for recognition *in* the judgements of others. And not merely recognition either. The demand that others recognise one's authentic self, recognise one's unique way of being according to one's inner nature, is also a demand that others esteem and respect that authentic individuality. Not because he is right or virtuous, or even because he is impressive, but simply because he is being true to himself.

The politicisation of authenticity, indeed the politics of authenticity, becomes the politics of recognition. And it is this that provides the ethical underpinning of all forms of identity politics, from multiculturalism to more recent expressions, such as transgenderism. There is little doubting its moral force, as stunted as it is. As Sonia Varga puts it, 'Seeking answers to the question of how to live a good life, the vocabulary of authenticity has in our contemporary cultural context become what the notion of autonomous subjectivity was to early modernity' (Varga 2013: 5). The sense of having some inner nature or essence, some internal law that needs to be realised, recognised and respected by others becomes a lifelong mission. It is sustained not simply by the drive to be oneself, but through the often active seeking out of others' misrecognition, others' disrespect, even their so-called microaggressions. It is, as Rousseau would understand, an extreme unfreedom, a lifelong dependency on others for esteem, affirmation and praise, indeed a massive inflation of *amour-propre*. And this new form of dependency, generated by the ethic of authenticity, has another name: narcissism. After all, what else is the demand that others constantly recognise your true self, your authenticity, other than the demand that they reflect back to you, unchallenged, your own sense of yourself.

In the end, then, authenticity, this close twin of autonomy, turns into its opposite. For the autonomous individual, raised to moral freedom by his active participation in society, by his capacity to relate himself to universal rationality, and to will what all ought to will, promised a form of civic humanism, of active democratic citizenship. The authentic individual also participates in society, but he relates society to himself. He demands that it affirms the value of his feelings, of his inner nature. And as such he turns his fellows from being ends in themselves into mere means—raw material—for his self-actualisation.

References

Berman, M. (1971). *The politics of authenticity*. New York and London: George Allen and Unwin.
Cranston, M. (1991). *Jean-Jacques: The early life and work of Jean-Jacques Rousseau, 1712–1754*. Chicago: University of Chicago Press.
Diderot, D. (1976). *Rameau's nephew and D'Alembert's dream* (L. Tancock, Trans.). London: Penguin.
Durant, W., & Durant, A. (1967). *Rousseau and revolution*. New York: Fine Communications.
Ellingson, T. (2001). *The myth of the noble savage*. Berkeley: University of California Press.
Ferrara, A. (1992). *Modernity and authenticity: A study of the social and ethical thought of Jean-Jacques Rousseau*. New York: SUNY Press.
Goethe, J. W. (1962). *The sorrows of young Werther, and selected writings* (C. Hutter, Trans.). New York: The New American Library.
Gutmann, A., & Taylor, C. (1994). *Multiculturalism*. Princeton, NJ: Princeton University Press.
Hartman, A. (2015). *A history of the culture wars: A war for the soul of America*. Chicago: University of Chicago Press.
Hegel, G. W. F. (1896). *Lectures on the history of philosophy* (E. S. Haldane & F. Simpson, Trans., vol. 3). London: Kegan Paul.
Heidegger, M. (2000). *Being and time* (J. Stambaugh, Trans.). Oxford: Blackwell.
Marcuse, H. (2002). *One-dimensional man: Studies in the ideology of advanced industrial society*. London: Routledge.
Marx, K. (1961). *Economic and philosophic manuscripts of 1844* (M. Milligan, Trans.). New York: Dover Publications.
Rousseau, J. J. (1979). *Emile, or on education* (A. Bloom, Trans.). New York: Basic Books.
Rousseau, J. J. (1987). *The basic political writings* (D. A. Cress, Trans.). Indianapolis: Hackett Publishing.

Rousseau, J. J. (1997). *Julie, or the new Heloise* (J. Vache, Trans.). New Hampshire: Dartmouth College Press.
Rousseau, J. J. (2008). *Confessions* (A. Scholar, Trans.). Oxford: Oxford University Press.
Sartre, J.-P. (2003). *Being and nothingness: An essay in phenomenological ontology* (H. E. Barnes, Trans.). London: Routledge.
Taylor, C. (2007). *A secular age*. Cambridge, MA: Harvard University Press.
Trilling, L. (1972). *Sincerity and authenticity*. Cambridge, MA: Harvard University Press.
Varga, S. (2013). *Authenticity as an ethical ideal*. London: Routledge.
Williams, R. (1958). *Culture and society*. London: Bloomsbury.

8

Self, Society, Alienation: From Marx to Identity Politics

Josie Appleton

This chapter draws on works by Marx, and the Marxist theorists István Mészáros and Gyorgy Lukács, to examine the tensions existing within the self as it developed under capitalism. After examining Marx's theory of alienation, and specifically the alienated self, I continue to critique contemporary forms of politics and culture such as identity politics. I argue that contemporary forms of the self can be usefully explained in terms of Marx's theory of the alienated self under capitalism.

Marx's Critique of the Bourgeois Individual

Marx built on critiques developed by Hegel and others of the bourgeois individual. It is not that Marx is opposed to the individual or that he elevates the communal, the collective, over the individual. Rather, his concern is with the estrangement of the individual from his social being,

J. Appleton (✉)
Manifesto Club, London, UK

on the one hand, and the estrangement of forms of the social from individuality on the other.

That is, he is primarily concerned with the extremely narrow and *one-sided* forms taken by the individual and society under capitalism. These are not experienced as two, interacting, complementary elements: the two sides to the being of a person, such that they feel that their individual and social existence are equally essential, and equally 'them'. Instead, the two elements of individual and society exist as contradictory, mutually exclusory forms, which are opposed to and 'external' to one another.

On the one hand, there appears to be a particular individual, who is simply immediate, sensuous, and self-seeking. He sees others as means to the ends of his own self-betterment and seeks only his own self-betterment. Therefore, as Marx put it, society exists as a *mere means* for him: he 'regards other men as means' and 'debases himself to a means' (Marx 1975b: 220).

> In the rights of man it is not man who appears as a species-being; on the contrary, species-life itself, society, appears as a framework extraneous to the individuals, as a limitation of their original independence. (Marx 1975b: 230)

On the other hand, there is a realm of social abstraction: for the individual, society appears not as something the individual has made, but as a natural force, which he cannot fathom, and which is imposed upon him.

The realm of the market (the result of the collective labour of society) is experienced as a naturalised realm: moving like the wind, independent of the wills of men. In other ways, too, the demands of society are experienced by the individual as an imposition upon him, as something externally demanded which is a restriction upon him and hostile to his nature.

As Lukács puts it: the laws of the market 'confront him as invisible forces that generate their own power'. Man's own labour power—his own activity—becomes subject to the 'non-human objectivity of the natural laws of society' (Lukács 1971: 63).

The concept of labour in Marx's *1844 Manuscripts* presents the way in which an individual's own activity appears as the activity of an external force. His own labour is 'external' to himself: it is a labour of self-sacrifice, of mortification, serving some other force or person. 'External labour, labour in which man alienates himself, is a labour of self-sacrifice, of mortification' (Marx 1975a: 326). Something a person has made appears to have no connection to him: it appears as something outside of him, external to him, even hostile to him. His own physical and mental energy is experienced as something directed against himself.

The critique by Marx, and by Lukács and Mészáros, is not of the individual per se, but the way in which this individual appears to be (and effectively *is*) something partial, one-sided, and split asunder into conflicting elements. The argument in the *1844 Manuscripts* is that the individual life and species-life, or social life, are estranged in the following manner:

1. His species-life is a mere means for his individual existence.
2. His individual powers are a mere means for external forces.
3. The two elements are defined against each other—and sacrificed to each other.

Because of the contradiction between individual and society, there is a tendency for social forms to exist in opposed, estranged elements.

For example, in *On the Jewish Question*, Marx highlights *the question of the separation of man into two beings*. First, as a particular individual, in civil society, driven merely by egoism and material wants. And, second, as an abstract citizen, in the life of the state, where he is 'divested of his individual life and filled with an unreal universality' (Marx 1975b: 220). Therefore, there is a sphere in which he is a 'communal being' and a sphere in which he is active as a private individual.

As a private individual in civil society, man is merely selfish, sees others as means to his ends, and sees all objects in terms of their material value to him. At the same time, there is man as an abstract citizen—his life in the state—which is entirely divested of individual life. When he enters into the world of the state (e.g. working for the state, or serving it in some way), man leaves individual life behind him and sees things only in impersonal and abstract terms. So the bureaucrat is effaced of any individuality and sees only general terms, standards, and inhuman things; he is not a person but a cog in the machine and seeks to efface his individuality.

Therefore, one sphere is merely immediate, selfish; the other merely abstract, universal, communal. There is a separation between man in his immediate, sensual, individual existence (the egotistical individual) and abstract, artificial man, man as an allegorical, moral person (the abstract citizen).

Other Marxist theorists have identified a sharp split between the realms of the individual capitalist, or consumer, and the realm of the market (or the general realm, which is the sum of private exchanges, the place where private exchanges meet one another). That is, there is a realm where an individual acts only as a private citizen, in isolation from others; and another realm in which they are subjected to the decisions and actions of society as a whole.

Lukács argues that 'Bourgeois thought observes economic life consistently and necessarily from the standpoint of the individual capitalist and this naturally produces a sharp confrontation between the individual and the overpowering supra-personal "law of nature" which propels all social phenomena' (Lukács 1971: 63). He argues that this corresponds in consciousness to a split between subjectivism and naturalism: that is, there is a realm of arbitrary choice, at the level of the individual, within which you can do whatever you want to do; but at the level of society it is entirely given, natural, and the movements and demands of society face you as an inexorable and imposing force, not as something you have made or even contributed to making.

Similarly, Mészáros observes how the contradiction between individual and society leads to what he calls the 'false alternative' of naturalism and abstraction in art. Therefore, either art is naturalistic—representing the object as it is, unmediated by thought—or else it is purely abstract, colours and shapes, unrelated to real objects in the world (Mészáros 1986: 96). He also highlighted the contradiction between particularism and abstraction: the tendency to either look at the smallest details of things, at the level of a private person, interested only in private satisfaction; or else from the perspective of entirely impersonal abstraction and quantification, which is indifferent to qualities, details, or emotions.

The Origins of This Contradiction

The origin of this contradiction, according to Marx, is the following: the bourgeois individual is only *indirectly* social. The social comes into being behind the backs of individuals: as the sum of private exchanges of commodities. An individual's labour becomes part of the labour of society 'only by means of the relations which the act of exchange establishes directly between the products, and indirectly, through them, between the producers' (Marx 1977: 78). Therefore, there is no directly social, or personal, relation between individuals: their relation is mediated through the exchange of commodities.

> There is a definite social relation between men, that assumes, in their eyes, the fantastic form of a relation between things. (Marx 1977: 77)

The social exists as a realm apart from the calculations of private individuals, as something extrinsic to them. They might see it as oppressive, or they might use it pragmatically to their own purposes: but it has the status of something that exists outside of them and existing in contradiction to them.

This is in contrast to the Middle Ages, when social relations, including production, were based on 'personal dependence', or the personal rights and duties between lord and vassal. A man owed certain services to his lord because he was *his* lord and, therefore, exchange relations had the quality of personal relations. But for the very reason that personal dependence forms the ground-work of society, there is no necessity for labour and its products to assume a 'fantastic form' different from their reality. They take the shape of *services and payments in kind* (Marx 1977: 81). Therefore, 'the social relations between individuals in the performance of their labour, appear at all events as their own mutual personal relations, and are not disguised under the shape of social relations between the products of labour' (Marx 1977: 82).

Under capitalism, however, the social comes into being only in the act of exchange, between private individuals, who have no prior and lasting relation to one another. The way in which the social comes into being is as a different substance to the sum of the individual calculations made.

Marx's emphasis on the contradictions between individuals and society is in part a critique of Hegel's *Philosophy of Right*. In this, Hegel is concerned with showing the essential unity of apparently contradictory elements in social life. When Hegel highlights the different forms taken by the individual, or society, he shows that these always include the opposite term. So, in its deepest inner, the individual is a universal thing: for example, take the category of conscience, which is at once the deepest inner of an entirely internal experience, but also a universal concept of The Good. Hegel also sees the forms taken by the state, law, or war, not as impositions upon the individual, but as objective and universal forms that are reflective of his will. So when the criminal is punished, he is punished not merely by something outside of him, but also by his own will. Therefore, in Hegel, the particular always contains the universal, and the universal always contains the particular.

For example, Hegel describes the institution of the family as forming a unity: the family includes the 'moments of subjective particularity and objective universality in a substantial unity' (Hegel 2008: 224). He says that the realm of the state is one in which there is a 'thoroughgoing unity of the universal and the individual': the individual's action produces the state. He finds himself in it and willingly subordinates himself to it. 'The individual's destiny is to live a universal life' (Hegel 2008: 228).

Even when Hegel highlights contradictions between areas of life—between state and society, civil society and civil service—he is always concerned to mediate these relations, to show how they are actually united. And so he seeks to find institutions which provide the 'middle term', which means the resolution of the contradiction: for example, the legislature between civil society and the state, or the different parts of civil society.

Marx's *Critique of Hegel's Philosophy of Right* argues that these are false subsumptions, false mediations. Marx criticises Hegel's 'middle term' and says it is a blunt weapon: 'The middle term is the wooden sword, the *concealed antithesis* between the particular and the universal'. Marx argues that the middle term of the legislature 'is a hotch-potch of the two extremes of the monarchical principle and civil society, of empirical individuality and empirical universality' (Marx 1975c: 150).

The Hegelian universal is a 'pseudo-universal', Marx says; and the middle term is the embodiment of the contradiction. Therefore, Marx is saying there is an essential contradiction in relations which cannot be fudged: and that this contradiction is moving more and more in the direction of all-out war.

Marx is arguing vis-à-vis Hegel:

1. The contradiction between individual and society is an absolute contradiction: the supposed mediation is a false mediation.
2. The contradiction lies not in forms of thought but in social production relations. These relations determine contradictory forms of consciousness.
3. Transcendence is only possible through the practical abolition of the contradiction. In *On the Jewish Question*, Marx says that the transcendence of alienation will occur 'Only when real, individual man resumes the abstract citizen into himself and as an individual man has become a *species-being* in his empirical life, his individual work, and his individual relationships, only when man has recognised and organised his forces *propres* as *social forces* so that social force is no longer separated from him in the form of political force, only then will human emancipation be completed' (Marx 1975b: 234).

The Contemporary Contradiction Between Individual and Society

Critics such as Zygmunt Bauman, Jean Baudrillard, Ulrich Beck, and Anthony Giddens have identified our current phase of history as an exceptional late stage of modernity, in which the traditional capitalist institutions and laws have been substantially modified. This phase of 'late modernity' has dramatic implications, they argue, for the relation between individual and society.

In brief, what we are seeing at the moment is the erosion of the social mediations between individual and society: the 'middle terms' that Hegel identified. These social mediations, or middle terms—such as family, trade union, church, political party, estate—formed in the early period of capitalism and provided the mode for its operation. These institutions began to erode in the period of late capitalism.

As these social mediations erode, we see the extension of the underlying contradiction between individual and society, or the particular and the universal, the part and the whole, into more extreme forms. This means that a feature that was previously implicit or existed below the surface of life (and was covered up or disguised through social mediation) is now on the surface and explicit.

We are living now in what I call a condition of *unmediated polarity* or *immediate polarity*. This is a condition in which the polarities which had previously been inherent, but hidden, now exist in an overt and unmediated manner. That is to say, there are increasingly one-sided forms of immediacy or particularism, corresponding to the individual; and on the other hand, there are increasingly general levels of abstraction. And these elements of particular and universal appear as increasingly opposed to one another.

So, we can see how forms taken by individual life and consciousness are increasingly oppositional to and conflictual with social existence. This is particularly evident in the new forms taken by identity politics.

Much of identity politics is marked by an extreme individualisation: corresponding to the state of an individual who seems to find themselves at odds with the world and social experience. The phenomenon of 'microaggressions',[1] for example, shows how many people experience their everyday social encounters as a form of aggression, subtly targeted against their sex, sexuality, or ethnicity. For victims of microaggressions, the social encounter is experienced in itself as a slight, as an act of hostility, and as a demeaning of their personality, denying their individuality. Examples given of 'microaggressions' commonly include the asking of questions such as 'where are you from?' or 'do you speak Spanish?'

The sense of personal victimisation is something quite different to established structures of social or racial oppression, whereby a social group is excluded or maintained in lower status positions. Instead, identity begins to assume a quite individual connotation, whereby race or

---

[1] See, for example, https://www.facebook.com/microaggressions/.

sexuality and various other categories become aspects of the self. These do not denote one's membership of a group, but instead the way in which the self feels itself to be slighted by the social world, denied and not recognised fully.

Identity politics also includes a protest against any form of 'naming' by the social world: for example, the assignation of gender categories. There is a growing reluctance by individuals to be defined from the outside, to be put into any box or category, such as that of 'male' or 'female'. There is a growth of a gender-neutral identity (people saying they don't want to be called 'he' or 'she', that they don't identify as either gender). Behind this lies an objection to being touched by general social categories, such as language, which puts people in the boxes of 'man' or 'woman'. The opposition to gender binaries is really an opposition to social categorisation—to anyone else naming you, defining you—to entering into any system as that makes you a part of a whole. It is an objection to people making assumptions, seeing you in a particular way, or *naming you*. Therefore, gender-neutral individuals want their own unique language: they request that other people say 'ze' rather than 'he', or 'they' or 'co' rather than 'she'.

Therefore identity politics includes a retreat to a more immediate individual: *defined by the fact that they find themselves in contradiction with the social world as a whole*. This victim-state is the basis on which they stake themselves, and their identity.

At the same time, the elements of collective life increasingly take on more abstract, faceless forms, which are blank and indifferent to the individual. Previous collective forms—the nation, or law, or a class or party—included an element of individual volition. The nation was composed of citizens, who willed it and identified with it, the law was applied to legal subjects, and the political party was made up of members. Now, by contrast, the elements of social life—the functioning of the state bureaucracy, for example, or the role of social policy—are increasingly taking forms that are detached from individuals, from their wills and desires.

One early example of this was the category of 'globalisation', identified by Anthony Giddens and others as the replacement for the social categories of nation or region. Globalisation is the collective force of society—or the global society—personified as an external and indifferent force.

Globalisation is faceless; it makes things happen but is not perceived as a social agent as such but is more akin to a natural force or natural event. Therefore, we have seen the replacement of specific relations with the blank force, which rolls over things and makes things happen.

It is also the case that policy and legal life increasingly take forms that are distant from—even counterposed to—the wills of individuals. The policy of 'nudge',[2] for example, involves policymakers influencing the actions of individuals, guiding them towards what they perceive to be the common good. That is, individuals are encouraged to act in ways perceived to be beneficial for themselves (e.g. by saving more money) or to others (e.g. by giving blood), through the design of systems geared to encourage them down certain courses of action. The significant aspect of nudge is the way in which it works entirely at a subconscious level: individuals are not supposed to be aware that they are being influenced, they are *bypassed*. Therefore, the citizen is not appealed to or engaged with: they do not act rationally, or socially, because they have not consciously perceived the ends of their chosen actions. Instead, the individual acts only immediately, according to immediate stimuli; while on the other hand, policy exists at arm's length, like a scientist in a lab, prodding the mice down particular tunnels. The school of nudge shows the extent to which policy has become distant from the consciousness and wills of individuals; how they operate on different planes, and one is not brought to bear upon the other.

I have outlined a similar trend in my book, *Officious*, which argues that new forms of law and of state are stripped of the wills or wishes of individuals: they are blank, rules that exist only for the sake of rules, operating in a sphere entirely separate from people's desires or perspectives. So, many contemporary policies—such as child protection policies, or health and safety policies—include much that is irrational and counter-intuitive, such as rules that adults must always accompany children in pairs (i.e. need chaperones), or that parents may not take photos of their children at sports events. The policy is not a summation of common practice, or general belief, but a strange, almost foreign, document, that people struggle to understand or see the sense of. Officious rules and regulations are

---

[2] See Sunstein, C., & Thaler, R. (2009). *Nudge: Improving decisions about health, wealth, and happiness*. London: Penguin.

not forms of law or policy in which people recognise themselves: instead, they experience policy as restrictive, as 'trying to stop you doing things', as irrational ('red tape gone mad'). They experience law as incomprehensible to such a degree that people do not know anymore what is and what is not against the law. The system, rather than representing them, seems to be 'out to get you', or trying to catch you out. This is also often the quality of the new officials, such as private security guards or council officers, who patrol the streets looking for people to fine. The question is not whether a real criminal act has occurred, but rather whether the law can be stretched in order to 'get' someone. The role of criminal justice, and political authority, becomes something detached from—and in opposition to—communal life, and the wills and beliefs of citizens. This is what I have called a 'bureaucracy for itself': a bureaucratic system that develops rules out of its own body, in isolation from the rest of society, and views citizens with a disdainful contempt.

The content of officious forms of state is a blank and abstract hostility to free individuals in civil society: it has no basis other than that it is against them. Therefore, the implicit hostility between state and civil society, which Marx highlighted, has now become a bare and open contradiction that can be seen in new forms of regulation.

Therefore, in summary, there is a tendency of *separation* of the elements of individual and society, or the part and the whole, into increasingly estranged and oppositional elements. The mediation that Hegel highlighted in phenomena (in the examples quoted above, from the *Philosophy of Right*)—that the individual was in substance something universal, and the universal was something individual—has now dissolved. The two elements exist not in mediated social forms, but as separate and contradictory.

The Relation of the Particular and Universal Today: 'I Identify As'

When social forms include elements of both the particular and the universal, these tend to exist as one-sided forms, unrelated to one another. When you see social phenomena that contain the elements of the individual and the social, these exist as unrelated elements: they are pinned together, or sit alongside one another, but do not relate.

For example, someone might say: 'I identify as a queer woman of colour'.

This contains the element of volition—'I identify as'—and then the element of a reified category, 'QWOC'. Therefore, it contains the individual as something free, who can choose anything: but the choice they make is from categories that are impersonal, disconnected from the self. This is why they do not say 'I am'. To say 'I am' (e.g. 'I am working class', or 'I am Christian') is to unite the particular and the universal: it is to say that a particular universal form is experienced as something inner. It is to say, in my inner being, in my sense of myself, I am something universal and social. The social group is the basis for what I feel myself to be.

In the phrase, 'I identify as', the category is not internal to the self, but rather external. You are putting yourself in a box, or pinning something to a lapel, rather than expressing a social determination as an inner determination, which is the case when you say 'I am'. In saying 'I identify as', you are pinning these two levels of social reality together—they are pinned together—but *as separate* items.

Therefore, there are two distinct, separate elements in the identity category: the element of arbitrary volition, which is the individual who identifies or chooses the category; and then, the objectified, naturalised, form of the identity category.

Assuming an identity category is not about your relations to others. It does not mean that you join a scene, for example, you join a gay scene, a punk scene, or that you go to particular bars, or engage in particular practices or listen to particular music. These are the ways in which, 20 years ago, people still found their identities and place in the world. Now, a person is as likely to find their identity category on the internet, on websites that include lists of genders (agender, bigender, etc.) or sexualities (asexual, aromantic, pansexual).[3] It is the relation of the isolated individual, not to a subgroup, a particular association, but to a reified *category*.

Similarly, if you look at modern forms of radical Islam, you see the two elements of individual and social existing as extreme, one-sided, and

---

[3] For example, http://genderfluidsupport.tumblr.com/gender.

unrelated aspects of a phenomenon, which lie side by side and do not mediate with the other. For example, in his book on Islam, Olivier Roy noted that in Salafism, there are two elements: the elements of faith and the elements of sharia (Roy 2006). Therefore, there is the pure subjectivism of faith, which is only a matter of emotion; and the pure law of sharia, which is only a matter of following by rote. There is the pure emotion of the individual as one element; then the pure instruction to the individual as the other. Whereas, in Christianity, or in even in classical Islam, there is more mediation between the particular and the universal: as God becomes man, or reveals himself to man, and man is in some way, in his essence, God.

The Seeking of Alienated Forms

Yet this extension of an increasing antinomy between individual and society is not merely a spontaneous process, but something *sought*.

People act in ways that seek the deepening of social estrangement: they act in order to create ever more empty one-sided forms and deliberately attack the remaining social mediations.

For example, when individuals experience social relations as 'toxic', or as a restriction on the self, they might shy away from love, or relationships, seeing these things as inhibiting them as individuals. They might identify their problems as being the result of 'loving too much' and seek a greater independence from any ties or romantic relations. They seek to be footloose, free of obligations or claims upon them. In *Therapy Culture*, sociologist Frank Furedi observed how personal relations (such as love or family relations) had become increasingly identified as being abusive, the site of violence or sexual abuse (Furedi 2004). Anti-abuse policies are therefore targeted against the privacy of the family, or the intimacy of a love relation: these relations are opened up to outside scrutiny and surveillance, since they are seen as intrinsically abusive and risky.

Or in jihadi 'culture', we see a similar separation of the individual from all community ties. The state of becoming jihadi is one of maintaining oneself in a hostile relation to all social ties (family, nation, mosque): it is a matter of uniting oneself with the abstract brotherhood, whose only content is the destruction of any concrete social relation. In *Holy Ignorance*, Olivier Roy shows how jihadis are against all elements of social life, including religious community, modern life, and the nation (Roy 2010, Appleton 2016a, b). Meanwhile, the universal they seek (the ummah) is a complete abstraction, a made-up community, whose content is only a state of opposition towards social particularity and towards individual autonomy.

More and more the contemporary human condition is one in which we act to increase our alienation: to accentuate the contradiction between particular and universal. We *will* the alienated state. We seek to distance ourselves from those relations which in reality are our sustenance.

Marx discussed this phenomenon when he talked in the *1844 Manuscripts* about the question of inversion, or the way in which, as a result of alienated relations, things appear upside down: the alienated function appears genuine, and the genuine or human functions appear alienated.

In the category of alienated labour, for example, Marx says that labour is the human essence, the realisation of yourself. But in the form taken by labour under capitalism, it appears to be the wasting and estrangement of yourself. The more you act, the less you feel you are; the more you produce, the hollower you become. In the *1844 Manuscripts*, he writes:

> …man (the worker) feels that he is acting freely only in his animal functions—eating, drinking and procreating, or at most in his dwelling and adornment—while in his human functions he is nothing more than an animal.
>
> activity as passivity, power as impotence…the worker's own physical and mental energy, his personal life—for what is life but activity?—as an activity directed against himself, which is independent of him and does not belong to him.
>
> Hence the worker feels himself only when he is not working; when he is working he does not feel himself. He is at home when he is not working, and not at home when he is working. (Marx 1975a: 327)

It appears that you are yourself when you are not working, when you are at home, or when you are alone. Or it appears that you realise yourself when eating and drinking: there is an inversion, such that the animal faculties seem human, and the human faculties appear animal.

Because things appear in an inverted manner, you seek the alienated form as if it were your essence—and *decry the true form as the origin of your alienation.*

Today, it is the social mediation itself that is experienced as the source of alienation: it is experienced as toxic, or as *kafir* (unbeliever). Instead, we seek forms of generality and particularity that are *devoid of the social mediation*, and indeed set against them. We seek, following the inversion, forms of being that increase our alienated state.

The Increased Role of the Mediator

There is one final point. The accentuation of the estrangement between the individual and the social is also driven by the increased role of the mediator.

As quoted above, Marx emphasised the nature of capitalist relations as relations mediated through an object, which was external to that relation.

In the *1844 Manuscripts* he talked about money as a mediator—he called money the 'chemical power of society', with the power to bind or break bonds, to bring people together or split them apart. Money is both the agent of separation and the cementing agent:

> If money is the bond which ties me to *human* life and society to me, which links me to nature and to man, is money not the bond of all *bonds*? Can it not bind and loose all bonds? Is it therefore not the universal *means of separation*? It is the true *agent of separation* and the true *cementing agent*, it is the *chemical* power of society. (Marx 1975a: 377)

In *Capital*, he developed this idea in the theory of commodity fetishism, according to which relations between people appear as relations between things. That is, things appear as the bearer of the social relation as we have remarked earlier. Marx argued there that social relations only occur *by means of* relations in the act of exchange: *directly* between the products, and *indirectly, through them*, between the producers. The external party, the mediator (the commodity in this case), becomes the bearer of the relation: the thing that brings people together, defines their terms, breaks them apart.

Now, in our times, there has been a great extension of the role of the external mediator, and the mediator has become increasingly separate from and unrelated to the relating parties.

In many areas, there are growing demands for mediating parties: from therapists mediating marriages, or policies mediating work relations. Even spontaneous sexual encounters are being subjected to bureaucratic mediation. This can be seen in the policy of 'affirmative consent', according to which couples are required to state their consent to sexual acts through certain explicit, officially specified forms (in some US colleges, this includes signing forms, or repeating certain specified phrases). Here, the sexual relation becomes a mediated one. The most private realm of the bedroom becomes, not a form of direct communication—a question of making something clear to the other person—but a matter of communicating in the terms of a third party. In the policy of affirmative consent, a third party specifies what 'counts as' consent; and you have to convince *them*, the mediator, before you can go to bed. Hence, the unnatural forms of expression, such as saying everything out loud, or signing forms, or taking photos: an explicitness that is the direct consequence of the relation being mediated through an independent body.

'We are living in a new sex bureaucracy', said two married Harvard law professors in an edition of the *California Law Review* (Gersen and Suk 2016). Jacob Gersen and Jennie Suk lament 'the steady expansion of regulatory concepts of sex discrimination and sexual violence to the point that the regulated area comes also to encompass ordinary sex'. Some American universities have moved on, they point out, from merely defining affirmative consent to actually scripting sexual acts, including the words that prospective partners should use, and the way that they should say them. The University of Wyoming, for example, states that 'anything less than voluntary, sober, enthusiastic, verbal, noncoerced, continual, active, and honest consent is sexual assault'. Rather than using body language, which can be misinterpreted, the university says that consent should come in the form of a verbal 'yes', or possibly, 'Yes, Yes, Oh! Yes!'

The school suggests some phrases that students could use during a sexual encounter. 'What would you like me to do for you?' is among the tamer offerings.

The greater the role of the mediator, the more that the most natural of relations becomes 'unnatural': the unmediated sex act is conceived as an unnatural violation by one party of the other. It is only through specific apparatus, and supervision, that people can be brought into relation to one another.

The more that we depend upon mediators for our interrelations, the less we relate directly, the more individuals are estranged from one another. The social relation becomes something effected not directly, but only through this unrelated, foreign, medium.

Therefore, in Marx's terms, their own action, their own relation to one another, appears to them as the action of another party; it appears to them through the mediator which states how the action and the relation should be conducted. There are no longer only two people in the bed.

Conclusion

In conclusion, the increasingly one-sided forms taken by the self today can be seen as an extension of the underlying contradictions described by Marx. The current forms can be seen as an expression of an essential contradiction that exists in the self under capitalism: the contradiction between individual and social forms of existence.

This self-alienation is being deepened by the deliberate seeking of the alienated state and the elevation of the role of the mediator. As a result, it is not only a spontaneous process, but is also something willed and sought, through our culture, and as a state policy.

Therefore, by the same account, there is a potential to wilfully oppose this process. There is potential for us to defend spontaneous and direct social relations: the genuine communal ties, or one-to-one exchanges, whereby people seek solace and communality with one another. We should criticise the role of the ever-expanding false mediator, which estranges us from ourselves, and from each other.

References

Appleton, J. (2016a). *Generation jihadi*. [Online] Spiked-online.com. Retrieved December 1, 2018, from https://www.spiked-online.com/2016/07/01/generation-jihadi/.

Appleton, J. (2016b). *Officious: Rise of the busybody state*. London: Zero Books.

Furedi, F. (2004). *Therapy culture: Cultivating vulnerability in an uncertain age*. London: Routledge.

Gersen, J., & Suk, J. (2016). *The sex bureaucracy*. [Online] Californialawreview. org. Retrieved December 1, 2018, from http://www.californialawreview.org/wp-content/uploads/2016/09/Gersen-and-Suk-37-FINAL.pdf.

Hegel, G. W. F. (2008). *Outlines of the philosophy of right*. Oxford: Oxford University Press.

Lukács, G. (1971). *History and class consciousness*. Cambridge, MA: MIT Press.

Marx, K. (1975a). Economic and philosophic manuscripts of 1844. In *Early writings*. London: Penguin.

Marx, K. (1975b). On the Jewish question. In *Early writings*. London: Penguin.

Marx, K. (1975c). A contribution to the critique of Hegel's philosophy of right. In *Early writings*. London: Penguin.

Marx, K. (1977). *Capital: Volume I*. London: Lawrence and Wishart.

Mészáros, I. (1986). *Marx's theory of alienation*. London: Merlin Press.

Roy, O. (2006). *Globalised Islam: The search for a new Ummah*. New York: Columbia University Press.

Roy, O. (2010). *Holy ignorance: When religion and culture part ways*. London: C. Hurst & Co.

9

Anti-humanism and the Deconstruction of the Liberal Subject

James Heartfield

Over the years reactionary and radical thought alike have both attacked that ideal, or person, 'the Subject'. In the nineteenth century Nietzsche wrote scathingly about 'that little changeling, "the Subject"' (Nietzsche 1989: 45). His was an aristocratic (or pseudo-aristocratic) reaction to the emergence of mass society, with men now free of fealty and obligation. Free subjects were to Nietzsche 'changelings', that is, they were untrustworthy and not dependable because they had minds of their own. One can find a similar idea in Boswell's recollections of Samuel Johnson, when the man of letters says it is impossible to trust a man who is guided by his own inward light, because one does not know where to find him (Boswell 1923: 168). But Nietzsche is also using a common anti-Semitic trope. Jews were often seen as 'changelings', and in much reactionary German writing, one can see this same preoccupation with a democratic Subject who

J. Heartfield (✉)
London, UK

presumptuously assumes authority over his own affairs. Heidegger had written in 1926 that mass man 'is not something like a "universal subject" which a plurality of subjects have hovering above them' (Heidegger: 166).

Radicals, too, were dismissive of the Subject. Jacques Lacan, the French iconoclastic psychoanalyst, mocked the notion of a willing subject, the 'Cartesian cogito'. Lacan said that the cogito is a 'monster or homunculus' and ridiculed 'the presence inside man, of the celebrated little fellow who governs him, who is the driver' (Lacan: 141).

Reactionary and radical thought alike both grappled with the high tide of democratic bourgeois civilisation, and as they did, they homed in on its highest product: 'the Subject'—which is to say, the free agent, the willing subject, contracting party, the voting citizen. In their different ways, both radicals and reactionaries were uncomfortable with 'the Subject' because that was where the strength of liberal democracy was. Both elitist notions of aristocratic privilege, and radical ideas of total social transformation, seemed to find their limits in the robust and widespread reproduction of individual agency across much of Western society.

The attack on the Subject as agent also widened into an attack on Man as such. 'Man is dead', wrote Michel Foucault, parodying Nietzsche, who had written 'God is dead' (Foucault 1966). Foucault meant that we have worshipped man, rather as we had worshipped God, but that this God too had failed us. Foucault wrote in the same vein, arguing that man is artificial and transient:

> As the archaeology of our thought easily shows, man is an invention of a recent date. And one perhaps nearing to its end. … one can certainly wager that man would be erased, like a face drawn in the sand at the edge of the sea. (Foucault 1986: 387)

(This striking image is drawn perhaps from a fragment of Herakleitos: 'History is a child building a sandcastle by the sea, and that child is the whole majesty of man's power in the world' (Herakleitos and Diogenes 1979).)

9 Anti-humanism and the Deconstruction of the Liberal Subject

Claude Lévi-Strauss was thinking along similar lines to Foucault when he wrote that 'the ultimate goal of the human sciences is not to constitute but to dissolve man' (Claude Lévi-Strauss 1994: 247).

A generation earlier, and on the other side of the political divide, Martin Heidegger made *das Man* mean something like 'the inauthentic masses', so that in the English translations of Heidegger it is written as 'the They'—though of course the word *Man* in German is closest to the English 'One'. Heidegger faults *das Man* for his/their 'idle chatter' and 'publicness' (Heidegger 1990: 343, 165). Rudiger Safranski rightly says that Heidegger's characterisation of 'the They' shows he 'has no sympathy with the principle of a democratic public' (Safranski 1999: 168).

At this point some might recoil in horror, or self-righteous indignation, on behalf of 'Mankind'. Or take sides with those who would celebrate its ending. However, there is potentially more to the attack on the Subject than this polarisation of response might suggest. The critique of Man, after all, could be a critique of the false identification of Mankind's collective interests as being singular. It might be a way of objecting to a false consensus view that we are somehow 'all in it together': one big happy family of Mankind. An idea that obscures real differences, between classes, or perhaps between men and women, or between white and black.

The drive to deconstruct the central, received ideas of the age did after all seem to be the point of critical thinking. Was it obvious that liberal, market societies were the optimum for social progress? Critical thinking challenged that idea, deconstructing the case. Was it assumed that the family unit was the natural domestic form? Critical thinking questioned that assumption. Deconstructing those ideas that seemed to be most natural was the project.

In any event, I want in this chapter to trace just some of the intellectual journey that brought people to these conclusions, and I will concentrate on the generation of '68 and their debts to earlier ways of thinking.

Collectively they were known as 'post-structuralists'—or sometimes 'deconstructionists'—and the best known were the historian Michel

Foucault, the philosopher Jacques Derrida, the Marxist Louis Althusser, the psychoanalyst Jacques Lacan, and the political scientist Jean-Francois Lyotard.

Post-structuralists drew on some prior ideas.

Phenomenology

One was 'phenomenology' developed by Edmund Husserl, Alfred Schutz, Martin Heidegger (to a degree), and others.

The core idea of 'phenomenology' was a reform of philosophy. Prior philosophy, in particular that of Immanuel Kant, had divided the world into what could be seen, 'the phenomenon' and what could not be seen, 'the noumenon'. Before people had talked about the physical world, and the metaphysical world, that which was beyond the physical (Kant 1964, chapter 3).

Another German philosopher, Georg Hegel, thought that Kant's separation of phenomenon and noumenon was too rigid (Hegel 1975: 73). He proposed that the forms of things, the phenomenology, was an expression of the movement of the absolute Spirit through the world (Hegel 1977: Preface, §11 *et seq.*).

Husserl was not satisfied with Hegel's answer, and proposed to set aside, or bracket off, the whole 'Subject-Object' divide. It was a source of endless difficulty, he said, so better to put it to one side, and attend instead to 'the things themselves'. He meant the things as they appear to us, before we start to sort them into what is subjective and what is objective: one might say the things of consciousness as they present themselves (Husserl 1970, 2001: 101).

Ernst Mach's drawing of a view through the left eye gives some insight into how the world looked to phenomenologists paying attention to 'the things themselves'. Mach's hand, legs, and even the side of his nose, are in the world, just as the divan he is lying on is, the window, and the room itself. He was trying to show what we really see, not what we construct in our heads as being a picture of the world. (This is not to say that Mach was a phenomenologist, but he was thinking along some similar lines.)

9 Anti-humanism and the Deconstruction of the Liberal Subject

'Self portrait', also known as 'View from the left eye,' first appeared in Ernst Mach's *The Analysis of Sensations*, 1886.

Bracketing the opposition between Subjective observer and the Objective observed world also helps Husserl overcome what many people saw as a problem of *solipsism*. By that they meant that the reasoning mind seemed to be shut up in a box, without any sure way of knowing that other minds were not just automatons. With Husserl's 'bracketing' of the division between subjective and objective, just as the observer is in the world, so is everyone else in the world, and their comments and ideas, too. They all exist together in a 'life-world' or *Lebenswelt*.

Husserl's development of the phenomenological method was to argue for a different basis to 'objectivity' than the warrant of the external world, in what he called 'intersubjectivity': agreement between people, which builds up into a shared 'life-world'. So, he argued that we can see 'the objective sciences as subjective constructs', because 'the objective is precisely never experienceable as itself; and scientists themselves, by the way, consider it in this way whenever they interpret it as something metaphysically transcendent, in contrast to their confusingly empiricist talk' (Husserl: 129).

Husserl says that 'when we are thrown into an alien social sphere, that of negroes in the Congo, Chinese peasants, etc., we discover that their truths, the facts that for them are fixed, generally verified or verifiable, are by no means the same as ours.' So it is that the '"objective" a priori is grounded in the "subjective-relative" a priori of the life-world'. In this regard, 'we speak of the "intersubjective constitution" of the world' (Husserl: 139, 140, 168).

It is quite common today to find people in the humanities saying that something is a 'social construct'. They might say that 'pop music' is a social construct. Or they might say, more surprisingly to those who were used to thinking of those things as natural, that gender is a social construct, or that race is a social construct.

The concept of 'social construct' is so ubiquitous in colleges today that it is rather taken for granted as the background to much contemporary thinking. But just before it slips from view we ought to notice that it is itself a specific concept of how things are. First and foremost, it is Husserl's concept, the concept of the 'intersubjective constitution of the world'. Recognising that will forewarn us against some of the philosophical assumptions that we all make when we say, lazily, that 'such and such is a social construct'.

Husserl's phenomenology, with its themes of the collapsing of the subject-object distinction, of the intersubjective constitution of reality, was an important bridge between nineteenth-century philosophy and the post-structuralist thinking of the later twentieth century, laying the basis for much of the deconstruction of key assumptions, most importantly, the deconstruction of the Subject.

Another important influence was the reinterpretation of Hegel's theories of development in France in the mid-twentieth century. This also bore the name 'phenomenology', though confusingly Hegel's use of the word is distinct from Husserl's, as we shall see.

The Reception of Hegel in France

Georg Hegel's work had not had much impact in France, but between 1933 and 1939 Alexandre Kojève gave a series of lectures in Paris outlining Hegel's book *The Phenomenology of Spirit*, which among other things contains his well-rehearsed 'dialectic of the Master and the Slave'. The course was a great success and some important thinkers attended, including the surrealists André Breton and Georges Bataille, psychoanalyst Jacques Lacan, sociologist Raymond Aron, and the philosophers Maurice Merleau-Ponty and Jean Hyppolite.

Kojève tended to understand Hegel to be describing the development of human institutions 'in the guise' of describing a spiritual progression. Where Hegel's book is a 'Phenomenology of Spirit'—an account of the forms that Spirit assumes as it moves through history, Kojève's lectures describe an 'anthropogenesis' (Kojève 1991: 6). For Hegel, Spirit finds itself progressively in its realisation through different historical forms, such as the school of sceptics, the Church, and later in national constitutions. In Kojève's version the subject is Man ('Man is self-consciousness' Kojève 1991: 3), and in Hegel's the subject is Spirit. According to Kojève we have merely to shed the arcane language of 'spirit' in order to understand Hegel's real humanistic message. This approach ought to be fruitful, and in large part it is, but ironically the movement away from an idealist towards a humanistic reading of Hegel is only achieved at the expense of losing a fundamental aspect of Hegel's contribution.

In short, Kojève was making Hegel's *Phenomenology of Spirit* into a phenomenology more like Husserl's and much less Hegelian. Kojève's reading was influential. 'Most contemporary thinkers,' said Jean Hyppolite, 'accept Hegel's phenomenology but reject his ontology'. That is to say they accept his account of the development of the forms, but not the underlying force that drives the development of the forms, because that is 'Spirit' and so too religious in its explanation for mid-twentieth-century French progressives (Hyppolite 1974: 205).

The drawback to this approach was that it was precisely the spiritual side that was the transformative side. Hegel saw the passage of spirit reducing all its manifestations into merely relative transient positions. Without the driving force of transcendent Spirit, the different figures of

Hegel's phenomenology, Master and Slave, Self and Other, are hardened into lifeless and sterile opposition. Where Hegel foresaw the struggle between the Master and the Slave resolving itself in a happier mutual recognition, his later interpreters were gloomier, seeing no way out of the clash of overlord and subordinate. Hyppolite warned that 'if we just stayed with the Phenomenology, by separating it from its conclusion as well as from its preface, we would remain at a humanism, at a philosophical anthropology,' and the development of his thinking would be 'incomprehensible' (Hyppolite 1977: 34). The transformative and historical aspect of Hegel's thought would be abandoned.

In the first of his 'Theses on Feuerbach', Marx (1997: 92) says that:

> The chief defect of all hitherto existing materialism—that of Feuerbach included—is that the thing, reality, sensuousness, is conceived only in the form of the *object or of contemplation*, but not as *sensuous human activity, practice*, not subjectively. Hence, in contradistinction to materialism, the *active* side was developed abstractly by idealism.

This helps us to understand what is lost when, as Kojève and those following him did, one takes the Spirit out of Hegel's *Phenomenology*. The Spirit is the active side of the *Phenomenology*, the driving force for the transition from one manifestation of itself to another. Abstractly no doubt, but still in Hegel's *Phenomenology* the possibility that one could transcend any given form is possible because all forms are only partial manifestations of Spirit. Without Spirit there is no transcendence, or transition, from any one form into any other. They simply remain standing in opposition to one another.

So it was that Hegel's influence in France was as the author of a phenomenology, from which the spiritual transcendent side had been removed. Hegel dis-spirited was right for the thinking of the times, which was losing sight of the ideals that could take people beyond their circumstances. The drama of the Russian Revolution had descended into Stalin's opportunistic dictatorship, while the 'democracies' courted Hitler's Fascist regime: the poet Auden called it 'a low dishonest decade' (Auden 1939).

This reinterpretation of Hegel was important to Louis Althusser because Althusser was a Marxist, and Hegel was to some degree, Marx's inspiration. The dogmatist Althusser wanted to make sure that any lingering Hegelian idealism was not imported into the Marxist theory of the French Communist Party. In doing so he was turning Marxism into a lifeless 'determinism' that looked increasingly like the caricature of Marxism to be found in the screeds of Cold War ideologues.

Althusser appeals to Marxists not to reverse Hegel's priority of the Spirit over civil society, while hanging onto the Hegelian formula, 'the relation between an essence and its phenomena, sublimated in the concept of the "truth of …"'. Instead Althusser sees in Marx what he wants to see, namely a break from the 'Hegelian theme of phenomenon-essence-truth-of' (Althusser 1969: 111). Social orders are not in the grip of essential contradictions, he thinks—that would be far too idealistic an interpretation. In the place of the 'essential contradictions' favoured by Marx-inspired polemicists (see Mao Zedong 2009), Althusser argues for a more bloodless idea of 'overdetermination', according to which a situation

> may either be **overdetermined** in the direction of a **historical inhibition**, a real 'block' for the contradiction (for example, Wilhelmine Germany), or in the direction of **revolutionary rupture** (Russia in 1917), but in neither condition *is it ever found in the 'pure' state*. (Althusser 1969: 106)

'Overdetermination' was Althusser's alternative idea of how history moved. He took the ideal, the Spirit, out. But Spirit was the Subject of Hegel's philosophy, the moving force. In its place Althusser puts a mechanical relationship of 'overdetermination'. In Althusser's reading history was a 'process without a Subject' (Althusser 1994a: 218).

Structuralism

The other influence on the post-structuralists, which gave them their name, was structuralism. This is in large part a theory of linguistics, set out by Ferdinand de Saussure, which it would be difficult to do justice to here. Saussure's linguistics were notable for the way that he argued that meaning was derived from the system of signs: from how they related to one another within the system itself. That was rather different from 'nominalist' theories that saw a necessary, natural, connection between things out there, and the words with which we name things.

Furthermore, Saussure argued that 'language is not a function of the speaker; it is a product that is passively assimilated by the individual' (Saussure 2011: 14). Saussure was supported by N. Troubetzkoy, who argued that 'structural linguistics shifts from the study of conscious linguistic phenomena to the study of their unconscious infrastructure' (quoted in Lévi-Strauss 1968: 33).

One of the charms of the structuralist approach for cultural critics was that it was an alternative to a demand for activist or committed readings of literature. Though it seemed very formalistic to look at the way that meaning was created in the relations between signs, it did at least shut off the demands of radicals that art works should 'stand for' something, that they should be moral parables. In those activist readings, literary criticism was all about finding the truth of the text outside of the text, by reference to another moral realm—as Roland Barthes objects in his book *Writing Degree Zero* (Barthes 1983).

But what was appealing as a plea for the autonomy of literature in Barthes soon became something else. Saussure's structuralism became a model for a theory of society in which human agency was not just diminished but downgraded to being a mere effect or symptom of social structures.

So, Claude Lévi-Strauss, the anthropologist, interpreted systems of social organisation as if they were languages: 'language is at once the prototype of the cultural phenomenon and the phenomenon whereby all the forms of social life are established and perpetuated' (Lévi-Strauss 1968: 359).

'Linguistics thus presents us with a dialectical and totalizing entity but one outside (or beneath) consciousness and will,' he wrote. 'Language, an unreflecting totalization, is human reason which has its reasons and of which man knows nothing' (Lévi-Strauss 1994: 252). He conceived of 'social structures as entities independent of men's consciousness of them (although they in fact govern men's existence)' (Lévi-Strauss 1968: 121).

Lévi-Strauss found the approach useful in his understanding of the way that social ties worked with tribal peoples:

9 Anti-humanism and the Deconstruction of the Liberal Subject

kinship systems, marriage rules and descent groups constitute a coordinated whole, the function of which is to insure the permanency of the social group by means of intertwining consanguineous and affinal ties. They may be considered as the blueprint of a mechanism which 'pumps' women out of their consanguineous families to redistribute them in affinal groups, the result of this process being to create new consanguineous groups, and so on. (Lévi-Strauss 1968: 309)

The psychoanalyst Jacques Lacan also worked something like Saussure's linguistics into his theory of the formation of the subject: 'the subject… is constituted as secondary in relation to the signifier.' And with tribal notching and tattooing 'thus is marked the first split that makes the subject as such distinguish himself from the sign in relation to which, at first, he has been able to constitute himself as subject' (Lacan 1994: 141).

Structuralism, then, was a linguistic theory, which, carried over into anthropology, sociology, and psycho-analysis, gave an account of the Subject as an effect of discourse. Althusser gives an account of the way that a given address, 'Stop!' spoken by a policeman, makes the person so addressed into a Subject, because he is addressed. He says that 'Ideology interpellates individuals as Subjects' (Althusser 1994b: 128). Michel Foucault says something similar in his account of Jeremy Bentham's 'Panopticon'. Bentham proposed a surveillance system for convicts, in a planned prison where the warders would observe the prisoners who are always on display, always observed. Foucault sees Bentham's Panopticon as a model for other ways that people are observed and so made into subjects. As he says:

> What generalizes the power to punish, then, is not the universal consciousness of the law in each juridical subject; it is the regular extension, the infinitely minute web of panoptic techniques. (Foucault 1995: 215)

Foucault is basically uncomfortable with the 'universal consciousness of the law in each juridical subject'. That to him sounds like too much of a concession to the voluntary reproduction of liberal society. He wants instead to say that this Subjectivity is the product of domineering modes of observation that call forth in the bodies around a sense of themselves as Subjects. There is some element of truth in what Foucault says, but overall it is so one-sided as to be wrong. What he takes out of his account of the creation of the Subject, as does Althusser, is the self-actualisation of the Subject, the way in which people make their own history.

A Reform Project

From its origins, post-structuralism became a project of reforming philosophy, psycho-analysis, Marxism, literary studies, and the Human Sciences.

The project was to rid these endeavours of their lingering, pre-modern, metaphysics.

This is something that is said very frequently: so much so that the meaning of it is often assumed to be understood and shared. Often though we are being bamboozled. After all, who wants to put their hands up as being a defender of metaphysical mumbo jumbo?

Metaphysics in history was the book that Aristotle wrote that came after the Physics. Was it not Hume that told us to cast the book of Metaphysics into the fire? Kant says that Metaphysics is 'the consideration that certain of our cognitions rise completely above the sphere of all possible experience, and by means of conceptions to which there exists in the whole extent of our experience no corresponding object' (Kant 1964: 28).

Among the things that Kant thinks are metaphysical are some that today we might discount, like 'immortality', and some we might be sceptical of, like God, and others that are our subject here, namely free will. 'The science which,' writes Kant, 'has as its especial object the solution of these very problems is named metaphysics' (Kant 1964: 28).

For the post-structuralists, though, the campaign to exclude 'metaphysics' extended to a campaign against the metaphysics of the 'thinking self' (Lacan: 140–142), and the 'Metaphysics of Presence' (Derrida 1997: 74).

In his book *The Experience of Freedom*, the philosopher Jean Luc Nancy argues that our understanding of freedom is metaphysical. Freedom must be freed of its transcendent dreams, says Nancy, which we must do because we will only be disappointed if we try to reach for the stars. A better idea of freedom would be that it was just existence, he says:

> liberating human freedom from the immanence of an infinite foundation or finality, and liberating it therefore from its own infinite projection to infinity, where transcendence (existence) itself is transcended and hereby annulled. It is a question of letting freedom exist for itself. Freedom perhaps designates nothing more and nothing less than existence itself. (Nancy 1993: 13–14)

Freedom for Nancy, then, is just being. The transcendent yearning to be something else is illusory, he is saying. It will lead to the annulment of the existent self. Real freedom only comes with the abandonment of the metaphysical transcendent.

Jacques Derrida criticises the appeal to 'democracy or "human rights"—which directly or not comes back to this metaphysics of Subjectivity' (Derrida 1991: 40). Here, the narratives of freedom and democracy are being criticised because they imply the emancipation of a Subject (in this case a people). Subjectivity is 'metaphysical', which for Derrida means null, or false. Of course, he is right in the sense that democracy and rights are about being more than bodies, more than just existing. They are about reaching beyond the immediate or animal existence.

Derrida gave a name to the reform that would rid us of metaphysical illusions: deconstruction. Deconstruction would be different from other kinds of criticism because it would bring nothing new:

> The movements of deconstruction do not destroy structures from the outside. They are not possible and effective, nor can they take accurate aim, except by inhabiting those structures. ... Operating necessarily from the inside, borrowing all the strategic and economic resources of subversion from the old structure, borrowing them structurally, ... (Derrida 1997: 24)

This was critique, but it was not critique. Criticism that would articulate the structures of what was being critiqued, but without any aspiration that it would bring forth any new principle. Even the Subjectivity of critics was set aside as overreaching.

Jean-Francois Lyotard coined a more dramatic, and eye-catching name for the reform of the humanities that deconstruction was proposing, when he called the project 'post-modernism'. Lyotard explained his understanding of 'modernity', which we are leaving behind:

> I will use the term **modern** to designate any science that legitimates itself with reference to a metadiscourse ... making an explicit appeal to some grand narrative, such as the dialectics of Spirit, the hermeneutics of meaning, the emancipation of the rational or working Subject, or the creation of wealth. (Lyotard 1989: xxiv)

Rejecting these defining narrative structures of modernity, Lyotard announced the *post*-modern age in the following way: 'I define postmodernism as incredulity towards metanarratives' (Lyotard 1989: xxiv).

Incredulity was a good shorthand for deconstruction. So often when we read the deconstructions of the Self, or Socialism, or the Nation, they do not, as Derrida says, add very much to the causal links that are set out in the conventional theories of these things. The major difference is one of tone—instead of assurance, incredulity. There is a modern punctuation mark called an interrobang—an exclamation mark and a question mark combined, like this‽ It was invented by an advertiser, Martin Spekter in 1966. Lots of deconstruction simply sets out the conventional account, with all of its 'metaphysical' connections highlighted, and at the end there is an unspoken interrobang‽

They believe in freedom‽ Can you believe it‽

The Impact of Post-structuralism

Post-structuralism was quite a small, if creative, movement in France in the 1970s. In the 1980s and 1990s, though, it began to have a big impact in American and British Universities.

There are two ways to look at the impact that post-structuralism had. The first is rather against the grain of post-structuralist thought, and that

9 Anti-humanism and the Deconstruction of the Liberal Subject

is to point out that the interest in the idea came about because of something happening in the world.

To deconstruct the grand narratives of 'the free world', 'consumerism', 'patriarchy', 'the nation', 'white supremacy', 'colonialism', 'the subjugation of nature'—all of this seemed like a good idea on university campuses. In the 1980s students and lecturers were groaning under the yoke of Ronald Reagan and Margaret Thatcher's mix of free markets, patriotism, and family values. It was good to have a snarky way of ridiculing those ideas—more especially one written in a secret code so that any who questioned it could be dismissed as unenlightened.

These ideas were developed to help people in France to explain to themselves why the Socialist project of the emancipation of labour had failed. But with some adjustments to a new content they did equal service explaining why the free market was not bringing people the freedom, security, and satisfaction that they hoped it would. Deconstruction was a way of analysing failing ideologies. The truth of this text was, so to say, outside of the text.

On the other hand, deconstruction was good to Derrida's promise. It did not bring anything new to the table. Rather deconstructionists only laid bare the shortcomings of the conventional viewpoint.

The real pertinence of post-structuralism or deconstruction, though, was its deconstruction of the Subject. The rational self, seeking to understand and also to alter its destiny, was the target of the deconstructive urge. The Subject is at the core of the modern liberal order. Free subjects are the fulcrum point around which everything turns. Without reasoning subjects how are agreements possible? So much of life is contractual, promises are made and kept, services promised and paid for, and sales and purchases all rely on contracting parties.

What Foucault thinks of as an illusion is arguably the great success of the liberal order, namely 'the universal consciousness', not exactly of 'the law', but of the core assumptions of civil society, 'in each subject' (each 'juridical' subject if you will). Consider the alternative. Dictatorships generally fail even before they provoke revolts, because the dictator must substitute his will for the will of all. That is plausible in a small tribe—perhaps—but hardly in a modern metropolis. For the dictator to make all of the thousands of petty decisions that the populace makes every day would be as impossible for him as it would be intolerable for us. The freedom of the Subject, which is the internalisation of the order of free Subjects, is the condition for any kind of order at all.

Extrapolated upwards, the free Subject who is an individual becomes the free Subject that is a people. The logical structure of freely contracting Subjects is similar at the micro-domestic level as it is at the macro-societal-wide level. The Constituent Assemblies stand in the place of individual mind, as the reflective body of the Collective Will. States, too, set themselves goals and enter into agreements.

But the centrality of the Subject to the liberal order is severely tested today. The philosophical critique of the Subject has a resonance because of extensive doubts about subjectivity. Houria Bouteldja's *Indigenes of the Republic* mobilises a heady mix of radical Islamic thought and post-structuralism. For her it seems clear that the deconstruction of the Cartesian 'I' is part of the case against white domination:

> The Cartesian 'I' affirms itself. ... It is this 'I' that will from now on occupy the centre. I think therefore I am the one who decides. I think therefore I am the one who subjugates, pillages, steals, rapes, commits genocide. I think therefore I am a modern, virile, capitalist, imperialist man. The Cartesian 'I' will lay the philosophical ground for whiteness. It will secularize God's attributes and confer them to the Western God, who is, in fact, none other than a parable of the white man. (Bouteldja 2016: 34)

In Bouteldja's view the liberal subject is hopelessly implicated in imperialism and chauvinism. Her critique of subjectivity chimes well with a disdain for liberal democratic values.

When intelligent critics look aghast at the way that peoples exercise their democratic choices it is easy to hear the resonances of the post-structuralist critique of democracy and of self-government. The 'bad' choices that people make, like voting to leave the European Union or to put Donald Trump in the White House, invite a corrosive deconstruction from the critics. These choices are not freely made, we are told, so much is illusory. Plainly the people's choice was not determinant, but merely an effect of the (bad) discourses of Leave, or the Trump campaign.

9 Anti-humanism and the Deconstruction of the Liberal Subject

Or perhaps they were programmed to vote the way that they did by Russian twitter bots? In any event, the dismissal of popular choice is relatively easy for those who think that freedom is an illusion—like Jean Luc Nancy—and that simple existence, freed of transcendental freedom, would be real freedom. With that outlook it becomes simple to dismiss the illusory choice and follow instead what is presumed to be the better outcome for everyone's economic well-being.

One does not have to go to such grand public issues to see the way that choice, once the ideological bedrock of the liberal order, is seen today by many experts and officials as illusory. Taxes on sugary drinks and minimum pricing of supermarket-bought alcohol are both examples of the way that the government feels that it should nudge us into the right behaviour. There is an actual government department, known colloquially as the 'Nudge Unit' (or Behavioural Insights Team), with 150 staff that was initially within the 10 Downing Street Cabinet Office, and today still reports to it. The Nudge Unit is there to advise the government on how to modify the behaviour of the public. Plainly that is only possible because the people in the Team think that individual choices are not expressive of subjective agency, but merely effects of poor information environments.

Scotland's government is even more certain that it can dismiss the willed choices of its citizens. They have only recently had to backtrack on some striking attempts to subvert individual freedom. The 'Getting it Right for Every Child' policy had a clause in it that each and every child would have a 'named person'—somebody in an official capacity—that would act as a state guardian for the child (Scottish Parliament 2017). As the proposal shaped up, Scots rebelled against the provision, not least because it was as unworkable as any dictatorial system, but also because they felt that it was a usurpation of the rights of parents.

There are of course many examples of intrusive laws in recent years, from the Anti-Social Behaviour Order (now abandoned) to the restrictions on public gatherings made possible by the Harassment laws. These are all coeval with the philosophical attitude towards the Subject that fails to take freedom and choice seriously.

References

Althusser, L. (1969). *For Marx*. London: Penguin.
Althusser, L. (1994a). *The future lasts a long time*. London: Vintage.
Althusser, L. (1994b). Ideological state apparatuses. In S. Zizek (Ed.), *Mapping ideology*. London: Verso.
Auden, W. H. (1939, October 18). September 1, 1939. *The New Republic*.
Barthes, R. (1983). *Writing degree zero*. New York: Hill and Wang.
Boswell, J. (1923). *Life of Samuel Johnson*. Chicago: Scott, Foresman and Company.
Bouteldja, H. (2016). *Whites, Jews and us*. South Pasadena: Semiotext(e).
Derrida, J. (1991). *Of spirit: Heidegger and the question*. Chicago: Chicago University Press.
Derrida, J. (1997). *Of grammatology*. Baltimore, MD: Johns Hopkins University Press.
Foucault, M. (1966). l'Homme, est il mort? Arts 38, June.
Foucault, M. (1986). *The order of things: The archaeology of the human sciences*. London: Tavistock.
Foucault, M. (1995). *Discipline & punish: The birth of the prison*. New York: Vintage Books.
Hegel, G. (1975). *Logic*. Oxford: Oxford University Press.
Hegel, G. (1977). *Phenomenology of spirit*. Oxford: Oxford University Press.
Heidegger, M. (1990). *Being and time*. Oxford: Basil Blackwell.
Herakleitos and Diogenes. (1979). *Herakleitos and Diogenes*. San Francisco, CA: Grey Fox Press.
Husserl, E. (1970). *The crisis of the European sciences*. Evanston, IL: Northwestern University Press.
Husserl, E. (2001). *Logical investigations*. Oxford: Routledge.
Hyppolite, J. (1974). *Genesis and structure of Hegel's phenomenology of spirit*. Evanston, IL: Northwestern University Press.
Hyppolite, J. (1977). *Logic and existence*. New York: State University of New York.
Kant, I. (1964). *Critique of pure reason*. London: Everyman Edition.
Kojève, A. (1991). *Introduction to the reading of Hegel*. Ithaca, NY: Cornell University Press.
Lacan, J. (1994). *The four fundamental concepts of psychoanalysis*. London: Penguin.
Lévi-Strauss, C. (1968). *Structural anthropology*. London: Allen Lane.
Lévi-Strauss, C. (1994). *The savage mind*. Oxford: Oxford University Press.

Lyotard, J.-F. (1989). *The postmodern condition: A report on knowledge*. Manchester: Manchester University Press.
Marx, K. (1997). *The Marx reader*. Cambridge: Polity.
Nancy, J.-L. (1993). *The experience of freedom*. Stanford, CA: Stanford University Press.
Nietzsche, F. (1989). *Genealogy of morals*. New York: Vintage.
Safranski, R. (1999). *Martin Heidegger: Between good and evil*. Princeton, NJ: Princeton University Press.
de Saussure, F. (2011). *Course in general linguistics*. New York: Columbia University Press.
Scottish Parliament. (2017) *Children and young people* (Information sharing) (Scotland) Bill, Policy Memorandum.
Zedong, M. (2009). *Collected writings of Chairman Mao: Volume 3—On policy, practice and contradiction*. Texas: El Paso Norte Press.

10

Narcissism and Identity

Claire Fox

Introduction

Any reflection on narcissism today invariably starts with Donald Trump. It has become more than a jibe to discuss the American president as a narcissist. There is a serious debate amongst US psychiatrists and psychologists about diagnosing the president with a clinical illness, Narcissistic Personality Disorder (NPD), with a view to getting him deposed (HuffPost 2017). Trump's 'condition' has become a byword for everything wrong with the superficiality and selfishness of modern society. As Lynn Stuart Parramore noted on *AlterNet*:

> It took a while to fully manifest, but what many social critics, most notably Christopher Lasch (author of *The Culture of Narcissism*), noticed bubbling up from the painful social and economic conditions of the last third of the twentieth century has finally burst into full Technicolor glory in the image of America's president. In the form of Donald Trump,

C. Fox (✉)
Academy of Ideas, London, UK
e-mail: clairefox@academyofideas.org.uk

we have a bloated ball of toxic energy whose name, pasted on gaudy skyscrapers the world over, has become a byword for pathological narcissism. (Parramore 2017)

But it is not just Trump who is diagnosed as a narcissist. The selfie-obsessed young are also seen as 'suffering' from the condition. It is almost a cliché these days to talk about Generation Me, Me, Me. It is argued that millennials are uniquely self-obsessed, preening, full of self-regard and entitlement. Proof is provided by a range of mind-boggling statistics associated with digital natives: 80 million photographs are uploaded on Instagram, and 1.4 billion people publish personal details on Facebook, *every day*. In the UK in 2017 more than a million selfies were taken each day. In 2013, the *Oxford English Dictionary* proclaimed that 'selfie' was the word of the year, recording that its use in the English language had increased 17,000 per cent from the previous year.

While such 'evidence' may be impressionistic, narcissism is also becoming a fashionable subject for serious academic studies (see, e.g. Wilson and Sibley 2011). One particular book, *The Narcissism Epidemic: Living in the Age of Entitlement*, by Jean Twenge and W. Keith Campbell, made headlines around the world and—unusually for an academic book— headed the bestseller chart. This 2009 book analysed data to prove a seismic shift in America's cultural norms towards increasing self-admiration as a generational trend.

But before we start diagnosing a whole generation, or indeed sending Trump off to a psychiatrist, perhaps we need to take a step back and look at what narcissism is and is not. I make no claim to any psychiatric or psychological expertise, but then neither can many of those who regularly apply the label to twenty-first-century social and political trends. But taking a lead from Christopher Lasch's 1979 masterpiece, *The Culture of Narcissism*, which took the diagnostic pathologies of discrete narcissistic personality types and examined their cultural impact, I hope to make a modest contribution by updating some of his insights while debunking some myths that have grown up around his work. My argument, and it is an argument rather than an academic thesis, aims to sketch out new strains of pathological narcissism and how they express themselves via an obsession with performative identity, both personal and political.

Narcissism Emerges

In 1968, the term narcissistic personality disorder, or NPD, officially entered the diagnostic and statistical manual of mental disorders, emerging from the world of psychoanalysis. The term narcissism was first coined in 1898 by Havelock Ellis, an English doctor who studied human sexuality. The word is borrowed from the Greek myth of the beautiful young boy, Narcissus, who rejected the overtures of the mountain nymph Echo, and instead fell in love with his own reflection in a forest pool. Havelock Ellis used the formulation 'narcissus-like' to refer to a female patient who was masturbating 'too much'. Following this, in 1911, Austrian psychoanalyst Otto Rank wrote the first psychoanalytical paper on the subject: 'A contribution to the study of narcissism', focusing on a female patient for whom combing her own hair was so sexually arousing that nobody else's love could compete.

Freud followed with his 1914 essay *On Narcissism*. He split narcissism into two distinct categories. The first, 'Primary Narcissism', is a happy, harmless state in which a baby thinks it is the 'centre and core of creation'. For infants, it is indeed healthy to be selfish in order to ensure basic needs are met. Freud's 'Secondary Narcissism'—the problematic kind—was characterised however by the failure of adult patients to develop a capacity to direct the libido outwards: instead re-investing it in the self, where it festers.

What makes narcissism an elusive pathological category is that it is not an illness as such; rather, it can be a normal part of development, in which we gradually learn to separate our own viewpoint and needs from those of others. It is not entirely age specific either. Well past infanthood, elements of selfishness linger into adolescence (one reason why psychiatrists are reluctant to diagnose NPD in teenagers). While we all gradually shed intense self-absorption and self-centeredness over time, NPD may well be diagnosed if malignant self-involvement continues to dominate into adulthood.

Although NPD may be a diagnostic tool, it is not a scientific concept, and as such its definition can be fuzzy and imprecise (Ronningstam 2011). However, it does have some salient features that are regularly cited. For example, a core inner self that is overwhelmingly self-referential, desirous of attention, and desperate for the world to admire him or her, but only relating to others and society as objects to be used, with little or no capacity for empathy. Or someone who is incapable of self-refection, sees any criticism as a personal slight, and often views himself or herself as a victim in the face of the mistreatment of others. One can see from these broad-stroke descriptions why it is easy to diagnose Donald Trump, or Generation Snowflake, as people with NPD.

Lasch on Narcissism

Christopher Lasch avoided such crude labelling by deploying a more nuanced approach. In *The Culture of Narcissism* he warns us not to be too crude in our understanding of narcissism, as it may not be a simple matter of causation: 'The concept of narcissism provides us not with a ready-made psychological determinism but a way of understanding the impact of recent social changes' (Lasch 1991: 50). To give a flavour of his approach, I want to highlight some of his observations.

Lasch argued that aspects of clinical NPD were no longer markedly different from the personality type emerging from the culture of post-war American society. More broadly, Lasch observed that every age develops its own peculiar form of pathology which expresses itself in an exaggerated form, through the underlying structure of the character or personality type of its time. For example, the prevalent pathology of the day can present as a heightened sense of normality. In Freud's time, the central therapeutic problems were hysteria and obsessional neurosis, illnesses of the individual psyche that—it is argued—were born of too much repression and order, in extremis manifestations of the disciplining mechanisms of early capitalist society and the rigid nature of bourgeois morality. Lasch wanted to explore how one prevalent pathology of the 1970s—NPD—was reflected in new forms of psychological personality emerging in reaction to America's radical economic and social changes.

To remind ourselves of Lasch's contemporary world: his book was published at the end of a period of enormous political turmoil. Everything that had previously been known seemed to be in flux. It was written in the aftermath of the 1968 youth uprisings, which had overthrown past certainties. There was the emergence of the 'new left': student revolutionaries at home and anti-imperialist revolutionaries abroad. Feminism was challenging traditional notions of family, and a hedonistic counterculture challenged hierarchy and authority. This was the period of the Vietnam War, Watergate, and Woodstock, resulting in questioning of mainstream political arrangements. Huge technological changes had a massive disruptive effect on traditional patterns of work and production. Consumerism appeared to be creating a version of individualism many found threatening to a collective outlook.

This fragmentation hastened the collapse of older community ties through which individuals had traditionally realised themselves. Lasch believed that for the self to flourish it needed social ties, which allowed the individual to go beyond himself. The removal of those ties leaves the individual abandoned and needy. Lasch noted of his contemporary subject of study:

> His apparent freedom from family ties and institutional constraints does not free him to stand alone or glory in his individuality. On the contrary, it contributes to his insecurity. (Lasch 1991: 10)

Lasch also noted that the 'age of fracture' had left society stuck in a treadmill of the present, in which any sense of historical continuity had been lost, leaving us alienated from the past and looking instead towards an anxious and unknowable future. This affected the individual's sense of self:

> It makes sense to live only for the moment, to fix our eyes on our own 'private performance,' to become connoisseurs of our own decadence, to cultivate a 'transcendental self-attention'. (Lasch 1991: 6)

When Lasch described this new personality, grabbing greedily at any momentary sense of personal well-being, he identified the emergence of the 'therapeutic sensibility' (Lasch 1991: 7) alongside narcissism. This phenomenon is familiar to us now with the subsequent explosion of therapy culture, and this quote still rings true:

Having no hope of improving their lives in any of the ways that matter, people have convinced themselves that what matters is psychic self-improvement; getting in touch with their feelings, eating health food; taking lessons in ballet or belly-dancing; immersing themselves in the wisdom of the East; jogging, learning how to 'relate,' overcoming the 'fear of pleasure'. (Lasch 1991: 4)

Lasch says that these activities—although harmless enough in themselves—become wrapped up in the narcissist rhetoric of 'finding the real you'. This signifies a retreat from political change and collective endeavour.

The Culture of Narcissism was in many ways prescient and had an enormous impact in its time. Extraordinarily, this left-wing academic work was a bestseller and featured in a spread in *People* magazine. Its author had an audience with President Jimmy Carter, who used its themes in his famous 'Crisis of Confidence' speech. However, the book's popularity has bred subsequent confusion. Superficial reading has allowed both conservatives and liberals to claim it as supporting their political agendas. This indicates the richness of its themes; indeed, like all classics, it has become a pick 'n' mix treasure trove of insightful quotes. However, I think there are three key misreadings which have become barriers to allowing us to update Lasch's insights for today.

Lasch Misunderstood

First misreading: *narcissism as a clinical term is over-used to understand contemporary social trends and explain contemporary victimhood.*

Lasch seems to have unleashed a torrent of articles and books which use narcissism to describe and explain all of society's ills: often in a tone of cultural pessimism. A new book, Kirsten Dombek's *The Selfishness of Others: an essay on the fear of narcissism*, criticises Lasch in just these terms, accusing him of inciting a ubiquitous discourse of clichéd and lazy truisms that have ballooned into a sweeping and increasingly meaningless indictment of an entire culture. Similarly, psychologist and anthropologist

Michael Macoby believes 'narcissism has become a garbage can for every kind of egocentrism and selfishness' (Scharfenberg 2017).

Although this may be an accurate assessment, it seems unfair to blame Lasch's work for what Dombek terms the 'narcisphere': a thriving blogosphere of pop psychology that now routinely categorises entire swathes of the population as narcissists. She notes the ever-expanding swollen list of those so-labelled, with 'the disease of narcissism spreading like a virus' (Dombek 2016: 19). A taxonomy has emerged in which any and all brands of narcissism can be diagnosed by online tests: for example, *The Narcissist Next Door: do you know someone like this?* as well as niche forums and endless support groups, even for daughters of narcissistic mothers (Psychology Today 2017).

Interestingly, evidence of an alleged increase in narcissistic pathologies is supplied by counsellors and psychologists, who report that more and more people are seeking therapy for the trauma caused by narcissistic bosses and partners. To note, it is the very rise of the narcisphere (which claims Lasch as its mentor) that suggests a more modern model personality type: the psychologically needy and fragile victim with a heightened sense of grievance, who is always hard done by at the hands of others. And, ironically, the villain that is blamed by all these traumatised victims is narcissism.

Second misreading: *narcissism as the result of excessive individualism.*

The second misreading of Lasch is to take *The Culture of Narcissism* as a critique of excessive individualism, a reading especially prevalent in leftist commentators, such as David Brook's *The Road to Character* or Oliver James' *Selfish Capitalism*. Lasch's thesis is cited as evidence that neoliberal capitalism unleashed rampant and problematic individualism: creating a narcissistic and self-centred society of greedy consumers. However, Lasch was not attacking individualism at all. Rather his critique was that late capitalism *diminished* individualism into a mere hologram, robbed of independent agency, because the only way of realising one's ambition to be 'great' was to attract the attention and admiration of others.

His book was at least in part a counter to Tom Wolfe's 1976 *NY Magazine* cover story *The Me Decade and the Thrill of the Great Awakening,* which celebrated the cultural trends of the seventies as an outburst of vitality. Wolfe wrote of 'the greatest age of individualism in American history' (Wolfe 1976). Lasch saw these trends more negatively, arguing that a period of decadence threatened to destroy real individualism and replace it with toxic, narcissistic self-obsession. Lasch says that for the narcissist 'the world is a mirror'; whereas for the ideal 'rugged individualist' (whom he admired) the world is 'an empty wilderness to be shaped to his own design' (Lasch 1991: 10).

In this sense, Lasch's great insight was to reveal that the very basis of a healthy self was a strong, autonomous individual, whereas a culture that celebrated the individual, but lacked such a grounding, would ultimately have the unintended consequence of damaging the self.

Third misreading: *narcissism as a code word for excessive vanity and/or self-love.*

The third misunderstanding of Lasch is to conclude that narcissism is all about self-love. However, he repeatedly explained that narcissists have very little ego: they lack confidence in their own judgement, have a weak sense of self unless constantly admired, and have a shallow, insubstantial, personality.

This misreading of narcissism also misses some important nuances, even in terms of the origin of the word. Returning to the original myth, we see that when Narcissus fixated on the floating image in the water, he failed to recognise the image, but rather mistook it for a separate being, with whom he fell in love. When he tried to embrace his loved one though, the image disappeared in ripples. In this sense, Narcissus did not know himself well enough even to recognise his own mirror image. His self-love was illusory; the self that he loved was watery, insubstantial, and unobtainable, if not fatal.

Beyond Greek myth, therapists report that their narcissist patients experience a withered inner life and feel inwardly vacated or hollowed out. Thus, their malignant self-love (close to self-hatred) stems from a sense of emptiness and drives narcissists to hunger for authentic emotional experiences to fill their inner void. This drives them to compensate by creating an external false self, brimming with confidence on the surface, but dependent on the admiration of others and external recognition to prop up this façade.

It is this aspect of narcissism which I feel is most prevalent in contemporary society. My intuition is that the young of today are not satisfied with the hollowed out and meaning-lite version of the self which is on offer in the twenty-first century. It is this shift, post-Lasch, that I now want to explore.

Generation Body

Many have noted that the self-esteem movement is a major culprit in narcissistic trends amongst younger generations. From the 1980s onwards, adults were encouraged to heap praise on children and teenagers regardless of whether they had achieved or accomplished anything worthwhile. This was undoubtedly a well-meaning attempt to give the young greater confidence. But perhaps this approach has rebounded and added to their sense that their self-worth is only superficial. The popular critique of the self-esteem movement is that it has led to an overly pumped-up youth, full of themselves, with an entitled sense of self-worth. But this is only partly true in what is a more complex story.

In *The Self Under Siege*, Robert Firestone assesses the literature of self-esteem and shows that children who are offered compliments for skills they have not yet mastered or talents they do not possess, often feel as though they have received no praise at all (Firestone et al. 2013). Firestone notes they are in fact left feeling emptier and less secure than before. The more we massage egos indiscriminately, the more they doubt their abilities and crave real recognition for their true selves.

It seems to me that the conundrum is not that we have socialised a generation of egoists, but that we have a generation which yearns for a more rooted, anchored, and substantial sense of self. Although this drive to make more of themselves, to pursue what Charles Taylor calls 'the ideal of authenticity' (Taylor 1992), is a positive one, too often their efforts take alienated, warped, and deviant forms, hemmed in by narcissistic tendencies. Strikingly, this new quest for the authentic self is rarely focused on enriching one's interior life as a way of transcending self-preoccupation. Rather, it tends to take on an overtly exterior form, often as public performance. As US public intellectual Christine Rosen notes, the Delphic Oracle's maxim 'know thyself' has now become 'show thyself' (Rosen 2017). For example, the quest to make more of yourself often involves the conscious construction of a 'new you' that involves a focus on the body.

In some ways, the body has replaced the soul, heart, and mind as the site for moral enhancement of the self. American social historian Joan Jacob Brumberg gives a fascinating account of the changing self over a century by comparing diaries of adolescent girls (Brumberg 1997). For example, an 1892 diary entry is full of moral language about improving the diarist's own character:

> I resolved not to talk about myself or my feelings. To think before speaking. To work seriously. To be self restrained in conversation and action. Not to let my thoughts wander. To be dignified. To interest myself in others.

It is difficult to imagine the charming and quaint last sentence of this quote being written today. A 1982 diary entry, by a teenager of the same age, paints a different picture:

> I will try and make myself better in any way I can. I will lose weight, get new lenses, a new haircut, makeup, clothes and accessories.

Here the focus on making oneself better by focusing on externals, specifically the adornment of the body, is starkly demonstrated.

Today's construction of the self, however, is far more drastic and visceral even than getting new lenses or dieting. So, for example, plastic surgery and body modification have increased exponentially since the 1990s. Breast augmentation, liposuction, filler and Botox treatments are now more common than therapy (see Williams 2016). And patients are getting ever younger. A report by the Nuffield Council of Bioethics notes the emergence of cosmetic surgery apps targeted at nine-year olds (*Guardian* 2017). Teenagers are no longer worried about wearing braces; there has been an explosion in cosmetic dentistry amongst under-18s in the US, thought to be due to children wanting good teeth for selfies. In

2017, according to the American facial plastic surgery industry, 55 per cent of facial plastic surgeons saw patients who want to look better in selfies in their practices (up 13 per cent from 2016) (Facial Plastic and Reconstructive Surgery 2018).

These exterior-focused examples are not about finding the real self, but are often about appropriating someone else's body. This trend is not about self-love but is driven by dissatisfaction with one's own body and the imperfections which come with it. According to Dr Neelam Vashi, director of the Boston University Cosmetic and Laser Centre: 'A new phenomenon called 'Snapchat dysmorphia' has emerged where patients are seeking out surgery to help them appear like the filtered versions of themselves' (Oddity Central—Collecting Oddities 2018). Advocates from psycho-analysis suggest that cosmetic surgery can address body-confidence issues, but admit that patients are rarely satisfied, and end up coming back for more and more work; they do not feel at home in their own bodies (sciencenordic.com 2018).

Complaints about cosmetic surgery can often have a whiff of class snobbery, especially when feminists sniffily disapprove of those aspiring to a Barbie figure, boob jobs, or acquiring a Kim Kardashian bottom. But even the more 'progressive' backlash against everything from plastic surgery to selfies can be equally body obsessed. The feminist meme of posting ugly selfies seems to be in defiance of body-beauty standards, proving that looks can be deceiving. Yet once more they make the physical manifestation of self their focus (Mail Online 2018). Is it really the 'authentic' you, to post pictures of yourself without make-up, using the #nofilter hashtag to signal just how honest you are? Even political activism has become body obsessed. In her book *What Women Want: fun, freedom and an end to feminism*, Ella Whelan offers hilarious examples of feminism's obsession with genitalia, in which 'Pussy hats are not a euphemism' and women's marches feature placards of 'hand drawn signs showing uteruses, vaginas, boobs and chants that rhyme with pussy and cunt', to illustrate a historic shift in feminism. If once the movement was about the 'fight for a woman's right to leave behind dishcloths, baby bottles and kitchenware of the private sphere and be as much part of the public world as any man' now we are 'pushing women back into the bathroom with a mirror in hand. Encouraging them to find meaning in staring up their own arseholes' (Whelan 2017: 27–53).

Discussing the new phenomena of 'Gross-out Feminism' and how it is dragging women back 'to the state of visceral, biological creatures', Whelan quotes Caitlin Moran's semi-autobiographical novel *How to Build a Girl* in which Moran boasts, 'There is no such thing as oversharing'. And this over-sharing makes a particular virtue of talking about women's bodies; fast becoming a feminist orthodoxy:

> Women who don't discuss their bodily fluid on Twitter or write about it in articles are oppressed, restrained and exhibiting symptoms of internalised misogyny, apparently. (Whelan 2017: 41)

And while there may be pitying disdain for those who seek to change their bodies through nip-and-tuck, other examples of surgical intervention however are viewed as welcome, as a new form of liberation. Arguably, the increasing prevalence of transgenderism and the huge increase in children and teenagers being referred to gender identity clinics (the number has quadrupled in the last five years) are also focused on the body as a site of change. This, just like body enhancement, is about appropriating another body to be one's true self; the focus on the *real me* means doing drastic violence to one's own physical being (e.g. amputation of genitalia, etc.). Josie Appleton, in her excellent blog post on this, notes how the transgender phenomenon suggests that the true self takes a form that is entirely physical. To quote a number of transsexuals: 'I want to look like what I am'; 'I must transform the body I have so it fits as closely as possible to my image of myself' (Appleton 2017). Appleton notes that the person you are is no longer a matter of 'spirit, or vocations or actions or choices in the world.' Instead, who you are is reduced to altering physical form. Your true self is another body.

A further, dark side of this new search for self, as focused on the literal self (i.e. the body), is illustrated in exponentially growing modern pathologies such as eating disorders and self-harm. Some believe that modern maladies such as anorexia reflect growing narcissistic social trends. Dame Joan Bakewell got into trouble for making such a point when she argued in an interview with the *Sunday Times* that anorexia may well be 'a sign of the overindulgence of our society, over-introspection, narcissism really' (Bakewell 2016). She was forced to apologise, but much academic psychiatric literature concurs that there is a consistent link between narcissism and eating disorder symptoms.[1] One study by the *International Journal of Eating Disorders* (entitled *Narcissism and narcissistic defences in eating disorder*) makes the point that sufferers, in explaining their behaviour, often deploy the narcissistic 'poor me' defence. Seeing themselves as misunderstood martyrs, subject to intolerable demands, always victims of others, patients sarcastically conclude 'So it's OK for you to hurt me but I can't hurt myself?' (Waller et al. 2007).

More recently, the pathology du jour is self-harm, which involves a range of deliberate behaviours including cutting, burning, bruising, inserting objects into the skin, reopening wounds, and breaking bones. At the end of 2016, a report by the National Society for the Prevention of Cruelty to Children (NSPCC) in the UK, using data obtained through Freedom of Information Requests, discovered that 18,778 11–18 year olds were admitted to hospital for self-harm between 2015 and 2016. (Sputniknews.com 2016). Although we should be wary of NSPCC panics, every indication outside of hospital admissions is that the problem is widespread and growing. A recent *Times Education Supplement* survey of 1100 school leaders found that incidents of self-harm had risen to include half of *all schools*, including primary schools. Where self-harm used to be limited to girls in private schools, teachers now report that there is a cluster in every class in all types of schools (Tes.com 2017).

Self-Display

There has been another interesting shift in relation to self-harm. Despite the visible physicality of self-harm, it has traditionally been a clandestine activity: self-harmers previously went to great lengths to hide their scars, wearing long-sleeved tops and polo neck jumpers to cover their wounds. Recently, by contrast, self-harm has become a performance on social media, and there is a new craze for livestreaming self-harm. One

---

[1] See evidence presented by Kathryn Garden and Joseph Dombeck from the department of psychology at N. Dakota State University.

commentator has written about mothers worrying that such overt displays might produce a contagion, noting instances of their children's friends 'self-harming, then posting photographs of their injuries online for their peers to comment on...' (Funnell 2013).

Emily Tanner notes (Tanner 2015) that there is a 'disturbing subculture on Instagram in which young people are sharing messages which promote dangerous (even deadly) behaviours', sharing images and pictures which idealise suicide and anorexia, such as excessively skinny bodies under the notion of 'thinspo', an abbreviation for the internet slang 'thinspiration'. Lasch famously wrote, in an age long before selfies and live streaming, that 'we cannot help responding to others as if their actions—and our own—were being recorded and simultaneously transmitted to an unseen audience' (Lasch 1991: 47). But now, it is not only *as if* we are recorded; our pathologies are actually videos.

While experts are worried that these trends are normalising self-harming behaviours and leading to the proliferation of pro-anorexia or cutting online-chat rooms and discussion boards, there is a broader and alarming trend towards exhibitionism of psycho-social pathologies. Dr Stan Kutcher, an adolescent-psychiatry expert, argues, 'The pendulum has swung from "let's never talk about it and let's never educate ourselves about it" to "let's everyone blab about it"' (cited in Bine 2013). This can make psychological suffering seem an attractive, attention-seeking, condition to define oneself by.

The move from treating one's own psychological illnesses as covert and secretive to being publicly open may have positive aspects. One constructive interpretation of online communities of sufferers would be that they are an attempt to go beyond the empty self; to transcend *me* and find new forms of solidarity. But the problem with these safe spaces for self-harmers is that in order to be accepted into the group you need to advertise and illustrate your suffering in a variety of melodramatic ways. They encourage the young to parade their illnesses as a way of revealing 'the real you': one is incited to literally show one's scars.

This feeds into a broader trend in terms of how the project of the self has taken a glaringly narcissistic and performative turn, far beyond the psycho-social realm. The phenomenon has a mirror image in the world of social relations and political engagement. Take the preponderance of political selfies: these are no longer confined to the trivial. Today, no demonstration, riot, terrorist attack, or natural disaster is complete without accompanying selfie evidence that '*I* was there'. The pervasiveness of campaign-trail selfies in the build-up to the US 2016 presidential bid led the *New York Times* to christen it the 'Selfie Election':

> When candidates oblige so many people, some requesting multiple takes to straighten that smile, square a double chin or get a pesky photo bomber out of the frame, are they losing the chance to clarify a policy position, listen to concerns or even just look a voter in the eye? (The New York Times 2015)

Some try and talk up the phenomenon as positive, arguing, for example, that 'in selfie solidarity campaigns, the intimate encounter with the face and body is mobilized to reduce distance, to encourage identification, or orchestrate compassion' (Stanford University Press Blog 2015). Meanwhile, Derek Conrad Murray, Assistant Professor of History of Art and Visual Culture at the University of California at Santa Cruz, argues that individually, selfies often 'appear rather banal, commonplace, and benign.' But, seen through the lens of feminist representational politics, he wonders 'whether the urge to compulsively self-image is mere narcissism, or a politically oppositional and aesthetic form of resistance... a post-Third Wave feminist movement that reclaims the female body' (Murray 2015).

Regardless of such apologists attempting to dress selfie trends in positive terms as a new vehicle for 'self-fashioning', many intuitively realise that the contemporary political personality is marked by a shallow, superficial, and ersatz flimsiness. Again, this propels people into a search for greater substance and fuels a desire to add more authenticity to themselves. But once again, just as in Lasch's 1970s, twenty-first-century society seems unable to validate people for what they might become through achievement, work, social or political accomplishments: interaction with or on the world. Instead we have seen the growing prominence, social endorsement, and institutionalisation of identity politics, which celebrates people for their cultural, biological, and ethnic selves. And this really is where new forms of narcissism are most prevalent.

I Identify As

Asking how to make 'more of me' is a valid quest, but we need to critique a culture that rarely provides answers in terms of developing a richer interior life, reading and debating more, acting on the world, trying to transcend one's own preoccupations. Self-sacrifice has been usurped by victimhood. Against this backdrop, and abandoned to their own devices, for many young people searching for more depth, the best way to bolster the self often centres on dwelling on what makes them a 'real', standout, victim. And this can result in them appropriating others' experience, suffering, and even bodies.

Take the historic political fight for equal rights; today usurped by the discourse around identity politics and intersectionality. In this world, for the selfhood associated with various 'identity' communities to be valued, credibility is based on a hierarchy of political suffering, often demanding that victim-status is made visible, spelt out, and announced: 'as a woman', 'as a black man', 'as a Muslim', and so on. US writer Cathy Young argues this has led to a 'reverse caste system in which a person's status and worth depends entirely on their perceived oppression and disadvantage' (Young 2015). This has been caricatured as an 'oppression Olympics', one-upmanship that is often verbalised in debates to gain advantage and silence others based on the weight of the many intersectionalities of race, gender, socioeconomic status, disability, and so on, to determine who has it the worst. This can lead to the peculiar and undoubtedly unintended consequence of encouraging people to seek out performative selfhood as victims.

Or consider the grotesquely fascinating story of Rachel Dolezal, a white American activist who effectively 'blacked up' to pass as a woman of colour. Her defence, 'I identify as black', is an appropriation of a black physical persona to express her true anti-racist self. It seems that Martin Luther King's dream—that his children would not be judged by the colour of their skin, but by their character—has now been replaced by a physical and visible sense of self based on skin pigmentation.

This may be an extreme case. However, many gender-critical feminists accuse transgender activists of appropriating women's lives; cisgender feminists have long accused trans-women of 'appropriating female dress' or 'appropriating women's identities', often through demonstrations of caricatured femininity: reducing what it means to be a woman to attachments to stiletto shoes and make-up; small boys who like pink and dressing up in tutus are assumed to be signs of a girl struggling to get out of the wrong body.

This trend of appropriating the self from external sources is also apparent in the way that many 'Social Justice Warriors' treat the past and history: regularly plundering the hardships of earlier generations to claim as their own. In the 'Rhodes Must Fall' controversy at Oxford University, highly privileged BME students from one of the best universities in the world are happy to appropriate the suffering of colonialism and slavery into their contemporary personal stories. Annie Teriba, a history and politics student, declared that:

> There's a violence to having to walk past the statue [of Rhodes] every day on the way to your lectures, there's a violence to having to sit with paintings of former slave holders whilst writing your exams. (HuffPost UK 2015)

Making the brutality meted out to the bodies of ancestors part of one's own narrative can lend weight to contemporary political grievances. Dalia Gebrial and Chi Chi Shi write of:

> The festering, rotting wound [that the statue of Cecil Rhodes represents]… is the ideology of white supremacy…and the colonial apologism that refuses to heal it, can co-exist alongside our black and brown bodies. (Discover Society 2015)

These declarations of anguish, dependent on performative constructions which merge historic horrors with the present-day self-as-victim, may feel real to the individuals concerned but have a fake quality to them. They are forgeries of selfhood which, although attempting to personify the real thing, are objectively insubstantial. Perhaps it is a tacit or semiconscious awareness of the superficiality and inauthenticity of these claims that leads to the increasingly brittle defences of who owns identities. For all the fluidity seemingly available to a generation who now routinely start sentences with the phrase 'I identify as…', in fashionable disputes over cultural appropriation, identities are walled off and ferociously guarded by self-appointed gatekeepers. And these identity gatekeepers once again often centre on superficial aspects of self.

How ironic that a political culture in which many appropriate other bodies and personalities to bolster their own self-identity exists alongside a tendency to rigidly monitor others who dare appropriate 'our' symbols of cultural identity. But maybe it is telling that the defence of the self today often means policing the most trivial manifestations of identity, such as clothes and hairstyles. The script is familiar: denunciations of white (in the most part) celebrities for appropriation are now a regular part of the entertainment and fashion landscape. Singer Selena Gomez has been slammed for wearing an Indian bindi; fashion designer Marc Jacobs was attacked for styling models in colourful dreadlocks; fashion house Valentino and high-street brand Mango were both criticised for failing to use African models to promote African-inspired clothes.[2] But in this new ritual, when supermodels and popstars are castigated—for example, for dressing as geisha—is there not a danger of suggesting that the Japanese self is reducible to black wigs and white face make-up? Are those drinking tequila while wearing sombreros really stealing a core part of Mexican self-identity?

There has been something of a minor backlash against the trend. When white American teenager Keziah Daum posted a picture of herself dressed up for prom night wearing a sexy, figure-hugging, high mandarin collar *qipao* ('cheongsam' in Cantonese), an Asian peer tweeted 'My culture is not your goddam prom dress' and Daum became the target of tens of thousands of tweets accusing her of racism. However, before long it became clear that people in China saw her wearing the dress as a compliment, and writer Anna Chen pointed out that simply saying this was appropriation of Chinese fashion was actually rather crude anyway: 'if anything, the qipao represents power and class, not race, and certainly not the culture of some exploited underclass' (Chen 2018).

---

[2] Even eating has become a political minefield, with college cafeterias denounced for serving samosas, kebabs, or burritos. In the US, one of the highest profile cultural rows has centred on white girls in Oregon selling tacos; there is even a 'Feminist Guide to Being a Foodie Without Being Culturally Appropriative'.

Despite this recognition that cultural appropriation can be simplistic and often essentialising, it has still become a routine requirement of identity politics to proclaim and perform identity visibly, and to complain about usurpers. The body once more is the focus for political struggle. Tressie McMillan Cottom, an assistant professor of sociology at Virginia Commonwealth University, reacting to complaints from black feminists that Miley Cyrus has appropriated black dance ('twerking') at the MTV Video Music Awards a few years ago, went on to write a treatise in *Slate* arguing that 'To celebrate herself, Miley Cyrus used other women's bodies as a joke—women who look like me...' (McMillan Cottom 2013). Meanwhile Yomi Adegoke, co-author of *Slay in Your Lane: the black girl bible*, wrote a *Guardian* article tellingly entitled *Why does a black butt only look good in white skin?* In reaction to Jennifer Lopez and Iggy Azalea's big booty ditty, Adegoke complained that physical 'attributes that black women have so long been shamed for have finally been given...a new Aryan aesthetic...seal of approval due' (Adegoke 2014). Regardless of who is appropriating whose body in these public spats, it is depressing that anti-racism and selfhood seem so preoccupied with biological physique. Katy Perry, who can always be relied on to capture contemporary regressive trends, recently proclaimed her outrage at trendy new Braid Bar hair salons and combined this with a *mea culpa* for her own crime of wearing cornrows (Stolworthy 2017). In her cringe-worthy apology to the black and minority ethnic (BME) community she said that she realised her guilt when a 'politically woke friend' explained the 'power in black women's hair.' This sums up today's political degeneration: black power has been reduced to hair power.

Recognise Me

Just as we have witnessed the rise of identities constructed around the display of correct signifiers of cultural ownership, today's political activism is overly preoccupied with narcissistic demands for recognition in contrast to objective analysis or universal principles. 'Recognise my experience' demands that others acquiesce to a particular subjective narrative experience, and any debate can easily be characterised as a challenge to the very existence of different identity groups. For example, in debates about how to fight racism, it is now routine to denounce those who argue for a colour-blind approach (based on a commitment to universalism and equality) as perpetrating racist 'erasure' (Williams 2011). Writer and broadcaster Afua Hisch has complained: 'I've had enough of white people who try to deny my experience'. She concludes that those 'I don't see colour' commentators who disagree with her about the prevalence of racism in Britain today are really 'arguing over the very fact of my existence, the reality of my daily life' (Hirsch 2018).

Similarly, in the febrile transgender wars, it is never enough to accept that someone has transitioned to a new gender. It is demanded that we positively affirm their decision, change our linguistic rules to accommodate particular pronoun preferences, and anyone who dares to commit the crime of 'misgendering' is accused of 'denying transgender people's existence' or 'inflicting gender violence' on them. In an article entitled *The issue with misgendering* one commentator cites Charles Taylor's insight that 'Recognition is intimately tied to identity, and the understanding and validation of one's self' to critique the now (in)famous Canadian academic Jordan Peterson, concluding that his 'ridicule of and refusal to recognize gender-neutral pronouns implicitly asserts… "I don't respect you, I know better than you, you do not exist, you only exist on my terms, I tell you who you are"' (Imaizzle 2016).

Of course, as social animals, humans desire recognition from each other. Who wants to be ignored? But one thing that has changed in the narcissistic turn is that recognition has lost its indirect character. It is no longer based on the desire to have one's ideas admired, one's achievements lauded, one's hard work—even behind the scenes—appreciated; even having one's views argued against—a sign they matter even if disagreed with. Today—now that the self tends to be shorn of external achievements—recognition is more direct, literal, and visceral. Recognise my worth as me: no matter what. This can only open up a world in which the self is permanently wounded by criticism—always experienced as an existential assault on the self—and inevitably leads to a defensive retreat from any meaningful engagement with others for fear of encountering anyone who might challenge the core, fragile you resting on your superficial identity-based lived experience.

This is a cultural turn worth resisting and to conclude, let us consider some factors that remind us that the self can be enhanced in ways other than focusing on showing yourself and demanding public recognition for me, me, me. Historically, genuine self-worth may have often gone unnoticed. But this does not mean that people did not have an impact. To quote George Elliot, in her famous last line of *Middlemarch*, reflecting on the life of the novel's much-loved heroine Dorothea Brooke:

> [F]or the growing good of the world is partly dependent on unhistoric acts; and that things are not so ill with you and me as they might have been, is half owing to the number who lived faithfully a hidden life, and rest in unvisited tombs.

I understand that telling today's younger generations that they should aspire to living hidden lives is unlikely to inspire activity. Nobody actually wants to go unnoticed, or to be invisible. But there is something heroic in the act of doing right for the sake of doing right; not out of some desire to be recognised for having done so. Affirmation for achieving something that transcends the self is worth far more than affirmation just for being you. A few years ago, David McCullen Jr. gave a commencement speech to high school graduates, known as 'You are not special' (after it went viral). He ends his speech with the following words: 'Climb the mountain so you can see the world; not so the world can see you.'

McCullen was referring to the story of why there is no photograph, no selfie, of Edmund Hillary upon his conquest of Everest, while there is a photo of Sherpa Tenzing, ice-pick held aloft. Tenzing says that he offered to take Hillary's photo, but that Hillary declined, instead taking pictures of the surrounding mountains and planning routes over the peaks. As New Zealand writer Mike White asks: 'Can you imagine that today? Someone achieving something so momentous, but shrugging off the chance to immortalise it, not even turning the camera on himself to snap something of the occasion?' (White 2016). Of course, what immortalises Hilary is his action, not any photos of the achievement.

As we have seen, the problem when seeking recognition and admiration for the self without achievement is just how exposing it is. No wonder people experience criticism as such a threatening and raw assault on the self (rather than a creative engagement with their views or actions). It helps explain the preferred retreat to the contemporary halls of mirrors: echo chambers and safe spaces. In the *New York Times*, in the wake of Trump's election, Mark Lilla, Professor of Humanities at Columbia, wrote an article entitled 'The End of Identity Liberalism'. He said:

> We have produced a generation of liberals and progressives narcissistically unaware of the conditions outside their self defined groups, and indifferent to the task of reaching out to Americans in every walk of life. At a very young age children are being encouraged to talk about their individual identities, even before they have them. (Lilla 2016)

Perhaps that is true, but I suspect these self-defined groups are more engaged in protecting their flimsy identities: their indifference to 'reaching out' more a by-product of their insecure selves than attributable to arrogant narcissistic selfishness. Maybe in updating Lasch's thesis, we should think about how identity politics and its mirror pathologies can only thrive when bubble wrapped in safe spaces, populated solely by 'people like us' and 'allies' who agree with us. Maybe Narcissus is not the main problem from the myth. Rather, today's issues are best represented by the unrequited love of Echo, because it is the sealed-off echo chambers which are destroying the self in contemporary society.

References

Adegoke, Y. (2014). Why does a black butt only look good in white skin? *Guardian*. [Online] Retrieved November 24, 2018, from https://www.theguardian.com/commentisfree/2014/sep/23/why-black-bum-only-good-white-skin-cultural-appropriation.

Appleton, J. (2017). Transsexualism and the breakdown of personality. *Notes on Freedom*. [Online] Retrieved November 18, 2018, from https://notesonfreedom.com/2017/06/21/transsexualism-and-the-breakdown-of-personality/.

Bakewell, J. (2016). Anorexia is narcissism. *The Sunday Times*.

Bine, A. (2013). Social media is redefining 'depression'. *The Atlantic*. [Online] Retrieved November 18, 2018, from https://www.theatlantic.com/health/archive/2013/10/social-media-is-redefining-depression/280818/.

Brumberg, J. (1997). *The body project.* New York: Random House.
Chen, A. (2018). An American woman wearing a Chinese dress is not cultural appropriation. *Guardian.* [Online] Retrieved November 24, 2018, from https://www.theguardian.com/commentisfree/2018/may/04/american-woman-qipao-china-cultural-appropriation-minorities-usa-dress.
Discover Society. (2015). The violence of liberalspeak: Eulogizing Cecil Rhodes, the 'businessman' and 'munificent benefactor'. [Online] Retrieved November 24, 2018, from https://discoversociety.org/2015/12/01/the-violence-of-liberalspeak-eulogizing-cecil-rhodes-the-businessman-and-munificent-benefactor/.
Dombek, K. (2016). *The selfishness of others: An essay on the fear of narcissism.* London: Faber and Faber.
Facial Plastic and Reconstructive Surgery. (2018). AAFPRS—Media resources—Statistics. [Online] Retrieved November 18, 2018, from https://www.aafprs.org/media/stats_polls/m_stats.html.
Firestone, R., Firestone, L., & Catlett, J. (2013). *The self under siege.* New York: Routledge.
Funnell, N. (2013). Digital self-harm: Teens tap out an online cry for help. *The Age.* [Online] Retrieved November 18, 2018, from https://www.theage.com.au/opinion/digital-self-harm-teens-tap-out-an-online-cry-for-help-20130819-2s7av.html.
The Guardian. (2017). Protect children from online cosmetic surgery apps, say campaigners. [Online] Retrieved November 18, 2018, from https://www.theguardian.com/society/2017/jun/22/protect-children-from-online-cosmetic-surgery-apps-say-campaigners.
Hirsch, A. (2018). I've had enough of white people who try to deny my experience. *Guardian.* [Online] Retrieved November 24, 2018, from https://www.theguardian.com/commentisfree/2018/jan/24/white-people-tv-racism-afua-hirsch.
HuffPost UK. (2015). Oxford students call for 'racist' statue's removal. [Online] Retrieved November 24, 2018, from https://www.huffingtonpost.co.uk/2015/07/13/students-call-racist-oxford-university-statue-removal_n_7784810.html.
HuffPost UK. (2017). Is Donald Trump mentally ill? 3 professors of psychiatry ask President Obama to conduct 'a full medical and neuropsychiatric evaluation'. [Online] Retrieved November 18, 2018, from https://www.huffingtonpost.com/richard-greene/is-donald-trump-mentally_b_13693174.html.
Imaizzle. (2016). The issue with misgendering. *The Politics of Language.* [Online] Retrieved November 24, 2018, from https://politicsoflanguage.wordpress.com/2016/12/08/the-issue-with-misgendering/.

Lasch, C. (1991). *The culture of narcissism*. New York: W.W. Norton.
Lilla, M. (2016). The end of identity liberalism. *The New York Times*. [Online] Retrieved November 24, 2018, from https://www.nytimes.com/2016/11/20/opinion/sunday/the-end-of-identity-liberalism.html.
Mail Online. (2018). Images of pretty girls pulling ugly faces sweep the web. [Online] Retrieved November 18, 2018, from http://www.dailymail.co.uk/femail/article-4208130/Images-pretty-girls-pulling-ugly-faces-sweep-web.html#ixzz5FNd6XNaE.
McMillan Cottom, T. (2013). Brown body, white wonderland. *Slate Magazine*. [Online] Retrieved November 24, 2018, from https://slate.com/human-interest/2013/08/miley-cyrus-vma-performance-white-appropriation-of-black-bodies.html.
Murray, D. (2015). Notes to self: The visual culture of selfies in the age of social media. *Consumption Markets & Culture, 18*(6), 490–516.
The New York Times. (2015). Facing a selfie election, presidential hopefuls grin and bear it. [Online] Retrieved November 19, 2018, from https://www.nytimes.com/2015/07/05/us/politics/facing-a-selfie-election-presidential-hopefuls-grin-and-bear-it.html.
Oddity Central—Collecting Oddities. (2018). Snapchat dysmorphia—The trend of asking for plastic surgery to look like photo filters. [Online] Retrieved November 18, 2018, from http://www.odditycentral.com/news/snapchat-dysmorphia-the-trend-of-asking-for-plastic-surgery-to-look-like-photo-filters.html.
Parramore, L. (2017). 5 sensible things to do instead of obsessing about, and enabling Trump's narcissism. *Alternet*. [Online] Retrieved November 18, 2018, from https://www.alternet.org/trump-trauma/5-sensible-things-do-instead-obsessing-about-and-enabling-trumps-narcissism.
Psychology Today. (2017). The narcissist next door. [Online] Retrieved November 18, 2018, from https://www.psychologytoday.com/us/blog/your-personal-renaissance/201709/the-narcissist-next-door.
Ronningstam, E. (2011). Narcissistic personality disorder. *Journal of Psychiatric Practice, 17*(2), 89–99.
Rosen, C. (2017, Summer). Virtual friendship and the new. *The New Atlantis*.
Scharfenberg, D. (2017). Make narcissism great again. *Boston Globe*.
sciencenordic.com. (2018). Mental health problems worsen with cosmetic surgery. [Online] Retrieved November 18, 2018, from http://sciencenordic.com/mental-health-problems-worsen-cosmetic-surgery.
Sputniknews.com. (2016). Playground of abuse: Social media cause many kids to self-harm, says report. [Online] Retrieved November 18, 2018, from

https://sputniknews.com/society/201612091048372192-social-media-factor-charity/.

Stanford University Press Blog. (2015). The political consciousness of the selfie. [Online] Retrieved November 19, 2018, from http://stanfordpress.typepad.com/blog/2015/07/the-political-consciousness-of-the-selfie.html.

Stolworthy, J. (2017). Katy Perry apologises for cultural appropriation in past music video. *Independent*. [Online] Retrieved November 24, 2018, from https://www.independent.co.uk/arts-entertainment/music/news/katy-perry-apologises-for-cultural-appropriation-music-video-this-is-how-we-do-witness-a7785411.html.

Tanner, E. (2015). Girls, Instagram, and the glamorization of selfloathing. *Dissenting Voices*. [Online] Retrieved November 18, 2018, from https://digitalcommons.brockport.edu/cgi/viewcontent.cgi?article=1046&context=dissentingvoices.

Taylor, C. (1992). *The ethics of authenticity*. Harvard: Harvard University Press.

Tes.com. (2017). Self-harm has increased in almost half of schools, survey finds | *Tes News*. [Online] Retrieved November 18, 2018, from https://www.tes.com/news/self-harm-has-increased-almost-half-schools-survey-finds.

Waller, G., Sines, J., Meyer, C., Foster, E., & Skelton, A. (2007). Narcissism and narcissistic defences in the eating disorders. *International Journal of Eating Disorders, 40*(2), 143–148.

Whelan, E. (2017). *What women want: Fun, freedom, and an end to feminism*. London: Connor Court Publishing.

White, M. (2016). Me, me, me! The narcissism epidemic. *Noted*. [Online] Retrieved November 24, 2018, from https://www.noted.co.nz/currently/social-issues/me-me-me-the-narcissism-epidemic/.

Williams, M. (2011). Colorblind ideology is a form of racism. *Psychology Today*. [Online] Retrieved November 24, 2018, from https://www.psychologytoday.com/us/blog/culturally-speaking/201112/colorblind-ideology-is-form-racism.

Williams, Z. (2016). Me! Me! Me! Are we living through a narcissism epidemic? *The Guardian*.

Wilson, M., & Sibley, C. (2011). Narcissism creep?: Evidence for age-related differences in narcissism in the New Zealand general population—PDF. *Docplayer.net*. [Online] Retrieved November 18, 2018, from https://docplayer.net/36087811-Narcissism-creep-evidence-for-age-related-differences-in-narcissism-in-the-new-zealand-general-population.html.

Wolfe, T. (1976). The 'Me' decade and the third great awakening. *New York Magazine*.

Young, C. (2015). The strange world of social justice warriors—*Minding The Campus*. *Minding The Campus*. [Online] Retrieved November 20, 2018, from https://www.mindingthecampus.org/2015/06/18/the-strange-world-of-social-justice-warriors/.

11

New Forms of Alienation

Frank Furedi

The self can be considered (and has been in this collection) from a number of different aspects, and as a result, certain key themes resonate through the history of thinking about the self. There is one thing, however, that is the presupposition or starting point for many of these aspects of the self, and that is the fact that the very concept of the self is inconceivable without the self first feeling a need to assert itself: to attempt to find itself. The reason why the self needs to assert itself or try to find itself is because the self can only be a self thanks to its intuition of its own self-estrangement. The self knows itself as a self on the basis that it is estranged from itself and estranged from other selves. It is this that allows it to discern itself or pick itself out. In many important and fundamental ways this self-estrangement, this alienation of the self from itself and from its surroundings, is always lurking in the background of any discussion about the idea of the self. In many respects, people, as selves, for a very long time have understood that there is something that stands between them and the rest of world.

F. Furedi (✉)
University of Kent, Canterbury, UK

© The Author(s) 2019
A. Kennedy, J. Panton (eds.), *From Self to Selfie*,
https://doi.org/10.1007/978-3-030-19194-8_11

To take a contemporary example, the phenomenon of the selfie (see discussion in Chap. 10) is one of the most interesting examples of what I see as contemporary forms of alienation: at the very moment of snapping a selfie in the middle of a demonstration, while ostensibly participating in a public protest about some injustice, this act of taking a picture of oneself stands as a statement of one's alienation. The selfie says that in a very real way the picture of oneself is actually more important than whatever cause it was that was the motivation for going on the demonstration in the first place. The selfie represents, in this sense, a very clear accommodation to one's own state of alienation.

This willingness to embrace one's alienation is a very new development: one really without precedent. One of the fascinating, and hopeful, dimensions of human history up until now has been the existence of an ongoing, largely unconscious, struggle to settle accounts with self-alienation. People have written about it, they have struggled to overcome it, they have tried to find ways of neutralising its sometimes paralysing effects: when, for example, people are crippled with worry about how they are perceived, how they are seen, when they feel that only now and again can they slip off the social masks behind which, most of the time, they remain hidden.

There is a long and important history to be written of the struggle against self-alienation, and when it is, the message that must be recapitulated for the future is the truth that we do not have to accept and reconcile ourselves to the self: we do not have to exist in a distorted and limited fashion. On the contrary, we can try to change ourselves: self-changing is in itself critically important. In many respects one of the big differences between the way that the self is often perceived, both historically and now, and a more future-oriented vision of selfhood, is that the attempt to change oneself does not lead to us becoming obsessed with ourselves, but rather prompts us to think about creative ways in which we can leave ourselves behind. The difference is between the self as *given* or in some way assigned to us, and the self as something that we ourselves make or construct, that is, the self understood as a self-making being.

The act of self-making, however, cannot get off the ground without having some kind of external reference point to which we can relate (positively or negatively, as it may be). There is not enough space to consider this here in proper detail, but the question of the relationship of the self to external authority must be borne in mind because at the very moment that the self authorises itself (e.g. to embark on a project of self-changing), then at that moment the power of external authority disappears (for a full treatment, see Furedi 2013). To the extent that, by the 1960s and 1970s, people started to believe 'I am the authority' and no one else: they refused to recognise any external authority, anything beyond the self-determination of the self. This is positive, in one sense, in that it provides an illusion of liberation at least: an illusion that one is accountable only to oneself, not to anybody else. The problem, however, is that there must be a foundation, some kind of authority external to oneself, to provide meaning—a springboard—to the aspiration for liberation by grounding it in a way that provides some kind of existential security. If there is no anchorage for the self and it floats around, unmoored, looking purely within itself in terms of its own authority, lacking any external reference point on the horizon, then there is invariably a strong possibility that the self will sink, overwhelmed by insecurity and uncertainty. This phenomenon, a contemporary reality rather than a logical possibility, has been much discussed and referenced in a number of different ways in recent periods. (See in particular Lasch 1984.)

If we agree that it is authority that provides a context in which the self can be secure, then it follows, if the self has any kind of future in what I would call a liberal humanist sense (see below), that it is also very much linked to a quest for a new kind of authority: I think they go hand in hand. This is something I think we intuitively recognise in almost every contemporary social and political debate. The discussions and debates, to take one example, about fake news, on what is truth, are all in direct consequence of the fact that our culture contests authority to the point at which even the real and the fake become increasingly hard to distinguish and what divides them becomes more and more blurred.

I would argue that a liberal humanist notion of the self relies on self-changing, and also on a commitment to live freely. I think the commitment to live freely is really quite important: it is an ideal that was first developed by Aristotle in his idea of human flourishing where, in a sense, it is in the act of choosing and living freely that we become aware of what is good. According to one account:

for Aristotle moral virtue is a disposition to choose that is developed in the process of choosing. We do not do good acts because we are already good (at first anyway). We do good acts and in so doing become good. (Dworkin 1988: 42)

Humans are not born good but can become good essentially through making good choices about, and in, life and through living freedom. The idea of living freedom for ourselves in whatever modest, or immodest, way we choose to do it is fundamental. Human flourishing, which recognises that autonomy is both an end in itself, but also a means towards greater freedom and greater liberation, encompassed together, is really the context within which a liberal humanist conception of the self would like to see ourselves emerging and developing.

If we come back to the problem of alienation, historically there have been two important strategies developed to deal with it. One approach is the search to find oneself through the impulse to discover the *authentic* self: an impulse to clear a way through the various road blocks established by society and tradition on the way to becoming the 'real you'. Authenticity, and the search for it, has been a very persuasive way of dealing with alienation at certain points in time: principally the eighteenth century. At the same time, however, there was also the concomitant realisation that acting freely, and acting in accordance with the principles of freedom given by your autonomous self, was not only possible but necessary as a way of giving meaning to reason, rationality, and universal principles that all of humanity could live by. From this perspective, self-determination constitutes a process of discovery which enables us to flourish.

* * *

That said, it is important to realise that these are historically specific moments of realisation: insights into the self that are of their time. In the eighteenth century it is fair to say that, on balance, both the search for authenticity and also the desire to be autonomous were steps in the right direction: they were advancing together in a harmonious fashion. The apologetic or passive side to authenticity, which would emerge later on, was still relatively suppressed.

In this respect it might be interesting to consider Goethe's depiction of alienation in the *Sorrows of the Young Werther* (Goethe 1962), and just how different the approach Werther takes to his alienation through the struggle to be true to himself is to the way Werther's twenty-first-century equivalents tackle their alienation. Werther does not ask for respect or demand affirmation, he does not say look at me, pity me, accept me for what I am. Instead he ends up enacting a relatively heroic gesture—only a gesture, yes, but a relatively heroic one—in committing suicide. The literary theorist Georg Lukács argued that the enduring appeal of *Werther* was the protagonist's heroic refusal to compromise his principles, and that it was this unswerving devotion to his 'humanistic-revolutionary ideals' that was perceived as so subversive to the moral order (Lukács 1936).

Werther's letters to his friend Wilhelm tell of his joy in the simple society of the peasants of the village of Wahlheim ('forest home': a nod to Rousseau's noble primitive in the forest) and his love for Charlotte despite her engagement to Albert (who, being 11 years her senior speaks for the rules of society rather than the passions of youth). Excluded from the aristocratic circles of Weimar and kept at a distance from the now married Charlotte, Werther resolves the triangular dead end by shooting himself (with Albert's pistols) and is buried simply with no ceremony or mourners.

Now committing suicide in order to make a point—albeit a performative point—is not, of course, on par with taking a selfie, not on par with appearing wounded or taking offence, because there is something far far more meaningful communicated through that experience. The literature of the eighteenth century is best considered and approached, not just as simple fiction, but as what an imaginary eighteenth-century Foucault would have called 'the technology of the self'. For many people, literature, in particular the novel, was a way that enabled them, for the first time, to see the self for what it really was. The novel held up a mirror to what had previously only been intuited or hinted at, and it gave meaning to all those traces of oneself that one had been dying, up until then, to express or understand.

In this respect Rousseau's novel first published in 1761 *Julie, or the New Heloise* (Rousseau 1997) is particularly pertinent. Rousseau's novel was hugely popular at the time. Much like other epistolary novels of the age—*Werther* or

Richardson's *Clarissa*—the letters being written back and forth describe challenges to the conventional structures of bourgeois relationships. In Julie, the triangular relationship stands, again, in stark contrast to the basic bourgeois forms of stolid, limited, and limiting relations. On publication of *La Nouvelle Heloise* Rousseau was inundated with letters—written mainly by women, but also a couple of men—essentially writing to tell him that they felt he had written the novel just for them: that it was really about *them* in particular, that he had captured their inner selves in the novel, asking Rousseau if the main character was really him just pretending to be someone else (see Grogan 1999). The novel was something that allowed its readers, for the first time, to begin to see themselves.

This was a very important moment in the eighteenth century where two things were starting to happen at the same time. On the one hand, the novel was inextricably linked to the cultivation of the individual, particularly the cultivation of the individual self, because the novel provided a cultural medium through which that could occur. The characters in *La Nouvelle Heloise* and in *Werther* (and their readers) are involved in a psychological drama of reacting to society, but at the same time, also breaking with and rejecting the conventions of that society. The form of the break with convention is not strictly a simple rejection, but really a search for an alternative way of conducting their lives; it takes the form of a search for a new set of conventions. In this sense, at that historical moment, the attempt to find one's true self, to find out who one really is, has a very positive dimension. This is something that Lukács recognised in his *Goethe and his Age*, in his praise for the way novelists then were able to project a world in advance of where individuals were, and so encourage young people in particular to challenge themselves to be the authors of their own destiny, rather than the relatively passive objects of social convention (Lukács 1968).

In the literature of the period, then, there is still a clear connection between ideas of authorship and destiny as being something that one can embrace for one's self: it is possible to take responsibility. It is, I think, very important that both Werther himself and also other characters in the novel come to take responsibility for their lives. They might make very bad choices—suicide is clearly not a good choice—but they are making choices nonetheless and facing up to their consequences.

It is important to take notice as something else happens under the surface as the search for authenticity and the pursuit of autonomy evolve: two quite unexpected consequences begin to emerge.

First, little by little, the concept of autonomy acquires an increasingly psychological form: it is re-framed, re-packaged, in a therapeutic fashion so that it tends to become very much subject to therapeutic governance and to the governance of other individuals or third parties, in particular various forms of expertise (something that Lasch was perhaps the first to document: see Chap.10). Eventually, by the 1960s, we get to a point where one of the main goals of certain forms of therapy is to *help* the patient become autonomous. Autonomy is no longer the accomplishment of an individual but is instead to be realised through the assistance of external agency and support. Since that moment, helping people to achieve self-actualisation and self-esteem has become very much the business of professional experts (see Marx 1980). This turn towards assisted autonomy endows the concept of autonomy with a very new meaning.

Second—on the authenticity side of the equation—over time authenticity increasingly loses its romantic dimension. It is important to understand that the romantic dimension of authenticity, even in its most full-blooded Byronesque form, is not just escapism. There is an element of escapism, no doubt, but there is also an element of trying to make an imaginative leap forward through experimentation in art, literature, and lived experience. The imaginative dimension to authenticity is a crucial part of what makes it up. As with autonomy though, there is an analogous shift that occurs in the discussion of authenticity: generation by generation, there is a shift in emphasis away from the imaginative, aesthetic side. Less and less emphasis is placed on the attempt to find solutions to social problems in the domain of aesthetics, which for all its limitations at least has the merit of creating great art and great literature, and thereby providing other people with the artistic resources to imagine different possibilities for themselves.

As with autonomy, there is also a shift towards psychology; with psychology (e.g. in terms of authorial intent, the identity of the artist) starting to become ever more important in aesthetics, in the arts. What happens at a certain point is that the individual reaction to society, social norms, and social conventions, often promoted through the search for authenticity, mutates into a self-referential orientation. The self becomes its own cause and explanation, and contemporary culture adopts the attitude that it is worthy of uncritical, unquestioning, respect. This development has serious implications for the manner in which judgement is exercised.

For an individual to be an individual logically necessitates a degree of healthy scepticism on his part towards the judgement and opinion of others. But, until recently, the cultural value of judgement has not been questioned. What has begun to occur since the transformation of the self to becoming its own cause is that society has given the individual cultural permission to become estranged from the judgement of others. Many claim that, because I am not necessarily interested in the opinion of others, I might as well develop a different code of judgement for myself. In other words, I not only reject the conventions that exist, I will not be judged by, for example, those stolid bourgeois conventional norms: but I do not stop there. I also assert that there must be other criteria by which alone I can truly be judged, held to account, and deemed responsible.

Now, this is a method of proceeding (in trying to deal with self-alienation) that, while I do not endorse it necessarily, does have certain merits to it insofar as it still involves an assumption of responsibility. The ultimate direction, however, of the logic of authenticity, as it starts to unfold, should be clear: the next step is to move from saying I will not be judged by society to concluding that the reason I am not prepared to be judged by society is not just my whimsy, but down to the fact that social judgement is itself an inherently negative practice. In other words, at a certain point the refusal to submit oneself to public scrutiny, the desire to shield oneself from criticism, to shield oneself from exposure to what is essentially best understood as uncertainty, starts to be justified, no longer by saying that there are other or different criteria of judgement, but by stating that judgement is *in itself* a reprehensible phenomenon. At that point we arrive at non-judgementalism, which is now one of the key values of Western societies: the belief that society does not judge, everyone is free to do whatever they want, be whatever they want. At this critical point we find in non-judgementalism an artificial way of resolving the problem of self-alienation through artificially ridding the world of the uncertainty and risk that making any public judgement involves: of artificially ridding your own world of hurt and pain.

And, in the present moment, we see in the shielding of the self from the judgement of others effectively a request to accept me for what, whatever, I am. Accept me for who I am. It is in a real sense a plea or a demand for quarantine: for a safe space in which I can be myself. The most grotesque expression of this is to be seen in campus politics today, which is why there is so much discussion around it, but it is actually something that existed in society beforehand and has been in the water for a long time. At least since non-judgementalism became a value being taught to children in schools (see Furedi 2017): the very moment in which non-judgementalism trumps traditional values or the values of the previous generation. At that moment, judgement, which is a critical and fundamental element of autonomy, becomes pathologised to such a considerable extent that 'oh, you are so judgemental' is deployed as a routine social put down, a way of silencing others. The reason this is pathological is that society actually relies on judgement: without people who are prepared to be 'so judgemental' there is no way of us communicating within society, no society even. If we express ourselves in public, only to be met with polite indifference, not a genuine reaction in either a positive or a negative sense, but just inoffensive indifference, then there is no dialogue, no debate, no conversation, and no sociability anymore. Equally, and this is my main point here, there is no autonomy, there is no scope for people freely to make choices about other people's opinions, or about other people's attributes: it becomes pretty much a kind of free for all.

So, to recap, the nature of the development I am tracing is that of a shift, or a slide, from the romantic idea of self-authorship as something taken seriously, to a weak, fragile, conception that finds nothing to discover and no direction to take other than getting in touch with something that is already pretty much like myself. This is the problem and the crisis faced by those who still cling to a liberal humanist conception of the self. Just to reiterate one point that is implicit in the discussion here: there is a difference between rejecting convention and rejecting social judgement as such. It is of course quite legitimate to reject social norms, social values, the way society is: the obligation then falls on you, however, to develop a different set of criteria by which society will judge you.

At the heart of the experimental voyage of discovery to be found in *La Nouvelle Heloise*, and in the *Bildungsromane* of German writers, is the notion of a fundamental choice. That is the role of the novel at that time: it represents an experiment, a way of trying to reach a non-alienated state in which the self can be true to itself. But as we move through history to the present time, the developments I have discussed earlier lead us to a notion of the self which is peculiarly defined by the fact that it is estranged from the possibility of choice. Today that kind of choice, self-choosing and decision-making, is very much restricted. What starts to happen in these conditions is that the relationship between the self and choice mutates into something quite dramatic: the change is from a self that used to be developed through making choices about life (what we mean by the self-changing, imaginative, self) to a situation in which choice itself becomes almost an act of consumption and only an act of consumption. With the self no longer choosing between different courses of action, not choosing to make difficult decisions, the sort of decisions that inherently raise issues about uncertainty and risk, then the only choice the self does, or can make, is to choose itself. The self-changing self is now the self-choosing self. Which self shall I be today? This development is most clearly expressed in the dominance of identity politics in the current era.

The choices made are no longer decisions of a normative character or about fundamental issues to do with life. Instead of allowing oneself to take risks on the battlefield of life, caution has the last word, and all that is chosen is a self. This is a very dangerous development in the history of the self. It is very much easier to choose a self, a different self to the one you are: it is not choosing the self you want to be (that is self-changing), it is simply choosing a *different* self. It is a much more attractive proposition, an easier sell, than putting yourself on the line, testing yourself, and developing yourself in relation to difficult circumstances. What self-choosing amounts to is choosing an identity. Since the 1950s, identity has increasingly become the medium through which people interpret their self. Some social constructionists interpret this development as a process of 'selfing' (Weigert et al. 1986: 40).

The framing of the self through identity often endows it with a fragile and unstable character. A consumption-led identity, more accurately, because when someone says, 'I identify as this… or that' what is really being said is 'I identify as this particular type of person living this particular lifestyle'. What the self chooses in this case is the identity: rather than the self choosing for itself between different options (that will define itself) and deciding what is the way it can best develop in accordance with its own inner nature and with its inclinations. After all, one of the important elements in the exercise of autonomy is that people feel that they can act in accordance with the way they want to be. In this sense, it seems to me, that JS Mill's notion of autonomy[1] is more suggestive than the Kantian one, at least insofar as it is not really about some preconceived notion or sensibility which is expressed through being autonomous (see Furedi 2011). It is more of a recognition that it is being who you are in action that will result in the realisation of the positive potential of autonomy.

What I am trying to suggest then is that today we can see an important historical development as the self becomes increasingly passive, estranged from choice-making, and regards autonomy sceptically, if not cynically. As this development unfolds, the self increasingly attempts to find some reason for its existence by setting out to choose a different self. This is what counts as the heroism of the self today. The heroic moment becomes choosing a self, a ready-made identity, rather than the, by contrast, apparently mundane task of choice-making in the course of everyday existence. This choice of a new self is really best thought of as the purchase of a new social mask. The self goes to the supermarket, as it were, or Amazon, and takes a new self off the metaphorical shelf: a new social mask behind which to hide and which defines the self from then on. The self then seeks acceptance and recognition for this self from others: which, if not forthcoming, prompts an often furious and intolerant reaction. An understandable enough reaction given the self is in the process of trying to give meaning to and reason for its very existence.[2] The demand for acceptance is almost on demand, expected by right rather than earned: without the self having to put in the work that is normally involved in the struggle to confront the alienated state within which we live.

---

[1] See, for example, Mill (2008: 63), 'there should be different experiments of living... free scope should be given to varieties of character, short of injury to others'.
[2] I think this explains why, for example, trans activists believe they are at risk of death if they are not recognised by society. Symbolically at least they are right.

It is difficult to trace these developments at such short range; autonomy is not black and white and so the trajectory autonomy takes in the sense I have tried to map it here is difficult to follow. People who still hold onto an ideal of liberal humanism are likely to agree that the superiority of autonomy is based on recognising an inherent moral value in the act of self-determination. There is a moral value to be found in the very act of making choices: and this is because it is in the course of making choices that the moral imagination is exposed to the kind of experiences which both test and nourish it at the same time. No one can develop an autonomous self without exposing itself to that particular kind of experience. Even though this may seem self-evident to some, it is nevertheless crucial to engage and test oneself in this way and avoid the lazy route of mocking those who go out and shop their identity or say 'I identify as' something. It is all too easy to poke fun at the new language of pronouns and offence-taking, safe spaces, and so on, while remaining unable or unwilling to really engage in self-changing. It is not easy, after all, to be consistently for choice: to be consistently a self-determining individual. Just imagine the effort if *all* the choices in the course of a single day—getting up, brushing teeth, leaving the house—were made *freely* and only after due deliberation, rather than made *routinely*. It would be exhausting, and one can understand why most of us, at points, even most of the time, would rather allow other people to make choices for us: to be spared some of the burden and responsibility that free choosing involves.

This challenge, this difficulty, is something that has been understood historically by some people: it is, for example, one of the main merits of the existentialists. Certain sections of revolutionary movements in the past have also understood how important the act of will is. This is well known, but what is perhaps more interesting is the fact that even within Marxism, even in the Marxist tradition, there is something of a visceral reaction *against* the self being consistently self-determining. In Lukács' *The Destruction of Reason* there are passages of virulent hostility to what Lukács terms 'vitalism'. In one sense he is right because many of the vitalists were indeed fairly irrational: very mystical people.[3] In another

---

[3] 'In fine: the essence of vitalism lies in a conversion of agnosticism into mysticism, of subjective idealism into the pseudo-objectivity of myth' Lukács (1980: 414).

sense, however, Lukács is also reacting against an expression of a voluntaristic spirit or desire to self-determine, to take matters into one's own hands: that sort of vital principle. It is correct, of course, to criticise such thinkers (as Dilthey, Simmel, and Spengler) on the grounds that it is simply not possible for any given individual to determine his or her future. What makes this such a difficult discussion is the fact that the criticism is correct. Regardless, unless we do all make an attempt to choose and test ourselves out—even in the knowledge that we might never realise the objects of our choice—the only thing that is determined, for sure, is that we will be resigning ourselves to staying put in the intellectual, cultural, and political stasis in which we find ourselves today.

So, in the end, the most important lesson is that we must try and learn from the more balanced way that people have attempted to overcome their alienation in the past, and suggest to ourselves that, even though we may live in a world that is somewhat hostile to the struggle against alienation, more prone to embrace it, nevertheless we still have a weapon that anyone anywhere can take up: namely, our inherent capacity as human beings to make choices, to live with the consequences of those choices, and to test out our spirit, test out our imagination, and develop it in the process.

References

Dworkin, G. (1988). *The theory and practice of autonomy*. Cambridge: Cambridge University Press.

Furedi, F. (2011). *On tolerance: A defence of moral independence*. London: Continuum.

Furedi, F. (2013). *Authority: A sociological history*. Cambridge: Cambridge University Press.

Furedi, F. (2017). *What's happened to the university?: A sociological exploration of its infantilisation*. London: Bloomsbury Press.

Goethe, J. W. (1962). *The sorrows of Young Werther, and selected writings* (C. Hutter, Trans.). New York: The New American Library.

Grogan, C. (1999). The politics of seduction in British fiction of the 1790s: The female reader and *Julie, ou La Nouvelle Héloïse*. *Eighteenth-Century Fiction, 11*(4), 459–476.

Lasch, C. (1984). *The minimal self*. New York: Norton.

Lukács, G. (1936). The sorrows of Young Werther. Retrieved from https://www.marxists.org/archive/lukacs/works/1936/young-werther.htm.

Lukács, G. (1968). *Goethe and his age*. London: Merlin Press.

Lukács, G. (1980). *The destruction of reason* (P. Palmer, Trans.). London: Merlin Press.

Marx, J. H. (1980). The ideological construction of post-modern identity models in contemporary cultural movements. In R. Robertson & B. Holzner (Eds.), *Identity and authority: Explorations in the theory of society*. Oxford: Basil Blackwell.

Mill, J. S. (2008). *On liberty and other essays*. Oxford: Oxford World's Classics.

Rousseau, J.-J. (1997). *Julie, or the new Héloïse* (J. Vache, Trans.). New Hampshire: Dartmouth College Press.

Weigert, A. J., Teitge, J. S., & Teitge, D. W. (1986). *Society and identity: Towards a sociological psychology*. Cambridge: Cambridge University Press.

12

Conclusion: The Self and Its Prospects

Angus Kennedy

Identity-as Truth

Identity is one form in which we understand things to be true. A logical expression such as A = A or a mathematical expression such as 1 = 1 is a statement of identity and, on that basis, is true. It is true that A equals A because A is identical to A: A *is* A. And, equally, it is true that A does not equal B. 1 does not equal 0. Truth is found in identity: not in difference. This simply logical understanding of truth as identity is both profound and superficial.

When the self is reconceptualised as an identity ('I identify as'), one of the consequences is that the identity becomes understood as being true in this identity-as sense. In proclaiming that one is no longer a man, but is now a woman, what is being asserted is that the identity of woman is the 'true me', the 'real me'. To say 'I identify as a woman' is to say that 'I' *is* a woman or, to spell it out logically, that 'a woman is a woman'. In announcing one's identity in this way then, one appears to be speaking a profound truth: a truth that, being true, is not to be denied. The assertion can of

A. Kennedy (✉)
West Sussex, UK

course be challenged ('You are *really* a man, not a woman'), but the identity as such is not affected by this since *its* truth rests in the fact that 'I' have chosen to 'identity as': any biological 'facts' about what I (really) am have no bearing on such a conception of truth.

Such an account of identity represents a polar opposite to some of the more optimistic modes of selfhood that have been traced in the course of this book. Rather than putting primary importance on the idea of the self understood in terms of autonomy and self-transformation, this far more vulnerable identify-as self finds its validation in an identity which is externally fixed (as biology, skin colour, species), for which it demands public recognition, and in which identification-as it finds its truth. On the face of it the demand to be able to identity-as whatever one chooses appears to be an argument for fluidity, diversity, and freedom, but ironically tends towards a version of identity and selfhood that becomes far more fixed by the characteristics of the chosen identity than the self ever was by the normative standards of society.

This truth-in-identity is 'built-in' to any given identity. It is not something that one can be mistaken about; there is no room for doubt or maybe in 'I identify-as a woman'. It is a different kind of statement to, for example, 'I think I should vote this way'. Identities cannot be wrong or false for the bearer. Nor can they change, alter, or mature. They just are. This is not to say that people cannot discard an identity and take on a new one. Someone born a man may choose to identify as a woman but subsequently discard that identity and assume a new one: 'I used to identity as a woman but now I identify as genderqueer.' But at any one point in time, there is only one identity-truth about me and I cannot change that without exchanging my identity for another one. I find my truth in my identity: it is inside me, not something I have to pursue or debate or discover; it is rather something I can just feel and emote. For those operating within this identity-as concept of truth, it follows that what I assert to be true on the basis of my identity does not stand or fall on the basis of any empirical evidence, or history, or rational inquiry of any kind. It is not a matter of debate but rather a case of 'I speak my truth. Deny it and you deny me'.

Frank Furedi argued in his opening chapter that the Enlightenment project of allowing the self to self-authorise inevitably led to the de-authorisation of the self. The idea that the self could and should self-authorise was born from the growing de-authorisation of tradition and religion, exemplified by the Reformation, and amplified by the sweeping away of feudal hierarchy by nascent capitalism. Truth moved from being something 'out there' to being something 'in here'. As autonomy and self-determination became more achievable and more socially valorised, so too developed the idea—given the self was so important—that one had to be true to one's own, authentic, self. But there was a catch. As Furedi puts it: 'It is in the act of becoming de-centred—the result of the victory if you like of the authority of the self—that the self becomes aware of its own fragility.' So, the movement from the weakening of external authority that Luther put in motion ends with the self demanding protection for itself from external authority, from the state. As authenticity has decoupled itself from autonomy, the self has, paradoxically, reached a situation of demanding increased state regulation of the self through various forms of law, expert knowledge, and technocratic discourse. Certain of its truth, the self demands that 'lies' about it are stamped out.

It is in this light—particularly with respect to the growing extent of state intervention into personal life and the policing of identities—that the arguments made by Jamie Whyte in defence of selfish individualism are particularly poignant. The decline in voluntary associations such as trades unions, even of the family, is linked to the weakening of 'selfish individualism' by which we can understand the self-changing autonomous self. Whyte notes that there is little need to co-operate, to be social, if the individual has no freedom to, for example, purchase insurance or a pension but is compelled to do so by the state. Where such things are enforced by regulation, then the self does not need to look out for itself nor have to win others over to support its projects. The self need only 'win favour with those who wield the power to coerce.' The truth of this is to be seen in the increase in special pleading for resources by 'victims' and minorities demanding access to universities, jobs, and so on.

There are examples of this to be found every day in the media in the United States and United Kingdom. At the time of writing Surrey police were investigating an accusation of 'misgendering' levelled by Susie Green of the transgender charity Mermaids against Caroline Farrow, a Catholic journalist, who reportedly called her child, Jackie, her 'son' (Jackie had a sex-change at 16). The fact that this is taken so seriously—treated as a possible crime—is evidence of the degree to which truth, when it comes to questions of identity, is taken to be what one says it is (BBC News 2019a, b).

At the same time, Cambridge University withdrew an invitation to controversial Canadian academic Jordan Petersen who had been offered a visiting fellowship at the divinity school. Petersen shot to notoriety when he refused to use pronouns other than 'he' or 'she'. Protests following his appointment quickly had it reversed, with Cambridge University students' union saying: 'His work and views are not representative of the student body and as such we do not see his visit as a valuable contribution to the University' (Marsh 2019). The union appears to operate with a notion of truth that might be threatened, rather than advanced, by an encounter with views that are not those already held by the students. The union also assumes that there is a built-in majority of students that hold these views: that there is no need to canvas them or open up the issue to broader discussion or even a vote. Rather it is assumed that someone like Petersen can be shut down 'in the name of' students who would inevitably be offended or hurt by his views. The vice-chancellor, Stephen Toope, shares their view that free speech should not touch on questions of identity: 'Robust debate can scarcely occur, for example, when some members of the community are made to feel personally attacked, not for their ideas but for their very identity' (University of Cambridge 2019).

The politicisation of identity plays out in opposition to democracy insofar as democracy represents what the majority of individuals think is best as opposed to the truth of (often minority) identities. Politics has always been about competing interests but there is a difference between individual selves pursuing their interests—and in the process sometimes discovering what they have in common with others—and identities demanding recognition for what they are. Individuals can debate the pros and cons of issues and can also submit themselves to the will of the majority of individuals in a community. This kind of majority is not a majority formed, pre-formed in fact, on the basis that one identity is simply numerically superior to other identities. That would be a foregone conclusion, and there would be no point in a vote. It is rather a majority constructed at a specific point in time from individuals who each vote for something based on reasons. This is possible because individual selves can change: they can change their minds about something, be wrong, they can be persuaded of something, they can convince others. J.S. Mill was elected in 1865 on a platform including votes for women. It took until 1928 before women achieved democratic equality with men: following many years of debate, protest, and social change.

In the absence of values a priori, individuals choose values through their actions. It is through these individual existential choices that there arises a possibility of being together, 'human community' as Sartre has it (Sartre 2007: 65), because we can choose to agree on values which are then shared values. Identities, unlike individual selves, cannot enter into democracy except, ultimately, to destroy it. Unable to change their minds, identities enter into democratic contest only if they are going to win. It is assumed by many, for example, that African-Americans will vote Democrat simply because they are African-Americans, that gay voters will vote for gay marriage because they are gay (or have identified as 'allies'), that women will vote for quotas for female judges, that the old will vote for Brexit, and so on. If a given identity loses a vote, it is then explained away in terms of the hostility, ignorance, or prejudice of the majority and the result thereby disqualified.

Generation Selfie

In many attempts to define what is peculiar to contemporary conceptions of the self it is common to hear talk about a generation that is self-obsessed, narcissistic, given to finding realisation in its own self-imaging: in the selfie. Our own title—*from self to selfie*—can be seen to support such a view. But we have also tried to trace a historical process of the diminution of the self: from robust, Enlightenment, autonomous individuals to a much reduced selfie self, the self of contemporary identity debates. If we see the self in this way, as a reduced, 'little self', then it follows that this little self cannot be first and foremost characterised by *self*-reflection: the reason being that the boundaries of this identify-as self are fixed rather self-imposed. Again, there is something seemingly profound (Look at me! I can declare myself to be a woman although born a man: surely *that's* shaping my destiny) yet quite superficial (Look at me! I'm a woman). There is just less of a self in such a superficial expression of identity to reflect upon. Yes, even a shallow pool reflects, but what is lacking is *depth*. For the contemporary little self what matters more than self-reflection is immediacy and spontaneity: it is the emotional and therefore (it is argued) 'genuine' reaction that is considered authentic. The felt response that speaks to a true identity.

This passionate self-positioning—'I just cannot help being what I am, I *have* to speak out'—is characteristic of today's identitarians and a certain form of identity tribalism. What is less valued is the *thought-through* or considered response that is born from reflection and self-examination. Indeed, what is often considered progressive or manifest virtue today is allowing previously unheard or minority voices to dominate discourse in order to right historic wrongs and 'check privilege'. This emphasis on voice places a premium on the subjectivity of felt or lived experience. What matters is what one feels: not what one thinks. As a result, reason is discounted next to emotion. Demonstrable passion is a fashionable asset. It is striking that this cuts across left and right divides (for every trans-activist there seems to be a men's support group) and all manner of issues. It can appear that the more grandiose one's claim to victimhood can be, so much more authentic and legitimate one's identity claim becomes. This is what Frank Furedi describes under the rubric of embracing one's own alienation.

Self-definition that relies more on what one *suffers*, on what one happens to be, rather than on what one thinks and chooses, locks us, of course, into relatively one-sided forms of determination. With feeling: not logic. And, therefore, in not thinking. Real self-reflection, on the other hand, would involve an acceptance of one's limitations and a willingness to work in and around them. By contrast the selfie-self sees itself as flourishing through the denial of such limits.

Furedi ends his chapter looking at alienation in its historic development with a suggestion that we will not move out of the current moment of 'intellectual, cultural, and political stasis' unless people are willing to take risks in making life-defining choices rather than assuming identities 'off the shelf', which can only increase their alienation. In the two years since the lectures on which many of the chapters in this book were based we have seen the deepening and entrenchment of identity politics as a new great divide in Western society. We have also seen something of a backlash in terms of what is called populism or nationalism: from Trump to Matteo Salvini in Italy to the Yellow Vest protests in France.

Identity on the Front Line

It may appear strange in a time when nothing much is standing still to characterise the contemporary moment as defined by stasis. In its original sense, however, in Greek political history, it described disturbance rather than equilibrium. It spoke to internal discord in both individuals and city-states, effectively periods of civil war leading to the ascendancy of either oligarchy or tyranny. Politics today is reduced to the narcissism of small differences. What increasingly passes for politics is hatred for those imagined as threatening to our identity, and our concept of the political seems to owe more and more to Carl Schmitt's explication in terms of a friend-enemy distinction. Being political can be seen as a matter of raging against one's enemies on Twitter, seeking to 'own' or 'stomp' them or calling for their prosecution for hate crime.

If we take the contentious example of immigration and the related question of open borders, we can see how the debate necessarily speaks to a bitter internal division. To the extent that a US Democrat like Alexandra Ocasio-Cortez denies the territorial integrity of the United States,[1] so she opens up a new front against those of her fellow citizens who still believe that being a US citizen means something special and should, therefore, not be open to all. This is maybe why President Trump has started to push, at the time of writing, for birthright citizenship to be rescinded. A desperate measure, of course, since if citizenship is not defined by birth

---

[1] 'Alex believes that if we are to uphold civic justice, we must abolish ICE [The Immigration and Customs Enforcement agency] and see to it that our undocumented neighbors are treated with the dignity and respect owed to all people, *regardless of citizenship status*' (my emphasis) (Ocasio-Cortez 2019).

then it becomes purely and only defined by politics. Which means today by identity. Which deepens the conflict.

Stasis, yes, but not in the sense of being stuck in the mud. Stasis in the civil war sense. Sales of books about politics are up 50 per cent in the United Kingdom over the last year (Flood 2018). Books with titles reflecting variously on the end of freedom (Timothy Snyder, *The Road to Unfreedom*), the death of politics (Chantal Mouffe, *On the Political*), the end of the liberal order (Niall Ferguson and Fared Zakaria, *The End of the Liberal Order?*), and the destruction of democracy (David Runicman, *How Democracy Ends*) increasingly dominate the market.

Labour membership has leapt threefold in the last five years (Audickas et al. 2019). New political parties, such as *die Linke* and the *AfD* in Germany, the Five Star Movement and rebranded Lega in Italy, the rebirth of the Front National in France, or the Brexit Party in Britain, speak to a destruction of the middle ground, which is equally reflected in the one-sided, mutually exclusive positions, such as in the stand-offs on budget, taken by Republicans and Democrats in the United States. There is little room for nuance or overlap between Red and Blue: it is now hard to imagine any pro-choice Republican senator being elected (Kilgore 2019). There are no more Rockefeller Republicans and Blue Dog Democrats are a fast dying breed. And debate is polarised. The key reason being that the ascendancy of identity politics has been at the expense of any remaining authority in society, in the sense of there being shared normative values that could provide a common framework for being together.

Instead of being willing to submit the self to the judgement of others in society—to social norms—the self has instead had recourse to choosing an identity in order to try and come to terms with its alienation.

Much is at stake. If others in society do not recognise, do not accept, this newly assumed identity then the self faces an existential abyss. This is why there are such bitter debates about pronouns. This is why some extreme Vegans call for the death of farmers (BBC News 2019a, b). All of this increases the demand for policing: whether to protect farmers; or stop fox hunts; or to throw open female changing rooms, or prisons, to men who identify-as women (BBC News 2018). Selfies that hate other selfies line up to demand their prosecution for hate crime.

Policing the Subject

The contributions by Josie Appleton, Claire Fox, Jon Holbrook, and James Heartfield all examine, in different ways, the growing involvement of the state in questions of selfhood. For Appleton, with the increase in mediation by bureaucracy the self becomes increasingly one-sided: a change mirrored in society. For Fox, what she sees as a retreat from the model of the heroic self that set out to change the world has led to a diminished, privatised, self: as she puts it 'black power has been reduced to hair power.' In her model, the self's retreat from the public arena has left it open to regulation: noting that the policing of identity has become more and more widespread. While we are told we have complete freedom to 'identify as' anything we like, there is a rigorous policy to make sure—and the irony is heavy—that no 'fake' identities can insert themselves into the safe spaces. No room on campus, as Jordan Peterson discovered, for professors who adopt an identity based on non-recognition of newly declared pronouns. Similarly, Holbrook describes how the identity-focused present forces changes in the law, which focus less on justice and more on stopping identity denial in order to safeguard the selves behind them.

In his recent short book, *Identity*, Francis Fukuyama rightly identifies the tension in the self that some of the chapters in this book have conceptualised in terms of autonomy and authenticity. Autonomy, for Fukuyama, is about obeying or rejecting the moral rules of society. But there is another side to autonomy (which we have called authenticity) which flourishes in Rousseau, and in the arts, and seeks for 'full expression of the feelings and emotions that constitute the authentic inner self' (Fukuyama 2018: 54). The difficulty that arose, once the shared moral horizon that Christianity had afforded Europe lost much of its normative force, was the tendency towards what we could call authenticity autarky: a more radical understanding of authenticity as giving each individual the right to determine what existence means. But, 'without a minimal common culture, we cannot cooperate on shared tasks and will not regard the same institutions as legitimate; indeed, we will not even be able to communicate with one another absent a common language with mutually understood meanings' (Fukuyama 2018: 56). The proliferation of pronouns is perhaps one of the clearest example of this, but at root the problem is to be found in the idea that it is possible to 'identify as' without *any* form of restraint. Individuals on their own simply do not get to decide the way things are by themselves. Identity is not merely a matter of subjective whim or choice but something forged through social engagement rather than a mask assumed every morning.

Where Fukuyama is less convincing is in his understanding of contemporary populism and support for the nation as a reaction on the part of autonomy against authenticity. He argues that for many people the freedom of choice afforded by the end of shared moral norms is experienced as distressing rather than liberating: unlike great artists inspired by it maybe, they 'feel an intense insecurity and alienation because they do not know who their true self is' (Fukuyama 2018: 56). To combat insecurity, he thinks, they crave the security of a collective identity: nationalism or political Islam, which he sees as 'two sides of the same coin… expressions of a hidden or suppressed group identity that seeks public recognition' (Fukuyama 2018: 58).

The contributors to this collection argue something different. Enthusiasm for group identities is really almost entirely on the 'authentic' or 'selfie' side of the tension. Consider the zeal with which nonconformity to the group is prosecuted: through Twitter mobs, campus censorship, and the ever-expanding category of hate crime against protected groups. The alienation Fukuyama outlines is felt most intensely by those who do not see any need to restore moral norms, but instead want to establish new ones or destroy any remnant of old ones. Appleton, for example, traces the links between the figure of the transgender and the jihadi. Extreme, exclusive, nationalism is indeed a product of individual alienation, but nationalism itself relates more directly to the 'autonomy' side of the equation. Contemporary populism can be read, it seems to me, to express the frustration of individuals with the way things are and represent a desire for change, as much as it can be seen to express a nostalgic desire for a return to a lost identity. Either way, if there is to be hope for a humanist conception of society and politics, then it must be based on a conception of the self as sovereign: the individual must have precedence to and security within the group. We are simultaneously free as autonomous selves but at the same time embedded in the way society is.

No Way Out

James Heartfield, tracing the post-war intellectual history of the 'death of the subject' most notably in French (post-) structuralist thought, highlights that for Foucault the freedom of the subject was fundamentally an illusion. He denied the existence in each subject of a 'universal consciousness' of the core assumptions of society. Jerrold Seigel's account of Foucault's thinking about the self ends with a similar claim. His early work—such as *Madness and Civilisation*—tended to emphasise the inability of the subject to overcome the power, discipline, and institutions of existing social arrangements. For Foucault autonomy was best considered as something of a trap for Western society:

> the demise of freedom took place through historically identifiable social practices that subjected people to the conditions in which their subjectivity was formed. Paradoxically, these practices were part of the modern project of gaining autonomy for individuals by liberating their reason from the coils of tradition and arbitrary authority; for Foucault, the result was a new kind of self-enforced subjection. (Seigel 2007: 609)

In this, Foucault can be seen as making an argument that has a certain commonality with those of Furedi in this volume: the destruction of tradition has not led to the liberation of the subject but has instead led the subject (and this is the difference between the two accounts) to call for the state to take on the work of policing identities seen as being in conflict for recognition and resources.

In his later work on 'the care of the self' and 'technologies of the self', however, Foucault drew on classical Stoic notions of the necessity of practising the art of self-government, of 'individuality, forming itself in private, and gaining freedom by a withdrawal into itself' (Seigel 2007: 624). The self was, he thought, able to achieve this independence from existing structures of power in society through self-reflection, looking at itself in a mirror, and caring for itself, practising an 'aesthetics of existence', shaping one's self to be pleasing to the self, to be 'an object of pleasure': a self 'that achieves its special mode of "care" wholly by way of reflectivity' (ibid.: 626). The common point here is that the self-reflectivity in question is capable of acting without being constrained by the limits of any external authority, moral, or social norms. His conception of the possibility of the purity of such reflective self-fashioning is obviously open to the critiques of such notions advanced in the chapters by Fox and Appleton: in at least as pure self-reflectivity lacks by definition any external standard, and as such is prey to self-obsession and narcissism.

Foucault, however, in an essay 'What is Enlightenment?', written in the last year of his life, on the two-hundredth anniversary of the publication of Kant's original, appeared to align himself, as Seigel reads it, more to the liberal tradition than in many of his earlier writings. He advocated subjecting ourselves to a 'permanent critique' in order to rid ourselves of our self-imposed immaturity. Yet he goes on to argue that such a critique must be in the manner of Baudelaire's *flâneur* (a passive spectator or loafer on the edge of society), rather than in a modern understanding of the active subject, since he felt that humanism came with too much religious and political baggage in the sense that it imposed external standards that would impede the 'pure relation of the self to itself' (Seigel 2007: 629). The self would not be able to self-invent, in any true or authentic or novel sense, if it had to self-invent within the limits of a humanism: it would always end up inventing, not a new self, but a form of a *humanist* self. Foucault, all too aware that his work on the disciplining and shaping effects of discourse and power relations on the formation of the self within their horizon offered no exit, sought a way out of the dead end, but was unable to articulate one except in the imagined purity of a transcendence of limits. He could:

> countenance no mean between extreme subjection and radical liberation… Either reflection was wholly absorbed into the relations that brought it into being, serving only to perpetuate them, or it operated to form a self on which social powers and cultural norms had no purchase. (Seigel 2007: 631)

In the end his care of the self, in its one-sidedness, ends up tantamount to a denial of the real subjectivity that only exists in and through the *limits* of society. No worthwhile account of the self can even get started if it holds onto the possibility of *radical* liberation: human subjectivity and human freedom is always limited, always provisional, contingent, and, above all, relative. Seigel, in maybe the best contemporary account of the need for a balanced accounting of the self, ends his critique of Foucault and Derrida's attempts to transcend the limits of the self with a useful reminder of the critical importance of Kant's insight:

> the self that constitutes itself through reflection necessarily institutes a division in its being. It makes itself present to itself only by dividing itself into two parts, a subject and an object, and in doing so it loses the original quality of being prior to objectification that gave it the promise of freedom in the first place. That is, the pure reflective self can become present to itself only in an operation that makes it absent, depriving itself of the full self-presence it seeks to achieve. (Seigel 2007: 647)

Kant is arguing that alienation is something we bring about ourselves—we quite literally *object* to ourselves—and which we can never escape. Alienation is a result of thinking about ourselves. But so too is (the) distinction. The self that constitutes itself through thinking about itself, what it wants, and does not want, is a self that stands out and becomes noticeable. It is recognised on the basis of what it has made of itself, not what it was, and it can recognise other selves like it: selves with which it can disagree, or agree, oppose, or join in solidarity.

The Limits of the Self

Alienation may appear deeper and more intractable than ever before. Identity politics, we have suggested, amounts to embracing one's alienation, wallowing in it, with the ideas of self-changing and overcoming alienation written off from the start. The prospects for the self appear bleak. As Tim Black argues, the posing of 'self-authentication' as a solution to the 'problem of self-authorisation' has been a Pyrrhic victory at best. As long as authenticity remained wedded to the idea that the authentic self should be free *from* the judgements of society, it retained a relationship to autonomy in a struggle for independence. As it has developed, it has become 'a desire for recognition *in* the judgements of others': in effect, a *narcissistic* demand for recognition whatever one is; on the fulfilment of which the self has come to depend.

Alienation today often takes the form of an immature, almost childish denial, of limits: it asserts that whatever we care to imagine is possible, and let no one dare to deny it. Yet the self continues to be constituted through real constraints, not least, and at the limit, the inevitability of its mortality. We can, like one identity-entrepreneur in Belgium—69-year-old Emile Ratelband—go to the courts to have one's identity as a man 20 years younger recognised (The Telegraph 2018). We can self-identify as a different gender or race; we can assert that we are no longer even human (and demand to be known as 'Otherkin'). We can deny the relevance of social constraints such as the family, work, and the nation. These constraints remain real, however, as does, however degraded a form of selfhood it adopts, the very subjectivity that denies them. Much as we may try to deny the reality of our selves, much as we may seek ever more diverse forms of protean, gender-fluid, and transient identity, in the end we must remain inescapable to ourselves. And, much as we deny the reality of gender—dismissing it as a mere social construct when in fact there is nothing *mere* about what society constructs—we should not overlook the irony that new divisions and limits are busily being constructed in society. There are new rules on what can and cannot be said—at least not without the risk, in some cases, of suffering very real consequences including prosecution for hate crime—and entering public life is very much more challenging for those who continue to resist the orthodoxy.

Some—many—react sensibly by keeping quiet and adopting a neutral mask, looking to go unnoticed. Some take up the masks that will be most readily rewarded with recognition. Both forms of masking effectively amount to bad faith and serve only to increase the pressure on the self to settle accounts with its alienation. Either by going further down the route of embracing it or in experiments with self-changing. Those that choose the latter course may find it easier to stand out than ever before, although

12 Conclusion: The Self and Its Prospects

the reaction—judgement in fact—against them will be that much more severe.

* * *

Many of the contributors to this volume note the increasing degree of regulation of the self in contemporary western societies: in contradistinction to the historical importance afforded to the idea or possibility of self-regulation. Theories of self-liberation today speak to the denial or irrelevance of traditional social limits and norms while being blind to the extent to which new limits are being enforced on thought and speech in society. Certain sections of society (e.g. anti-racist activists, #MeToo feminists, right-wing nativists) presume to dictate approved modes of conduct to other sections of society or to proscribe their silence. What is clear in reading the contributions to this book is that the prospects for the self depend in great part on how we understand the nature of the relationship of the self to the question of limits. Not to the limits it imposes on itself through the purity of self-reflection—through the narcissist imagination—but on the real limits that the self finds through self-examination and self-criticism conducted on the basis of standards that are more widely shared. The self needs to judge itself and ask itself where it has failed, and why; what are its projects, are they good ones? Where has it fallen short of what is expected of it? This kind of self-criticism is quite removed from the dandified self-regard of Foucault's 'care of the self'.

In this respect, the arguments made in *Icarus Fallen* by the Arendtian philosopher Chantal Delsol are worth repeating. She suggests that the contemporary human condition is characterised by resentment towards our 'own history' of errors and by disappointment with our failure to 'make destiny submit to our hopes' (Delsol 2003). The utopian philosophy of progress (she roots it in Rousseau) hoped for the abolition of politics and an end to social conflict. It has instead brought about an existential crisis in which we deny the existence of any objective goods and relativise truth in order to excuse our failure to bring an end to contradiction. Delsol, however, sees it as necessary to face up to the reality of life as ineluctably mired in contradiction. We have to:

> live in a world where evil and death are lurking, where uncertainty impertinently provokes reason, and where war is always waiting in the wings of peace… [the son of Icarus] will stop cursing this incertitude when he has finally understood that the tragic is a bearer of meaning. Life has value in the antinomies among which it struggles. (Delsol 2003: 241)

Today, to the extent that we can direct our attention back to our selves, and to our limitations, to our lack of self-sufficiency, to the inevitability of conflict and division in society, and face up to the unpredictability of the results of our actions, so much the greater any chance of the re-emergence of the centrality of individual conscience, of the self-conscious self, and the recognition of humanity. This focus on the self must go hand in hand with what Furedi calls a 'quest for a new kind of authority'. This will itself require a reconceptualisation of the self given its history of understanding autonomy and authenticity as being in conflict with authority. We have learned how to argue, but what can give authority to Kant's imperative that we also *obey* is the key question for the contemporary self.

This quest for a new authority will need to search for answers to the question of where can the self today find a home, how can it accommodate itself, how can it learn to care for what is, and what it has inherited, as well as considering what it can build. The first step, as Heidegger argued, is *thinking*:

> as soon as man *gives thought* to his homelessness, it is a misery no longer. Rightly considered and kept well in mind, it is the sole summons that *calls* mortals into their dwelling. (Heidegger 2013: 159)

References

Audickas, L., Dempsey, N., & Keen, R. (2019). Membership of UK political parties. [Online] *Researchbriefings.parliament.uk*. Retrieved January 6, 2019, from https://researchbriefings.parliament.uk/ResearchBriefing/Summary/SN05125.

BBC News. (2018). Trans inmate jailed for prison sex attacks. [Online]. Retrieved January 6, 2019, from https://www.bbc.co.uk/news/uk-england-leeds-45825838.

BBC News. (2019a). Police investigation over 'misgendering'. [Online]. Retrieved March 26, 2019, from https://www.bbc.co.uk/news/uk-england-surrey-47638527.

BBC News. (2019b). Vegans call me murderer and rapist. [Online]. Retrieved April 7, 2019, from https://www.bbc.co.uk/news/uk-42833132.

Delsol, C. (2003). *Icarus fallen: The search for meaning in an uncertain world.* Wilmington, DE: ISI Books.

Flood, A. (2018). 'Scary new world': Political book sales explode as UK readers seek answers. [Online] *The Guardian.* Retrieved January 6, 2019, from https://www.theguardian.com/books/2018/nov/07/scary-new-world-political-book-sales-explode-as-uk-readers-seek-answers-waterstones.

Fukuyama, F. (2018). *Identity: Contemporary identity politics and the struggle for recognition.* London: Profile Books.

Heidegger, M. (2013). Building dwelling thinking. In *Poetry, language, thought.* New York: Harper Perennial.

Kilgore, E. (2019). The near-extinction of pro-choice republicans in Congress. [Online] *Intelligencer.* Retrieved April 7, 2019, from http://nymag.com/intelligencer/2018/06/pro-choice-republicans-in-congress-are-nearly-extinct.html.

Marsh, S. (2019). Cambridge University rescinds Jordan Peterson invitation. [Online] *The Guardian.* Retrieved March 26, 2019, from https://www.theguardian.com/education/2019/mar/20/cambridge-university-rescinds-jordan-peterson-invitation?CMP=twt_gu.

Ocasio-Cortez, A. (2019). Ocasio 2018: Vote November 6th. [Online] *Ocasio2018.com.* Retrieved January 6, 2019, from https://ocasio2018.com/issues.

Sartre, J.-P. (2007). *Existentialism & humanism.* London: Methuen.

Seigel, J. (2007). *The idea of the self: Thought and experience in Western Europe since the seventeenth century.* Cambridge: Cambridge University Press.

The Telegraph. (2018). Dutch man, 69, who 'identifies as 20 years younger' launches legal battle to change age. [Online]. Retrieved January 6, 2019, from https://www.telegraph.co.uk/news/2018/11/07/dutch-man-69-identifies-20-years-younger-launches-legal-battle/.

University of Cambridge. (2019). Rescindment of visiting fellowship | statement from Vice-Chancellor Professor Stephen J Toope. [Online]. Retrieved March 30, 2019, from https://www.cam.ac.uk/news/rescindment-of-visiting-fellowship-statement-from-vice-chancellor-professor-stephen-j-toope.

Index[1]

A

Agency, 69, 148, 156, 163, 173, 199, 213n1
Alienation, 3–11, 53, 122, 129–145, 193, 194, 196, 197, 200, 205, 212, 214, 216, 219, 220
Althusser, L., 9, 150, 154, 155, 157, 158
Authenticity, 46, 56, 59, 63, 70n1, 105–127, 175, 181, 196, 199, 200, 209, 215, 216, 220, 222
Authority, xiv, 20, 22, 23, 32, 45, 49–51, 54, 55, 60–64, 78, 82, 83, 87, 92, 108, 115, 124, 139, 148, 171, 195, 209, 217, 218, 222
Autonomy, 11, 17, 19, 22, 25, 59, 61, 63, 70, 71, 86, 95, 96, 107–110, 114–119, 121–126, 142, 156, 196, 199, 201, 203, 204, 209, 215–217, 220, 222

C

Class, social, 87, 89, 98, 137, 140, 177, 179, 184
Culture, xiv, 16, 21, 24, 66, 107, 113, 129, 141, 145, 170–172, 174, 180, 182, 184, 195, 200

D

Delsol, C., 61, 221, 222
Derrida, J., 9, 150, 158–161, 219
Diderot, D., 52, 109, 113

---

[1] Note: Page numbers followed by 'n' refer to notes.

Diversity, 80
Durkheim, E., 18
Duty, 62–64, 79, 92, 93, 116, 119–121, 124

Enlightenment, 20, 45–66, 50n5, 77, 83, 107–110, 114, 120, 125, 208, 218

Fichte, 19, 56
Foucault, M., 148–150, 157, 161, 197, 217–219, 221
Freedom, xiii, xvi, 17, 18, 21, 22, 25, 39n6, 41, 42, 45, 46, 48, 50n5, 51, 54, 56–65, 96n31, 98, 107, 108, 110, 111, 114–118, 120–126, 158–163, 171, 177, 179, 196, 214, 215, 217, 219
  of speech, 77
Freud, Sigmund, 9, 19, 21, 107, 169, 170
Fukuyama, F., 85, 215, 216

Gender, 137, 140n3, 152, 178, 182, 186, 220
Goethe, J. W., 122, 123, 197, 198

Hegel, G. W. F., vii, 20, 56, 65, 111, 118, 129, 134, 135, 139, 150, 152–155

Heidegger, M., 106, 107, 125, 148–150, 222
Hume, D., 19, 19n1, 55–57, 61, 158
Husserl, E., 150–153

Identity, 9, 11, 24, 25, 56, 61, 106, 124, 126, 129–145, 168, 178, 181, 182, 184–186, 188, 199, 202–204, 212–216, 220
  identity politics, 137, 219
Imagination, 17, 18, 204, 205, 221
Individual, xv, 17, 22, 28–30, 33, 47–49, 49n2, 52, 54–56, 59–64, 66, 69–78, 81, 82, 91, 95, 97, 99, 107, 108, 110–112, 111n2, 114, 116–118, 121–123, 126, 129–141, 143, 145, 148, 156, 162, 163, 170, 171, 174, 188, 198–200, 204, 205, 215, 216, 222
Individualism, 27–43, 71–73, 78, 82, 171, 173, 174

Judgement, 61, 113, 174, 200, 201, 214

Kant, I., 46, 48, 56–66, 70, 77, 114, 116, 118, 124, 125, 150, 158, 218, 219, 222
Kojève, A., 153, 154

L

Lacan, J., 9, 148, 150, 153, 157, 158
Lasch, C., 167, 168, 170–175, 180, 181, 188, 195, 199
Law, xvi, 40, 40n7, 54, 57, 61, 66, 72, 85–101, 88n3, 111, 114, 117–119, 121, 123, 125, 126, 132, 134, 137, 138, 141, 144, 157, 161, 215
Limits, 14, 17, 18, 46, 61, 62, 74, 76, 77, 82, 148, 218–222
Locke, J., 15, 16, 18, 30, 108
Lukács, G., 19, 129–132, 197, 198, 204, 204n3
Luther, Martin, 22, 23, 49, 50, 182, 209
Lyotard, J.-F., 150, 160

M

Marx, K., 15, 20, 22, 25, 107, 124n3, 129–145, 154, 155, 199
Mészáros, I., 129, 131, 132
Mill, J. S., 69–83, 203, 203n1

N

Narcissism, 126, 167–175, 179, 181, 218
Nietzsche, F., 147, 148

P

Post-structuralism, 160
Psychology, 35, 173, 179n1, 199

R

Race, 110, 136, 152, 182, 184, 220
Recognition, 14, 25, 53, 56, 62, 63, 70, 72, 77, 113, 126, 154, 175, 185–187, 203, 215–217, 220
Reformation, 23, 49, 50, 63, 83, 107, 209
Regulation, xvii, 42, 82, 139, 209, 215, 221
Religion, 51, 209
Rousseau, J. J., 45, 48, 51–57, 59, 64, 65, 69, 108–127, 109n1, 197, 215, 221
Confessions, 22, 51, 52, 119
Emile, 54, 55, 57, 64, 110, 111, 114–118, 120, 125
Julie, 54, 113, 119–125, 197, 198

S

Safe spaces, 180, 188, 204, 215
Sartre, J.-P., 106, 107, 125
Schelling, 19
Scruton, R., 58, 61, 90
Seigel, J., 16, 17, 61, 66, 217–219
Self, vii, 11, 13–25, 19n1, 45–66, 53n6, 69, 70, 72, 75, 77, 93, 94, 94n27, 106–110, 112, 114–118, 120–124, 126, 127, 129–131, 137, 140, 141, 145, 149, 153, 158, 159, 161, 162, 168–184, 186–188, 193–204, 208, 211, 212, 214–222
reflection, 17, 18, 21, 50, 167, 169, 211, 212, 218, 219, 221
self-authorisation, 20, 23, 25, 108, 219

Self (*cont.*)
  self-changing, 15, 16, 194, 195, 202, 204, 219, 220
  self-conscious, 15, 222
  self-determination, 14, 17, 20, 25, 108, 120, 123, 195, 196, 204, 209
  self-regulation, 221
  transformation, 13, 15, 16, 23, 148, 200
Selfie, 168, 181, 187, 194, 197, 211
Society, xiv, 14–16, 18, 36, 39, 41, 43, 45–49, 51–55, 59–66, 69, 72, 74–83, 85–90, 95, 96, 98–101, 107, 110, 112, 113, 115–118, 122–126, 129–145, 147, 148, 155–157, 161, 167, 170–173, 175, 179, 181, 188, 196–201, 203n2, 213, 215–222

Soul, 18, 20–22, 45, 49, 50, 61, 120, 176
Stoic, 217
Subjectivity, 17, 45, 49, 50, 52, 60, 61, 126, 162, 212, 217, 219, 220

Tradition, 21, 22, 49, 63, 65, 70, 122, 125, 196, 204, 209, 217, 218
Transcendence, 62, 64–66, 135, 154, 159, 218
Trilling, L., 106, 107
Trump, Donald, 162, 167, 168, 170, 188, 213

Voltaire, 109, 110

GPSR Compliance

The European Union's (EU) General Product Safety Regulation (GPSR) is a set of rules that requires consumer products to be safe and our obligations to ensure this.

If you have any concerns about our products, you can contact us on

ProductSafety@springernature.com

In case Publisher is established outside the EU, the EU authorized representative is:

Springer Nature Customer Service Center GmbH
Europaplatz 3
69115 Heidelberg, Germany

www.ingramcontent.com/pod-product-compliance
Lightning Source LLC
LaVergne TN
LVHW020344260326
834688LV00045B/1513